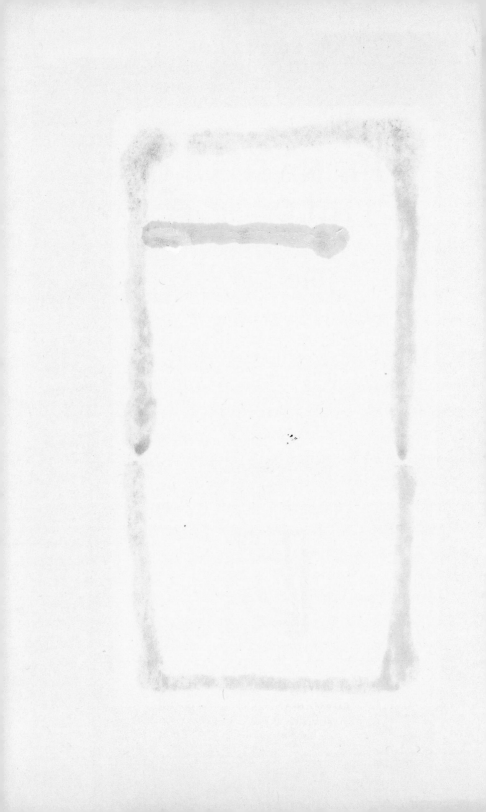

APQ LIBRARY OF
PHILOSOPHY

THE NATURE OF PHILOSOPHY

JOHN KEKES

1980

ROWMAN AND LITTLEFIELD

TOTOWA, NEW JERSEY

ISBN 0–8476–6247–0

Printed in Great Britain

for

Jean Y. Kekes

TABLE OF CONTENTS

PART THREE: PHILOSOPHICAL JUSTIFICATION

PART FOUR: PHILOSOPHY AND SOME OF ITS RELATIONS

PART FIVE: THE NATURE OF PHILOSOPHY: CONCLUSION

ACKNOWLEDGEMENTS

This book is a sequel to my *A Justification of Rationality* (Albany: State University of New York Press, 1976). In the previous book I develop a theory of rationality; in this book I apply that theory to philosophy. This results in some inevitable repetitions. In Chapters Three, Five, and Eight I draw on material from Chapters Eight and Twelve of the previous book. The two books, however, stand or fall independently of each other.

In Chapters Two and Five I incorporate the partial and revised contents of two of my articles: both were first published in *Idealistic Studies,* one in 1977, the other in 1979. In Chapter Three I use portions of an article I first published in the *Philosophy of the Social Sciences* in 1977. In Chapter Seven I rely on an article first published in *Inquiry* in 1979. Finally, Chapter Nine overlaps with an article first published in the *American Philosophical Quarterly* in 1979. I am grateful for permission to make use of these articles.

William Hay, Joel Kupperman, Jack Meiland, and Stephen Nathanson have read through the penultimate version of the manuscript. My debt to them is immense. They commented in detail, they gave me the benefit of their time, energy, and judgment, and they encouraged me. I have not always taken their advice, but the book benefited enormously from the comments I have heeded.

I am indebted to Max Black for suggesting the key term, perennial argument, around which the book revolves, and for helping me to think along the way. Stuart Brown, Josiah Gould, and Susan Haack read parts of the manuscript and I am grateful for their comments and criticisms.

The Research Foundation of the State University of New York provided two summer research grants, the College of Humanities and Fine Arts and the Office for Research of the State University of New York at Albany underwrote typing and duplicating expenses. I gratefully acknowledge their support. Helen Somich typed two versions of the manuscript; her intelligence, patience, tact, and precision are beyond the call of duty, and I thank her for everything.

I dedicate this book to Jean Y. Kekes, my wife and friend. She is more to me and has done more for me than I could possibly ask. If this book has merit, it is to a great extent due to her, for she has not only created the conditions in which I can work, but also helped to do the work by being first an audience, then a critic, and then an editor.

INTRODUCTION

This book is prompted by a concern about the absence of a satisfactory worldview in contemporary Western society. A worldview combines a reliable account of the nature of reality and a system of ideals. Having such a worldview makes the solution of problems possible, gives meaning and purpose to life, and thus creates the conditions under which life can be good.

The problem, as I see it, is not about our knowledge of reality. The growth of scientific knowledge has been steady. As a result, we live longer, we are in better health, and enjoy higher living standards than ever before. These improvements, however, merely create some of the conditions under which life can be good: by themselves, they cannot make it so. We also need a rational system of ideals; and it is this we lack.

Since our society does not provide them with such ideals, and since they do not generate them for themselves, most people live hollow lives. To fill them, they turn to mindless entertainment or drugs, they rediscover the thrills of magic by flirting with mysticism, witchcraft, astrology, religious revivalism, and other flowers of unreason. Many, rejecting these unworthy options, are left with a choice between despair, cynicism, and more or less obsessive pursuit of some sysiphean activity.

The difficulty is not the absence of ideals. The Western tradition has ample supply of them. The difficulty is the rational justification and systematization of those ideals. What we lack is a coherent system of reasonable ideals. It is this lack which is mainly responsible for many lives not being good.

The ideals we hold should be rationally justified. If they are not, we have no way of knowing whether the policies we adopt in accordance with them can be satisfactory solutions of our problems. Thus the rational justification of ideals is in the best interest of those who hold them. And the systematization of rational ideals is required by the desirability of having a coordinated policy for dealing with problems, rather than responding to them piecemeal with the risk that one effort may jeopardize another.

Though we have to cope with problems whether we like it or not, having a system of rational ideals makes it possible to cope in ways that shape our lives in directions we have chosen. It is this effort to shape our lives in accordance with a system of rational ideals that gives meaning and purpose to life. And success in the effort is what makes life good.

The thesis of this book is that it is the task of philosophy to show how to live well by the construction and rational justification of worldviews. It is to philosophy that one should look for a coherent system of rational ideals that gives meaning and purpose to life and in accordance with which its problems can be solved.

This view of philosophy is traditional. Its statement would have been a commonplace until around the beginning of this century. Part of my reason for restating it now is that, while the view I am defending is old, I have some new things to say about the nature of philosophy and philosophical justification. Another part of the reason is that many contemporary philosophers have come to reject this traditional view; when people turn to them for help, they fail to get it.

The book is divided into five parts. The first states the case against philosophy which the rest of the book is designed to meet. The charge, heard frequently from both philosophers and laymen, is that philosophy is incapable of discharging its traditional responsibility. The history of philosophy, they charge, reveals no progress and no knowledge; it is a history of futile, endless, and recurrent discussions of the same kind of questions. This, they say, explains both the gradual recognition of the insignificance of the subject and the disinclination of philosophers to continue in the useless old manner.

The second part begins to meet this case by describing a type of argument which I have come to call perennial. The practice of philosophy occurs mainly through perennial arguments. They are indeed endless and recurrent discussions of the same type of questions, but they are not futile. Their perenniality is a virtue not a fault. For perennial arguments aim to solve those enduring human problems whose persistent presence is an inevitable feature of human existence. The solution of such problems cannot result in their disappearance; it can only continue to produce policies for coping with them in changing circumstances. Of course, the policies we come to accept should enable us to cope with problems in accordance with our ideals. What ideals to be guided by, how to interpret available ideals, and how to develop policies which solve enduring problems as they occur in changing circumstances and yet accord with acceptable ideals, are the questions to be answered by perennial argumentation.

The forms in which these enduring problems occur, the rationally justified ideals available for solving them, the policies at our disposal, change from age to age. Therefore each society must form and reform its worldview. This, and not any inherent defect in the subject, is what explains the crucial importance, as well as the endlessness and recurrence, of philosophical arguments.

The third part provides a new theory of philosophical justi- fication. Its key idea is that there are two contexts of justification, not one, as is generally supposed. Each context has an objective standard of justification, and these standards are shown to be independently justified. A justified philosophical theory is the best solution of an enduring problem in a particular problem-situation. What makes it so is that it is more likely to be true than any of its rivals. An ideal worldview is composed of a cluster of philosophical theories thus justified; it offers a rational policy for solving enduring problems in accordance with rational ideals. The aim of philosophy, according to the traditional view I am defending, is to develop such a worldview in each age.

The fourth part is devoted to examining the relation between philosophy and common sense, science, and history. It is an effort to further elucidate the nature of philosophy by contrasting it with other pursuits. The contrast yields some conclusions about the kind of considerations that must be stressed or played down in the construction and rational justification of our worldview. These conclusions are that the worldview which will provide ideals for a good life must redress the present imbalance by stressing common sense, historical understanding, and cultural concerns against the inflated claims made on behalf of scientific understanding, and that the importance of science to a good life has been overrated in contemporary philosophy.

The fifth part gathers the threads of the previous discussions. A final account is given of the construction and justification of worldviews and this account is defended against its main contem- porary rivals. The picture that emerges is of philosophy as a humanistic enterprise whose conduct is in the common good. For participation in a rationally justified worldview provides a necessary condition for the achievement of a good life.

The whole of this book is informed by what prompted it: the diagnosis that we are in urgent need of a systematic and rationally justified worldview and that a humanistically interpreted philosophy is our best hope for providing it. In addition to this overall concern, there are several themes running through the book.

One is that philosophy cannot be done in isolation from the historical, political, scientific, social, literary, and other cultural influences upon it. The appreciation of cultural influences, however, requires historical understanding. And this means that the construction of worldviews inevitably involves an anthropocentric element. The importance of these humanistic considerations, however, does not change the fact that worldviews must and can be rationally justified. The recurring emphasis upon the necessity and possibility of rational justification in philosophy is another theme of the book.

The book is addressed to three groups. The first is composed of my colleagues, professional philosophers. I want to persuade them to return to the traditional view of the subject. The other group includes troubled nonphilosophers who turn to philosophy for answers and then are turned away again by philosophers. I want to assure them that they are right in their expectations, that philosophers are wrong in not meeting them, and that they should continue to demand what an improved philosophical practice will yield. I hope to show them here how philosophy is still capable of discharging its traditional responsibility. My highest hope, however, is for the last group: students of philosophy. Students often come to philosophy because they worry about the meaning and purpose of life, the point of being rational, the nature of morality, freedom, social justice, and so on. I want to show them that they have come to the right subject, even if its present state is unsatisfactory. I hope that this book will contribute to the education of a new generation of philosophers who will do better than my own.

PART ONE

THE PROBLEM

Chapter One

The Case Against Philosophy

"What is the use of studying philosophy if all it does for you is to enable you to talk with some plausibility about some abstruse questions of logic, etc., & if it does not improve your thinking about the important questions of everyday life."

LUDWIG WITTGENSTEIN[1]

I. *The Failure of Philosophy*

Philosophy has traditionally aimed at providing a rationally justified worldview. Such a worldview combines an account of the nature of reality and a system of ideals which give meaning and purpose to life. The first makes coping with our surroundings possible, the second makes it worthwhile. A good worldview accurately depicts the world, it provides a framework for understanding and appraising human experience, and it leads to successful action. It is useful, rational, and true. But it is also more, for a good worldview takes into account the feelings, desires, aspirations, and motives of people and also their capacities and limitations. It provides a way of harmonizing the dictates of human nature with the facts surrounding mankind.

It does not matter whether we refer to this as a worldview, *Weltanschauung*, metaphysics, philosophy of life, or just philosophy. What matters is that its possession defines a society. Those who share the outlook accept the same fundamental assumptions, have the same sense of values, they understand and appraise things by and large the same way, and so are parts of the same culture. The outlook also gives them a sense of continuity. For those who share it trace their tradition to past ideals and achievements and are agreed about what would constitute improvement and progress in the future. So a good worldview provides continuity in time and a sense of belongingness in the present.

The great benefit a person may gain from immersion in this worldview is wisdom. Wisdom involves the possession of knowledge and the capacity to use it well. It gives a man good judgment in intellectual and practical matters. As a result, he can live a better life. The wise man lives in harmony with himself, others, and the world. And what assures this harmony is the rationally justified and emotionally satisfying worldview which it is the traditional task of philosophy to provide.

The trouble with contemporary philosophy is that it is failing in this task. Its failure does not consist in falling short of the attainment of an ideal worldview. It would be unreasonable to blame philosophy alone among all human enterprises for not having achieved perfection. Blame attaches to philosophy because it has abandoned the effort to approximate the ideal. Philosophers hardly do any more what their predecessors have been doing. And in those cases where past and present problems and interests do coincide, the motivation for trying to solve the problems and the reasons for having the interests have radically changed. In the past, philosophical problems and interests were directed at finding meaning and purpose in life in terms of a rationally justifiable worldview. This is no longer so. The disappearance of philosophers would make no difference to the intellectual life of our society.[2] I regard this as tragic. Contrary to most contemporary philosophers I think that philosophy can and ought to perform its traditional task, its performance is desperately needed, and I deeply regret their refusal to actively engage in it.

Something bad has happened to philosophy. If this has been produced by a defect in the very nature of philosophy, then the subject is doomed. It is my view, however, that the sad contemporary state of philosophy is just a present-day aberration which may be remedied in time. However, the fact remains that many strong arguments favor the view that the contemporary defects stem from certain features which have always been implicit in the subject, but have surfaced only now. If this is true, philosophy simply cannot give what is wanted of it. I shall make my case for the subject in response to this charge against it. But my present concern is to state as forcefully as I can the case for the prosecution.

Essential to philosophy is the claim that it provides knowledge. For the development of a worldview must rest on knowledge of the world and the evaluation of what is known is possible only if something is known. Now philosophy has a 2500 year history, and yet it is impossible to find a single instance of philosophical knowledge. This devastating observation needs to be qualified. Philosophers, of course, know the theories and arguments of other philosophers. But this is knowledge of the history of philosophy, comparable to knowledge of the history of science. However, while the history of science includes scientific truths and scientific errors, the history of philosophy contains only philosophical errors.

Philosophical knowledge would consist of truths discovered by philosophy. Such knowledge might tell us, for instance, whether there is a spiritual element in reality, what things are good or bad, how to live well, whether anything exists that we can not observe, whether human beings are determined or free, what sort of society is the best, and so on. But while the history of philosophy is crowded with the views of philosophers on these and other subjects, there is no knowledge to be found. What one philosopher builds, others tear down. There is not a single truth about reality, not a single example of philosophical knowledge which is not repudiated by as many philosophers, using very convincing arguments, as there are philosophers championing it. Descartes complained in the seventeenth century that "I shall not say anything about Philosophy, but that, seeing that it has been cultivated for many centuries by the best minds that have ever lived, and that nevertheless no single thing is to be found in it which is not subject of dispute, and in consequence which is not dubious."[3] There has been no improvement since this passage was written.

In one respect, it must be admitted, philosophy has made advances. It has achieved a high degree of methodological sophistication. Formal logical techniques, methods of analysis, sharp and clearly drawn distinctions, provide powerful tools for contemporary philosophers. The availability of these tools, however, merely facilitates the inbred activity of philosophers: refuting each other's arguments. The results of methodological sophistication are a shortened life expectancy for philosophical theories and the inaccessibility of philosophical argumentation to nonphilosophers. A literate nonphilosopher cannot inform himself of what is going on in philosophy unless he invests much time in mastering a jargon and learning the symbolism in which it is couched. The history of philosophy abounds in impenetrable prose; the contemporary achievement is precision in an arcane tongue. As a result, even if the odd philosopher says something of interest for nonphilosophers, he is not likely to be understood.

Another way of approaching what is wrong with philosophy is by reflecting on what philosophers do. Philosophers fall into three not very sharply distinguishable groups. There are scholars and teachers whose job it is to inform those who are interested of the contributions made by philosophers who are not merely scholars and teachers. The other two groups contain the underlaborers and the masterbuilders, to appropriate these apt labels of Locke from a slightly different context.[4] The underlaborers work in a tradition established by the rare masterbuilder. The masterbuilders are the original, great philosophers who establish a new tradition, a new way of thinking about reality, who enrich us by constructing a worldview. The task of the underlaborers is to show how recalcitrant aspects of reality can be accommodated by the system, to defend the framework from external attacks, and to refine the original vision by working out its details. The vast majority of philosophers who describe themselves as *doing research* are underlaborers.

This threefold classification including the scholar and the teacher, the underlaborer, and the masterbuilder characterizes most disciplines whose aim is the enlargement of knowledge. There is, however, a distressing feature which makes philosophy unique among knowledge-seeking endeavors: most original philosophers start anew. Kant's introductory statement to his *magnum opus* is typical: "My purpose is to persuade all those who think metaphysics work studying that it is absolutely necessary to pause a moment ... regarding all that has been done as though undone."[5] Original philosophers usually begin by declaring the history of philosophy bankrupt and then go on to offer their contribution which solves most of the outstanding problems. Wittgenstein's engaging assertion that "I therefore believe myself to have found, on all essential points, the final solution of the problems,"[6] makes explicit the claim which can be found implicitly in the works of most great philosophers. After them only mopping up operations are required, if one is to believe the architects of yet another final solution.

The history of philosophy shows its most prominent figures half right and half wrong. The arguments for the bankruptcy of what preceded them are usually well-founded, but the claim to have solved the remaining problems is as little substantiated as were similar claims of the now chastised predecessors. The next critic of the latest philosophy waits in the wings.

Another way of putting this is that other knowledge-seeking inquiries are cumulative, philosophy is not. Great scientists advance knowledge and subsequent generations build upon their discoveries. Great philosophers do not advance knowledge and subsequent generations do not build upon their discoveries. The usual fate of great philosophers is to become labels for a style of thinking in which students of philosophy are enjoined not to engage. There is no progress, no growth of philosophical knowledge, only an increase in the number of mistaken paths. There is only a succession of false options expressed with greater and greater technical facility in a more and more specialized vocabulary.

Yet there is an illusion of progress in philosophy, and its first victims are philosophers. Both scholars and underlaborers can claim to have made progress over their predecessors. Scholars, by presenting yet another interpretation of some philosophical classic, and underlaborers, by further refining the tradition in which they happen to work. Clearly, however, whether these activities constitute progress depends upon the merits of the classic which is being interpreted and the tradition which is being refined. And if the masterbuilders—the authors of classics and the creators of traditions—merely produce false options, then the so-called progress made by scholars and underlaborers is no more than embelishment upon the blueprint of a castle built on air.

If this is true, then there must be some explanation for the high regard in which philosophy had been held for so long. The explanation has to do with filial piety. All knowledge-seeking disciplines began as philosophy, were nurtured by it during their adolescence, and declared their independence upon maturity. Astronomy, physics, and biology were, if not invented, then first seriously practiced by the ancient Greek philosophers; philosophers were the first mathematicians and geometers; sociology, political science, psychology, and linguistics were all born of philosophy.

During their infancy these disciplines were swathed in myths, speculations, superstitions. Maturity meant independence from philosophy; and it was made possible by the achievement of clarity about the questions and by precision in method which are the necessary prerequisites of knowledge. The production of knowledge and the attainment of independence from philosophy thus have gone hand in hand.

Many problems that start out as philosophical are marked by their apparent profundity and the attendant feeling of being at a loss as to how to answer them. As these problems are better understood, they become less intractable and a method of solving them begins to take shape. Thus it might be said that the progress from ignorance to knowledge is accompanied by passage from philosophy to science. Philosophy yields knowledge only in the very peculiar sense of having nurtured disciplines which do so.[7]

The significance of this is that the philosophical ambition to produce knowledge is doomed. If an investigation is philosophical, then it is not yet systematized and so it cannot yield knowledge; if it yields knowledge, it must be systematic, but then it is not philosophical. The domain of philosophy is thus those parts of reality of which we realize our ignorance. We but dimly perceive their existence, but we do not know how to investigate them. As Russell tells us: "Those questions which are already capable of definite answers are placed in the sciences, while those only to which, at present, no definite answer can be given, remain to form the residue which is called philosophy."[8] No wonder, therefore, that the history of philosophy fails to provide examples of philosophical knowledge.

What makes matters worse for philosophy is that it is very difficult to point to some aspect of reality that is not already subject to systematic investigation. Cosmological speculations are the province of astronomy, the properties of matter of physics and chemistry, living things are studied by biology, human beings and society by the many social sciences, language by linguistics, and even for events that might not exist there is already the budding science of parapsychology; our myths, obsessions, fears, and ecstasies are latched on to by psychoanalysts and anthropologists. The past has been claimed long ago by history, and prophesy has been cornered by psephologists and futurologists. It is said that the result of all this specialization is that we learn more and more about less and less. The corollary for philosophy is that it has less and less right to address itself to more and more questions.

Perhaps the time has come to retire philosophy? Its historical merits are great, for it prepared the ground for science. But now that we have the sciences, why do we need philosophy? What does it do that cannot be done better by science?

II. *The Weakness of Excuses*

One popular response philosophers give is that the difference between philosophy and science is arbitrary. As Russell puts it: "Philosophical knowledge ... does not differ essentially from scientific knowledge; there is no special source of wisdom which is open to philosophy but not to science, and the results obtained by philosophy are not radically different from those obtained by science."[9] According to this view, there is a continuity between scientific and philosophical problems. These problems are a mixture of factual and conceptual components. Problems that are mainly factual we can regard as scientific for the sake of convenience, while those which are predominantly conceptual are identifiable as philosophical. Conceptual problems tend to be more general and less amenable to experimental answers than factual problems, but the differences between them are a matter of degree. Philosophy and science thus do not have different domains.

Hundreds of philosophers, understandably anxious about their subject, rushed to embrace this reassuring answer. It allows philosophy to bask in the prestige of science, it relieves philosophers of the obligation to provide experimentally testable answers, and it makes use of the historical connection between philosophy and science.

It must not escape notice, however, that the acceptance of this answer amounts to the abandonment of the traditional conception of philosophy. The expedient of hanging on the the shirt-tails of science might save the claim that philosophy provides knowledge. It may be argued that since science provides knowledge, and philosophy is indistinguishable from science, therefore philosophy provides knowledge. But nothing saves the traditional aspiration of providing a worldview in terms of which wisdom and the meaning and purpose of our lives can be found.

The result is that "[w]hen reason is overturned, blind passions are rampant, and urgent questions mount, men turn for guidance to scientists, psychiatrists, sociologists, politicians, historians, journalists—to almost anyone but their traditional guide, the philosopher. Philosophy, in revolt against the past and against its traditional function, looks inward at its own problems rather than outward at men."[10]

Another response philosophers offer is that philosophy is a second-order activity, while science is a first-order one. They are not in competition, for they have different interests. We should "distinguish inquiries about the items which can fall into classes from inquiries about the classes into which they can fall, and for the sake of clarity call the former 'first-order' inquiries and the latter 'second-order' inquiries. The first-order inquiries are typical of the natural sciences, e.g. is this, or this kind of, chemical substance both soluble and magnetic? Are the effects of inflation also the causes of unemployment? ... [Philosophy is] a type of second-order inquiry whose interest ... is ... in the interrelation of the classes. For example, does being believed to be so involve being so? Is what is caused to be compelled to be? Can negligence only

be inadvertent? ... The distinctions, discriminations, and classi-
fications we make are the concepts ... we use. To have a particular
concept, e.g. that of justice, recklessness, or mass, is to be able and
disposed to assimilate or distinguish in certain ways whatever we
encounter. Examining the relations between the various ways we
classify things ... is examining the concepts we use. We can use
the traditional word 'analysis' for this examination of concepts."[11]
Thus, on this view, the task of philosophy is analysis or descriptive
metaphysics, as it has sometimes been called.[12]

Descriptive metaphysics "has a long and distinguished history,
and it is consequently unlikely that there are any new truths to be
discovered. ... But this does not mean that the task of descriptive
metaphysics has been done, or can be, once for all. It has
constantly to be done over again. If there are no new truths to be
discovered, there are old truths to be rediscovered."[13] The aim of
philosophical inquiry, so Wittgenstein ruled, is thus not to learn
something that was previously not known, but to describe the way
the concepts we all share work. "Philosophy may in no way
interfere with the actual use of language; it can in the end only
describe it. ... It leaves everything as it is."[14]

If philosophy is analysis, then it is not in competition with
science, for it has other interests; it is not to be blamed for failing
to provide knowledge, for that is not its task; and it does indeed
perform a task that no other discipline performs: the analysis of
concepts that everybody knows and uses. But this is a terribly
self-stultifying view of philosophy. It claims respectability at the
cost of importance. If some philosophers are interested in analyzing
what everybody knows without analysis, there is no reason for
stopping them. Should they, however, be supported and
encouraged? Should their courses be part of university curriculum?
Should scarce resources go to them?

The point is not the mercenary one that only those inquiries
should be supported that will repay the investment. There are
many subjects which deserve support because they are repositories
of ideals without which life is not worth living. History, literature,
the classics, and the arts are not going to make a profit. In the
past, philosophy would have been listed alongside these other
subjects in the humanities. The question of support is justifiably
asked now, because philosophy is no longer discharging its
traditional obligation.

For what is expected of philosophy is not to describe concepts
while taking care to leave them as before, but to challenge them,

rethink them, criticize or justify them. We do not want to be given an analysis of what we already know. We want philosophers to explore our fundamental assumptions about the world, ourselves, our ideals and lives. And we want them either to justify these assumptions on rational grounds so that we can continue to hold them with clear intellectual conscience, or to criticize them and show us that they are defective and need replacement. And we want them to propose replacements when needed and to argue the merits of new candidates. If the Western civilization is to endure, it has to be capable of flexibility, fundamental changes, and must have the ability to meet profound challenges presented by Marxism, Maoism, the gradual disappearance of religious values, and the rejection of liberal democracy by the overwhelming majority of the world. The activity of criticizing, defending, and developing worldviews is an essential part of this process. If philosophers are not willing or able to engage in it, others will. The question is not whether it should be done, but who will do it. The abdication of philosophers merely removes the most likely leaders, and thus jeopardizes the success of this crucially important endeavor.

"Philosophy, in the current Anglo-American vein, has largely relinquished—indeed it has scorned—those central areas of metaphysics, of ethics, of esthetics, of political thought, that constituted the mainstream and splendor of the philosophic tradition. It has left reality, the obstinate, messy sovereignty of the everyday world, to witch doctors on the one hand, and to intellectual terrorists on the other. What it offers instead is dry tack for teeth on edge."[15]

The Anglo-American tradition stresses one component of the traditional conception of philosophy: rational justification. There is another tradition, stressing another component: the construction of worldviews. This other tradition is exemplified by much Continental philosophy, existentialism, Marxism, oriental and occidental religious philosophy. Its hallmarks are relativism, historicism, fideism; concentration on bad faith, alienation, inauthenticity; exploration of the social, cultural, economic, or historical determination of philosophical ideals.[16]

Philosophers in the Anglo-American tradition regard as misdirected the demand that they should supply a worldview in terms of which wisdom, meaning, and purpose can be found. This, they say, is the proper activity of the sage. Whether what the sage does is philosophy is a controversial question; but there is no controversy about the fact that the typical science or analysis oriented philosopher and the typical sage are engaged in quite different activities. The sage presents to the world a point of view and recommends its adoption because it is emotionally satisfying, yields a result the sage finds desirable, and it is capable of giving a satisfying life to those who accept it. In this, the sage is not very different from the great philosophers of the past. The difference enters because philosophers recognize the obligation of supporting their worldviews by rational argument, the sage, on the other hand, believes that in the last analysis the adoption of worldviews rests on a *leap of faith*, or it is a matter of *engagement, commitment*, or *authenticity*.

The sage imports into contemporary philosophy an essentially irrational element. His approach rests on the belief that fundamental questions cannot be rationally answered. For rational answers presuppose some standards of justification and these standards would also have to be justified. But this justification cannot be provided because the process of justifying one standard by another must either be endless or lead to an arbitrary commitment to some standard or another. And so the sage recommends arbitrary commitment.

If it were true that fundamental assumptions could not be rationally justified, then all honestly held convictions would have an equal claim upon general acceptance. So science and pseudo-science, history and myth, medicine and quackery, considered judgment and rabid prejudice, would be equally acceptable. The civilizing restraints of debate, criticism, and rational discussion would disappear and force and propaganda would take their places as the method for settling disputes. Life, then, as Hobbes said, would be "nasty, brutish, and short."

Thus the mainstream of contemporary philosophy presents two alternatives: the irrationalism of the sage and the abdication of the Anglo-American philosopher. The crucial philosophical task of this or any other age is the analysis, criticism, justification, and, if necessary, the replacement of worldviews. The sage sees this clearly, but he denies that it can be done rationally. The philosopher, who is committed to rationality, agrees with the sage, if only by fiat. For he either cannot or does not address himself to that crucial task. So in contemporary philosophy neither of the dominant schools seems to be both rational and deal with the most burning issues.

III. *What is to Be Done?*

My purpose is to present a view of philosophy which avoids the pitfalls just discussed. Worldviews can be examined rationally and when they are so examined it is possible for philosophers to present an outlook which teaches wisdom and gives meaning and purpose to life. This, of course, amounts to a reaffirmation of the traditional role of philosophy. Philosophy, it will be shown, can and should play that role and its contemporary failure to do so is a disease whose cure is one of the intended consequenses of this book.

In order to defend philosophy, however, the case against it must be answered. And that case is that philosophy provides no knowledge, makes no progress, accumulates no achievements. Science, it appears, has preempted the knowledge-seeking role of philosophy. Philosophers may transfer their allegiance to science or they may restrict themselves to the analysis of concepts. In both cases, however, they fail to perform their traditional role. A defence of philosophy must ask and give satisfactory answers to such questions as What kind of knowledge, if any, does philosophy provide? What does philosophy do that science does not do better? Is there progress in philosophy? How can worldviews be rationally defended? How does philosophy provide wisdom and give meaning and purpose to life? I shall answer these questions favorably for philosophy. The answers depend on a view of the nature of philosophy and it is to the task of presenting that view that I shall now turn.

NOTES

1. Ludwig Wittgenstein in a letter to Norman Malcolm, quoted in N. Malcolm's *Ludwig Wittgenstein: A Memoir* (London: Oxford University Press, 1958), 39.

2. Cf. "If the several thousands or more of professional philosophers in America were all assembled in one place, and a small nuclear device were detonated over it, American society would remain totally unaffected. ... No one would notice any difference, and there would be no gap, no vacuum, in the intellectual economy, that would require plugging." Ernest Gellner, "Reflections on Philosophy, especially in America," in *The Devil in Contemporary Philosophy* (London: Routledge, 1974), 37–8.

3. Rene Descartes, "Discourse on the Method of Rightly Conducting the Reason," *The Philosophical Works of Descartes*, tr. E. S. Haldane and G. R. T. Ross (Cambridge: Cambridge University Press, 1970), 85–5.

4. John Locke, *An Essay Concerning Human Understanding*, ed. A. C. Fraser (New York: Dover, 1959), 14.

5. Immanuel Kant, *Prolegomena to Any Future Metaphysics*, ed. L. W. Beck (New York: Liberal Arts, 1950), 3.

6. Ludwig Wittgenstein, *Tractatus Logico-Philosophicus*, tr. D. F. Pears and B. F. McGuinness (London: Routledge, 1961), 5.

7. Cf. "It is obvious enough that if every step forward which philosophy makes, every question to which an accurate answer is found, gets accredited to science, the residuum of the unanswered questions will alone remain to constitute the domain of philosophy. ... In point of fact this is just what is happening. Philosophy has become a collective name for questions that have not yet been answered." William James, *Some Problems of Philosophy* (New York: Greenwood Press, 1968), 22–3.

8. Bertrand Russell, *The Problems of Philosophy* (Oxford: Oxford University Press, 1967), 90.

9. Russell, *op. cit.*, 87.

10. Time Essay: "What (If Anything) to Expect from Today's Philosophers," *Time Magazine* (January 7, 1966), 24–5.

11. Alan R. White, "Conceptual Analysis," *The Owl of Minerva*, ed. C. J. Bontempo and S. J. Odell (New York: McGraw-Hill, 1975), 104–5.

12. By Peter F. Strawson, *Individuals* (New York: Doubleday, 1963), xiii–xv.

13. Strawson, *op. cit.*, xiv.

14. Ludwig Wittgenstein, *Philosophical Investigations*, tr. G. E. M. Anscombe (Oxford: Blackwell, 1958), 124.

15. George Steiner, "The Lollipopping of the West," *The New York Times* (December 9, 1977).

16. Cf. "[T]wo very different forms of activity now go under the name 'philosophy': one is essentially rational and critical, with logical analysis ... at its heart; the other ... is openly hostile to critical analysis and professes to arrive at general conclusions by a direct, essentially personal intuition." John Passmore, "Philosophy," *The Encyclopedia of Philosophy*, ed. P. Edwards (New York: Macmillan and Free Press, 1967), Vol. 6, 218.

PART TWO

PERENNIAL ARGUMENTS AND WORLDVIEWS

Chapter Two

Perennial Arguments

"Principles taken upon trust, consequences lamely deduced from them, want of coherence in the parts, and of evidence in the whole, these are everywhere to be met with in the systems of the most eminent philosophers, and seems to have drawn disgrace upon philosophy itself. ... [E]ven the rabble without doors may judge from the noise and clamour, which they hear, that all goes not well within. There is nothing which is not subject of debate, and in which men of learning are not of contrary opinions. The most trivial question escapes not our controversy, and in the most momentous we are not able to give any certain decisions."

DAVID HUME[1]

I. *Characteristics of Perennial Arguments*

My strategy for replying to the case against philosophy begins by considering a particular kind of philosophical argument, called perennial argument. Perennial arguments are about ideals and some of these ideals give meaning and purpose to human life. Thus perennial arguments concern those very questions whose neglect constitutes part of the case against philosophy which I outlined in the previous chapter.

The discussion of perennial arguments will lead to the conclusion that they are of great importance, that their occurrence is in the common good, and that though they are not scientific, they are perfectly reasonable arguments which can be settled one way or another. This conclusion will entitle me to claim the same merit for philosophy, insofar as it can be identified with perennial arguments.

In this chapter I shall offer a general characterization of perennial arguments which will fall short of a definition. I shall give a definition later, but only after much more has been said. Perennial arguments are, for instance, about morality, logical consistency, religiosity, education, aesthetic sensibility, rationality, culture, democracy, scientific or historical understanding, and knowledge.[2] The subject-matters of perennial arguments are thus ideals.

Ideals are goals that people have, and their behavior is directed

17

toward them. Indeed, one way of understanding why a person does a certain thing in a certain situation is to understand the goal of his behavior. Knowing the goals also makes it possible to judge the success or the failure of the behavior. Success consists in approximating or achieving the goals, failure means to have attempted but not to have gotten closer.

People's behavior may be directed toward many different goals, but only some of these are ideals. For a goal to qualify as an ideal, the person must value it. People may act to achieve goals they do not value. For instance, they may be forced; they may act out of revenge, rage, resentment, indifference, or boredom; they may pursue a goal they abominate in order to avoid one even worse; or they may be ignorant or unconscious of the goal they in fact pursue.

So, ideals are goals valued by the people who have them. For a person to recognize something as an ideal is tantamount to recognizing it as something desirable. That a person acts so as to achieve what he accepts as an ideal requires no explanation, for such behavior is natural and expected. What needs explanation is when a person is conscious of having an ideal, has the opportunity to bring it about, and yet refrains from doing so. Self-sacrifice, stupidity, laziness, scruples, may account for such behavior.

In saying that the subject-matters of perennial arguments are ideals, I do not mean to suggest that perennial arguments are about intrinsically worthwhile achievements. Of course, the person engaged in the pursuit thinks of the ideal as worthwhile. But he may be mistaken. What one person regards as an ideal, another may abhor. So my use of *ideal* is not meant to suggest that perennial arguments can occur only about pursuits that are rated high on some objective scale of values. In my sense, tyranny, racial superiority, total submission to God, are ideals just as much as democracy, equality, and personal responsibility are. One of the questions I shall examine is how such disagreements about ideals can be rationally resolved.

Another source of confusion is eliminated if the difference between ideals and their exemplifications is recognized. Democracy is an ideal, Periclean Athens is an exemplification of it; just as appreciation of particular works of art, instances of knowledge, or rational behavior are exemplifications of the ideals of aesthetic sensibility, knowledge, or rationality. Perennial arguments are about ideals, not about their exemplifications. Of course, the ideals are represented in individual instances and there may be all sorts of arguments about the representations or exemplifications. But these arguments are irrelevant for my purposes.

Now while perennial arguments are about ideals, there are at least two different kinds of such arguments. To illustrate these I shall take one ideal, rationality, and show how the two kinds of perennial arguments can occur in its case. I mean by *rationality* the ideal of basing one's actions and beliefs on reason. Having reasons as their bases makes it possible for a person to explain and justify his beliefs and actions. A person who accepts the ideal of rationality thus incurs the obligation of holding only those beliefs and performing only those actions which can be explained and justified on rational grounds. Such an explanation and justification consists in his ability to provide arguments for his beliefs and actions and arguments against rival beliefs and actions.

Perennial arguments may be external or internal. They are external if what is argued is the acceptability of an ideal and they are internal if the dispute presupposes the acceptability of the ideal and concerns its precise nature. In the first case, the opposing sides debate about the merits of an ideal; in the second case, they agree about its merits and debate about its interpretation.

External perennial arguments are about conflicting ideals. For instance, a person may reject the ideal of rationality on the grounds that it inhibits spontaneity, leads to the repression of feeling and emotion, curtails imagination, or because he regards it as a mistake to suppose that in the last analysis any belief or action can be rationally justified. On the basis of such doubts, faith, intuition, or creativity might be juxtaposed with rationality as the ideals by which beliefs and actions should be justified. External perennial arguments thus may concern the respective merits of rationality and faith, democracy and oligarchy, morality and total freedom, as ideals guiding people's lives.

Internal perennial arguments, on the other hand, occur only if the opposing sides accept the same ideal. They may agree, for instance, that rationality as an ideal of justification is preferable to faith, intuition, or creativity. Their disagreement might concern the nature of rationality. Both sides accept something like the general description of rationality I have offered. They disagree, however, when they attempt to establish just what is included in and excluded from the general description. Rationality is a complex notion, composed of many elements. Internal perennial arguments are about the necessity and respective importance of various elements involved in rationality.

A debate of this sort may center around what may be called the *pragmatic* component of rationality. Is it or is it not necessary for the rationality of a belief that it should be likely to be true or for the rationality of an action that it should be likely to succeed? Champions of one conception of rationality may hold that the connection between rationality, on the one hand, and truth and success, on the other, is essential. They think of rationality as defining the field of beliefs which *may* be true and the field of actions which *may* be successful. A competing conception of rationality, however, may regard conformity to a set of rules, such as those provided by logic or science, as the essential component of rationality. According to this view, only if a belief has been arrived at or an action has been performed in accordance with logical or scientific techniques is it rational.

The first conception of rationality includes the pragmatic component as an essential element, the second one does not. The dispute is not about what is a component of rationality, but about what is an *essential* component. Internal perennial arguments are about just such competing conceptions of the nature of an ideal. Similar arguments may concern the nature of morality, where it might be debated whether pity, charity, or self-denial are essential components of morality; or they may be about the nature of democracy, concerning the question of whether equality, the multiparty system, or the separation of powers are necessary for a society being democratic.

Thus, though perennial arguments may be external or internal, what does it mean to say that they are *perennial*? *Perennial* carries the suggestion of being endless, long-standing, recurrent, enduring; and I do mean that the arguments I am concerned with are endlesss and recurrent. But I want to underplay the implication that perennial arguments must have a long history. For the life-span of perennial arguments depends on the life-span of the ideal which is argued about. Some of the ideals are very old indeed; knowledge, morality, logical consistency, and rationality have at least as long a history as our civilization. But others, such as culture, scientific understanding, or freedom are quite recent. In my use of *perennial* I do not want to exclude relatively recent ideals. Therefore, it is not their duration, but their lack of finality and recurrence which I take to constitute their perennial aspect.

The various perennially contested ideals are vague and general. It is not surprising therefore that there is constant debate about their acceptability and interpretation. One significant feature of these debates is that participants are aware that what one side regards as a good argument for accepting the ideal or as a correct interpretation of it is opposed by other arguments and interpretations which other parties to the debate regard as convincing. Thus each party champions a particular ideal or a particular interpretation of it and consciously opposes the ideals and interpretations favored by others.

One would expect, then, that when the debaters realize the nature of their argument, they would diagnose it to be a fundamental disagreement which cannot be overcome by rational discussion, and the debate would end. But this is not what happens: these debates continue and each debater continues to insist that his ideal or interpretation is correct and the others are incorrect.

Consider as an illustration of their endlessness and recurrence some external perennial arguments about rationality. At the height of Greek rationalism "what chiefly preoccupied Euripides in his later work was not so much the impotence of reason in man as the wider doubt whether any rational purpose could be seen in the ordering of human life ... [i]f we must attach a label ... the word 'irrationalist' ... fits Euripides better than any other."[3] Greek rationalism of course persisted undeterred, but only to encounter Tertullian's uncompromising opposition: "A plague on Aristotle, who taught them dialectic, the art which destroys as much as it builds, which changes its opinions like a coat, forces its conjectures, is stubborn in argument, works hard at being contentious and is a burden even to itself. ... What has Jerusalem to do with Athens, the Church with Academy. ... After Jesus Christ we have no need of speculation, after the Gospel no need of research."[4] Luther responded to the Renaissance by condemning the "whore reason" for leading man astray by licensing false pride and the illusion that salvation is in human hands. The enlightenment and the tradition it established was castigated by Kierkegaard for rigidifying thinking by forcing everything into the Procrustean bed of "bloodless categories". Psychoanalysts assail the ideal of rationality as impossible of achievement and its pursuit as a neurotic aberration; existentialists convict it for leading to "bad faith" and to "inauthentic" life.

The argument about the merits of rationality has continued for at least 2500 years. The argument is endless and recurrent, apparently without resolution. Champions of one side or another die and so factions may lose effective representation. But the old case is always presented again in a new guise, couched in the then contemporary vocabulary, only to be opposed by the most recent restatement of the same old opposition. Critics of philosophy may indeed wonder about the point of continuing the enterprise.[5] But, as I shall show, it has an extremely important one.

The situation is not substantially different if we examine internal perennial arguments. Consider, for instance, disagreements about the interpretation of *democracy*. The claims of majority rule, universal franchise, equality before the law, the consent of the governed are notorious competitors for licencing the description of a society as *democratic*. A champion of majority rule and one of the consent of the governed may each realize that his own interpretation is contested by the other. Their disagreement goes deep and clarification will not make either side relinquish the claim to being the only true champions of democracy. Analogous situations exist in such internal perennial arguments as whether the possession of taste, the capacity to have aesthetic experiences, or the appreciation of a vision, really constitutes aesthetic sensibility; similarly, morality may be taken to involve primarily doing one's duty, acting altruistically, or making oneself a better person.

It cannot be denied that both internal and external perennial arguments occur. The question is what to make of them. Reasonable observers reflecting upon the history of these interminable controversies may well come away with a feeling of hopelessness. They may conclude that the arguments are pointless: one simply has to take a stand on these fundamental questions and live one's life as well as possible. In doing this, however, they abandon rationality. For they deny, unwillingly perhaps, that fundamental questions are capable of rational answers. They are acquiescing in the view that the choice of ideals by which one lives one's life is determined by taste, temperament, accident, authority, or instinct, but cannot be rationally derived from the arguments for and against them. And in resigning themselves to this opinion, they disqualify themselves from having a right to object to other people holding other ideals which are vicious, harmful, destructive, and abominable. For if all they have in favor of their ideals is unreasoned commitment, then they cannot very well object to other people's commitments.

It will be seen by now that very much more depends on the possibility of rationally settling perennial arguments than the mere defence of philosophy. Defending philosophy is important because to do so is effectively to show the possibility of tackling fundamental questions rationally.

I have maintained that in order to show that fundamental questions can be rationally answered, one needs to show how perennial arguments can be rationally resolved. The first step toward doing that is to acquire an understanding of perennial arguments. And so far we have reached this much clarity: perennial arguments are either about the conflict of opposing ideals, or about conflicting interpretations of the same ideal, and they are perennial in the sense of being recurrent and endless. Before I continue with the positive characterization of perennial arguments, I want to dispose of two misinterpretations.

II. *Two Misinterpretations of Perennial Arguments*

Consider the following line of thought: arguments may be about three things. They may be about facts, and such arguments can be settled if it is ascertained what the relevant facts are; many scientific arguments are typically of this sort. Or, they may be about meaning, and these can be settled if the parties to it become clear of the sense in which they use relevant words. After such clarification, the argument may be resolved by the participants' coming to see that even though they use the same words they are talking about different things and they do not disagree with each other. Or the argument changes from verbal to factual, for the participants come to understand that they disagree about the nature of the thing discussed and not about the meaning of the word they use to refer to it. The third thing they may be about is how participants feel about something. But since such things are largely matters of taste, there is not much scope for argument here.

Now perennial arguments are not factual, for what is argued is not what the facts are, but the nature of the ideals which should be used for evaluating the facts. There is a temptation to say that perennial arguments are simply expressions of how people feel about various ideals and that is why they are incapable of rational resolution. But this interpretation is resisted by a large number of people who think that while perennial arguments are not factual, they are not irrational either. For such people the suggestion readily presents itself that perennial arguments are verbal, and that if we could only get clear about them, then they would turn into nonperennial factual arguments. This suggestion, however, is quite mistaken, for perennial arguments are frequently not verbal and so clarification, while always desirable, will not always put an end to them.

The possibility that external perennial arguments are verbal need not detain us long. For there are very many arguments about conflicting ideals in which the participants are quite clear about what it is they accept and reject. Fascists and liberal democrats do not disagree about what democracy is, but about its desirability; rationalists and fideists understand perfectly well what rationality and faith are, yet they evaluate them quite differently; nor is the dispute about religiosity between atheists and theists handicapped by either side failing to understand the meaning of the crucial word.

When we come to internal perennial arguments, however, the plausibility of verbal confusion causing them becomes greater. For why should we not conclude that when people disagree about the correct interpretation of *rationality*, aesthetic sensibility, morality, and so on, then they just mean different things and confusedly use the same word to designate them? The answer is twofold.

The first reason for thinking that *rationality, morality,* and *aesthetic sensibility* each denote one and only one ideal is that there is available a general description for each of them. Thus rationality depends on the exercise of reason and that involves being able to explain and justify one's actions and beliefs. Morality has to do with virtuous, principled conduct, with aiming to do what is right. Aesthetic sensibility involves the exercise of imagination and taste in making oneself susceptible to aesthetic objects.

Such generalities, of course, irresistably call forth the Socratic questioner lurking in each philosopher. My point, however, is not that these generalities should be left unquestioned, but that they define a domain upon which the questioning must be concentrated. Thus they guarantee a common subject for participants in perennial arguments.

The other reason for thinking that each perennial argument deals with one subject only is the testimony of intelligent participants. It would be incredible to suppose that every time intuitionists and utilitarians debate about morality, classicists and modernists about painting, or Aristotelians and Hegelians about logical consistency, they are in fact talking about different things and just happen, confusedly, to be using the same words. Such debates are conducted by self-conscious and thoughtful people and their shared conviction that they have a genuine disagreement ought to count at least as *prima facie* evidence for their having a common subject. The point I am making is not the psychological one that thoughtful and analytical people are less likely to be confused, but the logical point that if someone sees the presence of confusion here, then the burden is upon him to establish it. The initial evidence tells against it.

The conclusion I am drawing is that neither internal nor external perennial arguments need to be verbal. They may, of course, disguise confusion, but it is no more a built-in feature of such argument than of any other. So it is a misinterpretation of perennial arguments to treat them as if a little clear thinking could render them tractable. The root of this misinterpretation is the rigid classification of arguments into factual, verbal, and those having to do with feeling and taste. For, while I certainly do not think that perennial arguments concern taste or that they are verbal, I still hestitate to conclude that they are factual. What is at the bottom of this is the unclarity of the *factual* category. That unclarity is responsible for a second major misinterpretation of perennial arguments.

To say that something is a fact is to commit oneself to the assertion that some state of affairs actually holds in the world. A fact is, then, what is the case and saying that something is a fact amounts to saying that something is true. Of course, in saying anything one may be mistaken. The recognition of having made a mistake results in having to acknowledge that what one thought was a fact, or what one thought was true, was not. So two people may disagree about whether something is a fact, that is, whether something is true. But they cannot both be right; one or the other or both must be mistaken, for what is a fact or what is true depends not on what people think, but on the nature of the world. This much, I think, is clear and uncontroversial. But now complications enter.

It is a fact that the Declaration of Independence was signed in 1776 and it is also a fact that the Declaration of Independence is an important, historically significant document. These are facts, but obviously not the same kinds of facts. The signing of the Declaration of Independence in 1776 is something that happened; that it is important and historically significant is an interpretation of something that happened. Both are true, but they are different kinds of truths.

No reasonable person can deny that the Declaration of Independence was signed in 1776; all the evidence we have is in favor of believing it and there is no evidence at all against believing it. Of course, the evidence we have may change, but unless it does, we can take it as a fact. Reasonable people, however, may deny that the signing of the Declaration of Independence was an important and historically significant event. For importance and significance are subject to the acceptance of certain assumptions. If we accept the assumptions that politics is basic to history and that America plays a crucial role in the world, then the signing of the Declaration of Independence was indeed important and significant. But a person who thinks that it is not politics but, for instance, the unfolding of God's plan that is basic to history may think of the Declaration of Independence as a trivial episode in the history of Protestantism. And so may a Chinese historian who continues in that tradition of historiography which ignores events occurring far from the Chinese frontiers as the irrelevant antics of barbarians.

The point of these rather obvious remarks is to permit me to ask the question of whether the category of factual arguments includes both the facts about something having happened and the facts about the interpretation of something that has happened. I ask the question, although it does not matter very much for my present purposes how we answer it. What matters is that we should be aware of the question and that we should answer it consistently. And this, I am afraid, has not always been observed in the past.

There has been a long-standing tendency to identify factual questions with questions about something having happened and to treat questions about the interpretation of what has happened as nonfactual. Now this in itself is merely a harmless preference for one labelling convention over another. But it becomes a tendency to resist when it is combined with two additional assumptions. The first is that what this convention regards as factual questions are best answered by science. The second is that since questions of interpretations are not factual, and as we have seen they are not verbal either, they must be questions of feeling and taste and so not open to rational discussion.

So there emerges the following very mistaken way of looking at things: questions of fact are best answered by science; verbal questions are answered by clarification of meaning and as a result they either turn into factual questions or cease to be questions; and what remains is a matter of taste, feeling, subjective preference, where rationality has no foothold. Thus all questions are either scientific or incapable of rational answer. Or, to put the same point differently, if a question can be answered rationally, then it must be answered scientifically, the field of rational questions and answers being identical with the field of scientific questions and answers. As Schlick puts it: "All real problems are scientific questions, there are no others,"[6] or as Wittgenstein declares: "We feel that even when all *possible* scientific questions have been answered the problems of life remain completely untouched. Of course there are then no questions left, and this is the answer."[7]

The significance of this mistaken view is that it follows from it that perennial arguments are irrational. For perennial arguments are about the interpretation of what happened, and as such they are, of course, not scientific arguments. This fact about perennial arguments is generally recognized. There are, however, two ways of responding to it. One is to dismiss perennial arguments. The other is to reject the view that all rational arguments are scientific and think of perennial arguments as both rational and nonscientific. It is obvious by now that I favor the second response and that very many contemporary philosophers favor the first response. That incidentally is part of the reason why contemporary philosophers refuse to deal with the issues raised by perennial arguments.

III. *Conclusion*

Taking either of these two responses presents a very serious difficulty. The difficulty encountered by the response that perennial arguments are irrational is that it follows that the choices of ideals by which people live their lives are also irrational. Fundamental commitments, then, are made, but they cannot be rationally defended and so anything goes, provided it is licensed by some fundamental commitment. I say that this is a difficulty, because if it is true, the prospects for civilized life are poor.

The difficulty faced by the other, my own, option is to show how there could be rational arguments that are not scientific. This amounts to showing that in addition to factual problems resolvable by science, verbal problems resolvable by clarification, and problems of taste, feeling, and subjective attitude incapable of rational resolution, there is also a fourth kind of problem having to do with the interpretation of facts and still being rationally resolvable. Perennial arguments can, then, be allocated to this last category.

The categorical scheme I am adopting for the sake of clarity in future discussions is to distinguish between two kinds of factual arguments: descriptive and interpretive. The distinction is not sharp, it is a matter of degree. Yet some factual arguments do tend to be straightforward questions about what the facts are, while others take the facts as given and argue about their interpretation.

Perennial arguments are interpretive factual arguments. I aim to show that they are rational, but first additional clarification is needed.

The result of this chapter, then, is the beginning of a better understanding of perennial arguments. Perennial arguments are about ideals. Ideals can be argued about externally, if it is a matter of choosing between conflicting ideals, and internally, if the argument is about conflicting interpretations of the same ideal. Perennial arguments are recurrent and endless and they are neither verbal nor scientific. They are typical philosophical arguments and if they can be shown to be rational, then the aura of ill-repute pervading contemporary philosophy may be lifted.[8]

NOTES

1. David Hume, *A Treatise of Human Nature*, ed. L. A. Selby-Bigge (Oxford: Clarendon Press, 1960), xix.

2. The history of some perennial argumentation about some of these ideals is available: for aesthetic sensibility, especially regarding painting, see Ernst H. Gombrich, *Art and Illusion* (Princeton: Princeton University Press, 1960); for morality, see Alasdair MacIntyre, *A Short History of Ethics* (London: Routledge, 1967) and Stuart Hampshire, *Two Theories of Morality* (Oxford: Oxford University Press, 1977); for freedom, see Gertrude Himmelfarb, *On Liberty and Liberalism* (New York: Knopf, 1974); for education, see Sheldon Rothblatt, *Tradition and Change in English Liberal Education* (London: Faber, 1976); for culture, see Raymond Williams, *Culture and Society* (New York: Harper, 1966).

3. Eric R. Dodds, *The Greeks and the Irrational* (Berkeley: University of California Press, 1971), 187.

4. Tertullian, "The Prescriptions Against the Heretics," *Early Latin Theology*, tr. and ed. S. L. Greenslade (Philadelphia: Westminster, 1956), par. 7.

5. Cf. "The historian of philosophy can scarcely but be struck by the recurrence of certain positions, or at least certain attitudes of mind, in the history of philosophy; he will not find it hard to identify a good many of these general attitudes on the contemporary philosophical scene. If he is at all inclined to scepticism, he may well conclude that philosophy is nothing more than the sham-battle of systems of rationalizations, a clash of personalities masquerading as rational discussion." John Passmore, "The Idea of the History of Philosophy," *History and Theory*, Beiheft 5 (1965), 26.

6. Moritz Schlick, "The Future of Philosophy," *The Linguistic Turn*, ed. R. Rorty (Chicago: University of Chicago Press, 1967), 51.

7. Ludwig Wittgenstein, *Tractatus Logico-Philosophicus*, tr. D. F. Pears and B. F. McGuinness, (London: Routledge, 1961), 6.52.

8. I am aware of two historical roots of my notion of perennial arguments. One is the idea of *dialectic*. This is, of course, a notoriously imprecise term and it is very difficult to say just how my view fits into the dialectical tradition which ranges from Plato and Aristotle to Kant, Hegel, Marx, and contemporary dialectical materialism. I certainly deny that perennial arguments have an ontological ground; nor do I think that there is a steady progress towards some ultimate goal. And I do not claim that perennial arguments are superior, in some sense, to other arguments. How far this removes me from the dialectical tradition, I just do not know. I accept

Karl R. Popper's criticisms of the dialectical method in his classic "What is Dialectic?", *Conjectures and Refutations* (New York: Harper, 1968), 312–35. Yet I find myself in great sympathy with such dialectical works as Michael Oakeshott's "The Voice of Poetry in the Conversation of Mankind," *Rationalism in Politics* (London: Methuen, 1962), 197–247 and Nicholas Rescher's *Dialectics* (Albany: State University of New York Press, 1977) and his "On The Rationale of Philosophical Disagreement," *The Review of Metaphysics*, 32 (1978), 217–251. For an account of dialectic and a good bibliography, see Roland Hall, "Dialectic," *The Encyclopedia of Philosophy*, ed. P. Edwards (New York: Macmillan and Free Press, 1967), Vol. 2, 385–9.

The other historical connection is with the idea of *essentially contested concepts*. This is William B. Gallie's idea, see *Philosophy and the Historical Understanding*, Chapter 8, (London: Chatto and Windus, 1964). Gallie's idea is itself related to the notion of *open concepts* whose history includes Wittgenstein, Waismann, Stevenson, Hampshire, Hart, and Weitz. For an excellent account, development, and bibliography see Morris Weitz, *The Opening Mind*, Chapter Two, (Chicago: University of Chicago Press, 1977). My difficulty with this approach is that I do not know what concepts are; that, in any case, I am interested in arguments which can be true or false; and that I do not see how relativism can be avoided if the discussion is conducted in terms of concepts. Nevertheless, it is probaly true that the key terms in my perennial arguments are essentially contested concepts. It was Max Black who pointed me in the direction of perennial arguments from essentially contested concepts and it is to him that I owe the term.

Chapter Three

Problems

"Every philosophy, and especially philosophical 'school', is
liable to degenerate in such a way that its problems become
potentially indistinguishable from pseudoproblems, and its
cant, accordingly, practically indistinguishable from mean-
ingless babble. This ... is a consequence of philosophical
inbreeding. The degeneration of philosophical schools in its
turn is the consequence of the mistaken belief that one can
philosophize without having been compelled to philosophize *by
problems which arise outside philosophy.* ... Genuine
philosophical problems are always rooted in urgent problems
outside philosophy and they die if these roots decay."

KARL R. POPPER[1]

I. *Introduction*

In this chapter I shall continue to clarify the nature of perennial
arguments by showing what kind of ideals form their proper
subject-matter. The key to answering this question is the
recognition that the ideals I am interested in represent desirable
solutions of problems the holders of ideals have.

But just as there are very many different ideals, so also there
are very many different problems. In order to get clear about
perennial arguments, I shall also have to specify the nature of those
problems to which ideals constitute desirable solutions. In this
chapter I shall concentrate on problems, in the next on ideals.

The view of perennial arguments I propose, then, is that they
concern the ideals in accordance with which problems shared by
the participants can be solved. The impetus for participation is
provided by the need to solve the problems. The arguments are
conducted to determine which solution is the best. And what
qualifies as the best depends on the ideals or the interpretation of
the ideals which guide problem-solving. The most favorable
outcome of a perennial argument is that the participants agree
about having a problem in common and about it requiring a
solution. They engage in the perennial argument to choose the best
solution and that choice is made by coming to agree on an ideal or
on the interpretation of the ideal. This agreement provides a
standard by which the best solution can be chosen.

Both external and internal perennial arguments fit this pattern. In each case, the participants share a problem and they argue because they differ about the ideal in accordance with which the problem should be solved. If they disagree about which ideal should guide their choice, then their perennial argument is external. If they agree about the ideal, but disagree about its interpretation, then the perennial argument is internal.

The remaining two alternatives leave no scope for perennial argument. For if the participants agree about a problem and about the ideal in accordance with which it should be solved, then there is no need for a perennial argument, for they face a merely technical question. And if they fail to share a problem, then they cannot benefit from an argument about how best to solve it.

II. *Problems² and Theories*

The discussion will begin by considering problems, theories, and arguments in general and it will come to focus on perennial arguments, philosophical theories, and problems to which philosophical theories offer solutions. The view I aim to defend is that there is a special kind of problem which requires philosophical theories as its solution.

Theories are held against a background. The background may include beliefs, prejudices, expectations, other theories, value judgments, myths, rituals, practices, and countless other cultural phenomena. The background is the tradition or the way of life in which the argument occurs. One important feature of the background is a problem. Many things may count as problems. On the simplest level, a person may want to do something he regards as desirable, but means to do it are not available. For instance, he might wish to cure cancer, but is incapable of doing so. Or the problem may arise because surprises, anomalies, inexplicable events occur. The problematic nature of anomalies stems from the traditional assumptions and expectations that are part of the background. For an event is anomalous only if it contradicts previous standards of normalcy. Given our present thinking, speed greater than the speed of light, telephatic communication, the discovery of an insect species with intelligence comparable to ours would be anomalous occurrences. But problems may also be due to the discovery that the background comprises mutually exclusive elements. Theories, expectations, practices may be so related that adherence to one amounts to the repudiation of the other. The practice of Christianity may be incompatible with the practice of war; the ideal of mental health may conflict with the ideal of creativity; high living standards provided by efficiently organzied industrial societies may greatly diminish personal liberty. Problems occur in many ways and the different types of problems form an endless list.

Problems, however, do have a common feature: they stand in need of solution. The role of theories is to provide solutions. To understand a theory, therefore, is to understand also the problem to which it is a solution. The problem, the theory, and the solution provided by the theory jointly explain the point of holding the theory.

Theories solve problems by offering an imaginative account of the nature of things in the relevant domain. What prompts the adoption of a theory is the recognition that if things were as depicted, then what was previously problematic would no longer be so. Theories aim to reconcile the tradition and the anomaly; or they attempt to confront the problem by bringing out what is implicit in the tradition.

Problems show that our understanding of the world is deficient. We may want to do something, but given what we think we know, we cannot do it; or something happens which on our existing view should not or could not happen; or we may have ideals and the means we have for achieving them actually frustrate their realization. In all such cases, we need an explanation to reconcile what we take to be the case with what is the case. Theories offer these manifold reconciliations.

Problems constitute the fundamental link between theories and the world. Problems occur when people, as it were, bump into reality. Since the point of theories is to solve problems, naturally the ultimate test of their adequacy is whether or not problems are solved. A theory offering a possible solution is worthy of serious consideration; one providing a successful solution is worthy of acceptance.

The role of arguments in this context is to decide which theory presents a possible solution and to choose the best of all available solutions.

III. *Problems of Life and Problems of Reflection*

There is, however, a difficulty in this account. It might be argued against it that to judge a theory by determining whether or not it presents a possible solution to the problem that prompted it is hopelessly question-begging. For what counts as a problem depends on the theory. The existence of evil, for instance, is problematic only to someone who believes that there is a good God. Or, the accidental nature of some historical events is taken to require explanation only if it is supposed that there are historical laws. There are no problems in nature: problems occur when facts disappoint one's expectations. Expectations, as well as what is to count as fact, are shaped by the very theories whose acceptability one is endeavoring to determine. Problems, it may be argued, are parts of theories, and so theories should not be judged by their capacity to solve problems to which they themselves give rise.[3]

My reply to this objection is to distinguish different problem-areas and then show that within each of these areas human beings encounter the same problems regardless of what theories they hold. Of course, there are problems that could arise only against a specific theoretical background. The objection, however, rests on the mistaken assumption that all problems are theory-generated.

One way of classifying problem-areas is to divide them into problems concerning a person's response to nature or his physical environment, to humanity, including other people and society, and to himself.

Within each of these problem-areas there occur two kinds of problems. One of these people have merely in virtue of being human. Such problems are not the by-products of any particular theory. They occur because the species has evolved in a particular way and because the environment is what it is. I shall call these *problems of life*. If problems of life are not solved, the agent is damaged. The damage may be fatal, or merely destructive. At any rate, solving problems of life is required by what a person regards as his well-being. Problems of life are common to most members of the species, but their solutions are extremely varied. Because there are different and occasionally conflicting ways of dealing with them, it is necessary to choose between alternative solutions. Making such choices requires reflection, and this yields a second type of problem: *problems of reflection.* The fundamental problem of reflection is to find a method of choosing the most suitable of a number of ways of solving problems of life without actually trying out the rival solutions in practice. The point of reflection is to minimize the risks involved in acting inappropriately.

The first problem-area, the human response to nature, comprises problems of life having to do with the satisfaction of various physiological needs, health, shelter, and protection; the problem is to safeguard one's physical security and well-being. Evolution from primitivism affords the luxury of choosing between different solutions. The choice requires theoretical understanding, and science and technology are born of the need to choose well. The theoretical problems of science and technology, then, are the typical corresponding problems of reflection.

The second problem-area concerns one's relations with humanity, that is, with other people and society. These problems arise because man is a social being. The typical problems of life in this context have to do with one's attitude to family, strangers, friends, sex, authority, violence, and other social phenomena. The source of these problems is the inevitable conflict between the satisfaction of one's desires and their frustration dictated by the rules of whatever society one lives in. The associated problems of reflection are the theoretical problems of politics, morality, and the law.

The third problem-area has to do with people's attitudes to themselves. Put simply, it is about being happy; it concerns the pursuit of a rich and interesting internal life, self-knowledge, and self-acceptance. Characteristic problems of life in this area are the conflicts between long and short range satisfaction, the attitude to one's death, pain, suffering, and to one's physical and psychological limitations and capacities. The appropriate problems of reflection arise out of the need to imaginatively expand one's horizons so that new options may be discovered. It is in accordance with these that people shape themselves. And it is by comparing their own with other people's lives that they come to a better understanding of themselves. One important aspect of the humanities, art, and literature is that they are likely to be helpful in this endeavor.

Thus the objection noted before, that all problems are theory-generated, arises out of a failure to distinguish between problems of life and reflection. Problems of reflection are indeed theory-generated, but problems of life are not. Problems of reflection arise because problems of life have competing solutions. So while it is true that problems of reflection presuppose a theory, it is no less true that the theory is held because it is expected to provide solutions to problems of life. Theories presuppose problems of life. And we come by such problems and of the necessity of solving them in virtue of being human, and not because we are ensnared by this or that theory.[4]

Two points should be noted in this connection. The first is that provided only that a person recognizes something as presenting a problem to him, he must recognize it also as standing in need of a solution. But the solution need not be the removal of the problem. A person may regard his own want as needing to be unsatisfied, because it is unworthy, unimportant, or unwise. Or a person may come to think that allowing his own problem to persist will improve his character, make him a better person, redeem past sins, elicit pity, inflict deserved punishment, or allow concentration on more important things. Thus solution may come to doing nothing about the problem. Celibacy and fasting are solutions to the problems of sexual frustration and hunger. What the connection between problems and solutions requires is having to make a decision or formulate an attitude towards the problem. But the decision or the attitude need not dictate the removal of the problem.

The second point is a corollary of the first. The aim of problem-solving need not be physical survival. I am not suggesting that successful problem-solving is an inevitable biological imperative. There are many cases in which people solve their own problems in ways damaging to themselves. What guides problem-solving is a person's own judgment of what is in his interest. But, of course, he may err. For instance, someone may damage his body, because he believes that the flesh is an unworthy receptacle of his immortal soul. His problem-solving is guided by this belief. If, however, there is no such thing as the soul, he is simply mistaken. He did try to solve his problem in accordance with his belief, but the belief turned out to be false. It is understandable why he did it, even though he was mistaken in doing it.

The difficulty that besets much of the contemporary discussion about the rational evaluation of theories is that various evaluative standards offered all presuppose an already established theoretical framework. Those who are dubious of the possibility of rational evaluation acknowledge that what is claimed to be rational is indeed rational in a given framework, in logic, science, religion, or morality, and then go on to question the rationality of the framework. And, of course, so long as the standards offered are internal to one framework or another, their doubt cannot be removed. The merit of the proposed standard of solving problems of life is that with its help the critics' challenge can be met. A framework is rational, *inter alia*, if it contributes a possible solution to problems of life. Since problems of life are independent of theoretical frameworks, so is the standard based upon them. We shall return to a discussion of this standard in Chapter Seven.

IV. *Removable Problems and Enduring Problems*

There is a confusion about problems which stems from the assumption that if a problem is solved, then it ceases to exist. It follows from the assumption that nothing can count as a solution unless it leads to the disappearance of the problem it was meant to solve.

The root of this mistaken assumption is the unjustifiable extension of the model of the scientific problem-solving to problems of an entirely different kind. The model has the following features. We begin by encountering an intellectual or practical obstacle: we want to understand or do something, and we cannot. This is followed in cases of successful problem-solving by an explanation. The explanation enables us to understand or do what we previously did not understand or could not do. As a result, the obstacle is removed and thus the problem disappears. If a problem is seen as an obstacle, then it is solved only if the obstacle is removed. The consequence is that a theory cannot count as a successful solution of a problem unless it leads to the cessation of the problem it was meant to solve.

It is a mistake, however, to suppose that finding a solution to a problem of life or reflection necessarily implies that the problem has ceased to exist. Some problems endure, endlessly persist, and solving them consists in making a continued effort of coping. I shall call such problems *enduring*. Other problems are merely short-term obstacles and solving them does indeed result in their disappearance; these I shall call *removable*.

As an initial illustration of this distinction consider a man wanting to drive a nail into the wall. He may have the problem of not having a hammer and a nail. But once he finds them, he no longer has this kind of problem. Suppose, however, that he is also short-sighted and clumsy. These problems are enduring features in his life and he cannot make them disappear. He must learn to do as well as he can with these handicaps. Solution, in this case, consists in finding a way to live with problems. The solution is a *modus vivendi*.

Some problems endure because human beings and the world are what they are; it is not lack of effort, ignorance, or stupidity that makes them persist, but the scheme of things. Scaling a mountain, understanding a joke, proving a theorem, discovering the cause of an event, are problems only until a solution to them is found. But respecting other people's dignity, distributing permanently scarce resources, controlling one's temper, being objective, are not problems capable of removal. They endure because there is a conflict and the conflicting elements are not easily changed. Solution consists in developing a policy which minimizes the undesirable consequences of the conflict.

Consider, for example, the problem of what attitude a person should have towards his illness. If I find myself ill, my course of action is obvious. I consult a physician and do as he says. My problem is removable, provided my illness is not serious. But suppose that a person is frequently beset by illness and infirmity is a constant feature of his life. He, then, has to develop a policy. He may become closely attentive to his health, spend much of his life monitoring danger signals, and live a cautious, moderate life. Alternatively, he may try to ignore as much as possible his illness and endeavor to live as normally as he can. Or he may become resentful, bitter, and treat each symptom as yet another sign of the unfair scheme of things. The problem of what policy to develop and, once developed, to maintain it is an enduring problem.

The distinction between removable and enduring problems applies within the problem-areas I have discussed. For regardless of whether a person's problem arises in connection with his attitude to nature, humanity, or himself, the distinction between specific problems calling for specific responses and patterns of recurring problems calling for a policy of action persists.

The relation, however, between problems of life and reflection, on the one hand, and removable and enduring problems, on the other, is less clear. It will not do to identify problems of life with removable problems and problems of reflection with enduring problems. For many removable problems are problems of reflection and many problems of life are enduring problems. Testing a theory by experiment, proving guilt or innocence in a law court, interpreting the symbolism or allegory in a novel are problems of reflection, yet removable. On the other hand, one's attitude to sex, authority, family are problems of life, but also enduring problems.

Yet there is a relation between these two sets of problems. The difference between problems of life and reflection is that the former are necessarily nontheoretical, while the latter must occur against the background of a theory. What establishes the connection is not the logical necessity but the fact that removable problems are more frequently solvable without appealing to a theory, while the solution of enduring problems, having to do with a choice of policies, usually requires theoretical considerations. Hence it can be said that enduring problems tend to be problems of reflection, while problems of life tend to be removable.

The difficulty caused by the mistaken assumption that solving problems leads to the disappearance of the problems is that problem-solving comes to be regarded as a technological question. It is viewed as an exercise in removing obstacles from the way of doing what one wants. I have argued that while many problems are indeed solved in this way, not all are. And this has an important consequencce for my analysis of perennial arguments.

It is necessary for the favorable evaluation of a theory that it should offer a possible solution to the problem that prompted it. In the light of the previous discussion, problem-solving must be understood as including both removable and enduring problems. However, the prevailing view is that problem-solving must lead to the disappearance of the problem and thus only removable problems are recognized. And since by far the most effective way of solving removable problems is through science and technology, scientific understanding and technological skill have become the ideals of all problem-solving.[5]

This view is shared by many philosophers. Popper, for instance, writes, "[T]he natural sciences with their critical methods of problem-solving ... have represented for quite a long time our best efforts in problem-solving."[6] Kuhn, at least on this point, agrees: "To suppose ... that we possess a criteria of rationality which are independent of our understanding of the essentials of the scientific process is to open the door to cloud-cuckoo land."[7]

The result of regarding science as the paradigm of problem-solving is that nonscientific theories suffer in comparison with them. It is, of course, true that science is the best way of solving many removable problems. But nonscientific theories attempting to solve enduring problems should not be adversely judged just because they fail in this misguided comparison. The prevailing feeling of hopelessness in the face of enduring political, moral, and aesthetic problems is traceable to the belief that these problems are noncognitive, emotive, and unsolvable. And that belief comes from regarding science as *the* paradigm of problem-solving. While it is true that enduring moral, political, and aesthetic problems are not scientifically solvable, it is not true that they are not solvable.[8]

V. *Enduring Problems and Perennial Arguments*

Perennial arguments are prompted by enduring problems. The problems arise in all three of the problem-areas. Typical enduring problems in one's attitude to himself have to do with the meaning and purpose of one's life, the importance and attainability of self-knowledge and the possibility and method of forming and shaping oneself. Some of the enduring problems which arise in one's relation to humanity are the nature of one's responsibility to and for others, one's attitude to authority, the resolution of inevitable conflicts between altruism and self-interest, and the extent of one's allegiance owed to institutions, friends, one's country. Characteristic enduring problems connected with the relation between a person and nature are whether one should attempt to live in harmony with or make use of his environment, or whether nature is properly viewed as hostile, benevolent, or indifferent.

Consider, for instance, the perennial argument about morality. To say that one should treat one's fellow men in a moral way represents a solution to the problem of what attitude one should have to others. But as it stands, it is hopelessly vague and general. The variations on this theme present different interpretations of the ideal represented by morality: teleological, deontological, and self-realizationist accounts pretty well exhaust the options. Of course, further options appear within each of these interpretations. The limits of morality, however, are virtually defined by fundamental questions about the object of morality, whether it is to make oneself a better person or to act altruistically, or about the grounds of moral judgments, whether it is conformity to rules or the pursuit of some goal.

There are no general answers to these questions. For the answer that one can reasonably accept seems to vary with the situation in which the question is posed. In a pure laissez-faire economy, altruism should be stressed; in times of revolutionary changes, emphasizing the importance of moral rules against the fervid pursuit of ideals is likely to serve the ideal implicit in morality. But in a static, ritualistic society, reminding moral agents of the ideals of moral behavior may redress the balance; just as in a tightly organized political system, the claims of individuality should be stressed.

This point can be generalized. It is simply a fact of life that one has to have some attitude toward oneself, humanity, and nature.

Perennial arguments concern the question of what these attitudes should be. The difficulty is that while one can count on the persistence of enduring problems, the choice of policy depends on innumerable factors. The state of scientific knowledge, technological sophistication, historical perspective, the prevailing political situation, the state of the economy, international relations, and many other considerations may all influence the outcome of the argument. And if one faction succeeds in presenting its side victoriously, the argument is only temporarily resolved. For the relevant considerations will change and the merits of competing claims will be pressed again. This is why perennial arguments are recurrent.

The reason why the existence of perennial arguments is in everybody's interest is that it lessens the chances of establishing an orthodoxy. The reason why an orthodoxy should not be established is that problem-situations continually change. No doubt, what now has a claim to orthodoxy was once a fresh and new solution. But its attaining the status of unquestioned authority prevents the search for new solutions to meet changing problem-situations. Since enduring problems are encountered by all human beings, the persistence of challenges presented by perennial arguments is a necesary antidote to dogmatism, sloth, and the hardening of intellectual arteries.

The enduring problems I have mentioned, and the many more I have not, call for solutions. But each problem has many solutions, for there are very many policies that may be reasonably advocated as representing ways of coping. Philosophical theories are reasoned and systematic explanations and defences of the various policies. Perennial arguments occur because the merits of conflicting philosophical theories, representing alternative policies of coping with enduring problems, must be rationally judged. The question of how this judgment can be made is, of course, the same as asking about the rationality of perennial arguments. It is now possible to give the beginning of an answer, which will be developed in Part III of the book.

First, we have to settle what counts as a contestant in a perennial argument and then to decide which is the best contestant. The first involves appeal to tradition. The second depends upon the comparative problem-solving capacity of the competing approaches.

The answer to the question of what counts as a contestant is that if a particular approach to the realization of an ideal falls within the domain upon whose general description the contestants agree, and if the approach is meant as a solution of the enduring problem that prompted the debate, then the approach in question is a legitimate contender in a perennial argument.

Tradition enters into this decision-procedure because only by examining it can one discover what the problem is that forms the background of various approaches in perennial arguments. It must be asked: in response to what difficulty, in order to meet what challenge, did a particular contestant abandon the options that were available to him and come to propose a new approach? Only by answering this question can one understand the point or significance of a particular approach. In addition, tradition must figure in proposing and testing the adequacy of the general description that identifies the domain of specific perennial arguments. Such descriptions are adequate only if they do justice to the historical sample. If obvious candidates are excluded or dubious ones are included, then the general description is faulty. But whether or not this is so can be decided only by being acquainted with obvious and dubious cases, that is, with the tradition.

The attempt to understand perennial arguments merely by examining the contemporary state of the debate and by offering a general description of the domain on that basis dooms one's conclusions to absurdity. For it would be naive to suppose that art, rationality, science, and logic, for instance, can occupy only the domain that we in the second half of the twentieth century assign to them.

Thus my answer to the first question posed above is that exclusion from and inclusion into the field of *bona fide* contestants in perennial arguments depend on an appeal to tradition. This appeal determines whether or not the contestants share a problem and a domain.

The second question concerns the possibility of finding a rational method by which the best approach can be selected from the field of *bona fide* contestants. Part of the general principle for rationally settling perennial arguments is that that approach should prevail which is most likely to lead to the solution of the enduring problem that prompted the debate. The reason why agreement about the resolution of the argument is possible is that participants are engaged in the debate because they share a problem; it is in their interest to accept the solution of what they regard as their problem.

Let us again consider arguments about democracy. For them to qualify as perennial arguments the participants must first agree in quite general terms about what democracy is. The participants are likely to endorse some statement such as that democracy is the form of government in which principal authority rests with the people and they exercise that authority directly or through a representative body. Additional common ground is provided by the participant's recognition that society must be organized in some way and that this requires that some group or person should have ultimate authority. The debate starts either by various factions stressing such different forms of government as democracy, oligarchy, or monarchy, or by agreeing about the merits of one, say of democracy, and dispute the importance to democracy of such elements as universal franchise, rule of law, equality, and so on. Each faction claims that its own solution represents the best solution of the underlying enduring problem. The argument is about how to solve the problem which the participants share. It is this community of interests that makes perennial arguments rationally solvable.

If the participants recognize a common enduring problem and they agree about the general description of particular policies, then their disagreements can be rationally settled. For it is in their own interest to solve their problems as well as possible. If, however, they do not share a problem, or fail to agree in their general descriptions, then they are not engaged in a perennial argument.

The rationality of perennial arguments depends upon the solution of enduring problems. But since circumstances change, there can be no general solution. It would be a great mistake, however, to conclude from the lack of general solutions that there is here also a lack of rationality. That conclusion follows in the case of removable problems; for in science a solved problem ceases to be a problem. But insofar as philosophical arguments are perennial, they deal with problems that need to be solved again and again.

VI. *Conclusion*

In this chapter the clarification of perennial arguments was taken a step further. Perennial arguments are bridges between a problem and an ideal in accordance with which the problem should be solved. I have concentrated on the nature of problems here, but the discussion is not complete until ideals also are considered in the next chapter.

Some of the ill-repute surrounding perennial arguments is due to the failure to distinguish between removable and enduring problems. Removable problems disappear if a solution to them is found. Science and technology are the best methods for dealing with many such problems. But it is a mistake to suppose that all problems are removable and consequently it is a mistake to suppose that science and technology are the best methods for dealing with all problems. Enduring problems are persistent features of human life and they stem from the need to have some attitude toward oneself, others and society, and nature. The solution of these problems does not lead to their disappearance; solutions consist in having found ways of coping with the problem, in having developed a policy. Philosophical theories champion various solutions and perennial arguments are conducted to decide between them.

The enduring problems whose solution is the purpose of perennial arguments may be problems of life or problems of reflection. That is, these persistent pressures demanding a policy to cope with them may originate in the context of a theoretical way of looking at the world or they may stem from the dictates of human nature and the world. In the former case, they are problems of reflection, in the latter, problems of life. Problems of reflection arise because problems of life are frequently solved by the development of theories which explain the feature of the world that gives rise to problems of life; problems of reflection emerge in the context of these theories. Thus genuine problems of reflection are always traceable to some non-theoretical problem-situation. So regardless of whether enduring problems are problems of reflection or problems of life, they owe their existence and persistence to the facts that human beings and the world are what they are. These facts impose their burden upon us and the task of perennial arguments is to decide between various candidates for easing this burden. The burden cannot be removed, for carrying it is a condition of life, but it can be eased. And that is what perennial arguments aim to do.

Perennial arguments, however, do more than provide intellectual succour. They are necessary components in forming a rationally justified worldview. Such a worldview is composed of philosophical theories which offer solutions to our problems. Perennial arguments provide a way of deciding between the claims of competing philosophical theories. The decision rests, in part, on the success with which the theory solves the problem which prompted it. The

other part concerns the ideal in accordance with which the problem
is to be solved.

NOTES

1. Karl R. Popper, "The Nature of Philosophical Problems and Their Roots in
Science," *Conjectures and Refutations* (New York: Harper, 1968), 71–2.
2. The literature on problems is meagre. John Dewey, *Logic: The Theory of
Inquiry* (New York: Holt, 1938), attributes central importance to problem-solving,
but his discussion is imprecise, verbose, and insufficiently argued. For a sympathetic
account, see Kai Nielsen, "Dewey's Conception of Philosophy", *The Massachusetts
Review*, 2 (1960), 110–134. Robin G. Collingwood's logic of questions and answers
does not discuss problems under that label, but his questions bear more than a
superficial resemblance to what I mean by problems; see *An Essay on Metaphysics*
(Oxford: Clarendon, 1962), Part I, and *An Autobiography* (Oxford: Clarendon,
1939), Chapter Five. Popper and his followers explicitly discuss the importance of
problem-solving to scientific inquiry. But they do not regard problem-solving as a
context-independent standard of justification, as I do; see *Conjectures and
Refutations, op. cit.*, Essays 1, 2, 3, and 10; also Joseph Agassi, "The Nature of
Scientific Problems and Their Roots in Metaphysics," *The Critical Approach*, ed.
M. Bunge (New York: Macmillan, 1964), and Imre Lakatos, "Falsification and the
Methodology of Scientific Research Programmes," *Criticism and the Growth of
Knowledge*, eds. I. Lakatos and A. Musgrave (Cambridge: Cambridge University
Press, 1970). Henry W. Johnstone, Jr. in *Philosophy and Argument* (University
Park: Pennsylvania State University Press, 1959), 35–9, argues that philosophical
arguments are understandable only against the background of problems which they
intend to solve. But from this he draws the relativistic conclusion which it is my
central purpose to refute. Nicholas Rescher's *Methodological Pragmatism* (Oxford:
Blackwell, 1977), is very close in its orientation to my own, but it does not treat
problem-solving as a standard of justification. Larry Laudan's *Progress and Its
Problems* (Berkeley: University of California Press, 1977), does recognize the
central role of problem-solving in epistemology. My only reservation about this
splendid book is that it does not consider what I take to be a crucial question:
whether problems can occur outside of theories.
3. Cf. "Problems arise only in the context of presuppositions; it is because some
phenomena or situations or concepts are viewed in the context of a particular set of
already accepted beliefs that they become problematic." Harold I. Brown, "Problem
Changes in Science and Philosophy," *Metaphilosophy*, 6 (1975), 177–92; the
quotation comes from 177.
4. The relation between problems of life, theories, and problems of reflection is in
some ways very much like Popper's frequently used schema of beginning with
problems, proceeding to tentative solutions, eliminating error, and encountering a
new problem that has emerged in the process. See, for instance, his "Epistemology
Without a Knowing Subject," *Objective Knowledge* (Oxford: Clarendon, 1972),
119. My main disagreement with Popper is that I believe that problems of life are
not theory-generated, whereas Popper would deny, I think, that there are any such
problems. Cf. "But the problem 'Which comes first, the problem or the theory?' is
not easily solved. ... *the first theories—that is, the first tentative solutions of
problems—and the first problems must somehow have arisen together.*" Karl R.
Popper, *Unending Quest* (La Salle, Ill.: Open Court, 1976), 133.
5. Cf. "In science problems can be solved and done with, but in philosophy they
cannot, and to bring philosophy in line with science in this respect, it has to be

assumed that most of its problems never really existed." George R. G. Mure, *Retreat from Truth,* (Oxford: Blackwell, 1958), 250.

6. Popper, "A Realist View of Logic, Physics, and History," *Objective Knowledge, op. cit.*

7. Thomas S. Kuhn, "Reflections on My Critics," *Criticism and the Growth of Knowledge, op. cit.*, 264.

8. Jose Ortega y Gasset in *What is Philosophy?* (New York: Norton, 1960), Chapter Four, talks about the connection between problems and philosophy. He distinguishes between scientific and philosophical problems, calls scientific problems solvable, and regards philosophical problems as deeper. I am sympathetic to what I can understand of his remarks, but, as is usually the case with Ortega, they are more suggestive than developed.

Chapter Four

Ideals

"The discussions of every age are filled with the issues on which the leading schools of thought differ. But the general intellectual atmosphere of the time is always determined by the views on which the opposing schools agree. They become the unsposken presuppositions of all thought, the common and unquestioningly accepted foundations on which all discussion proceeds."

FRIEDRICH A. HAYEK[1]

I. *Introduction*

One conclusion of Chapter Two has been that ideals are the subject-matters of external and internal perennial arguments. Ideals are valued human goals whose achievement is the purpose of much of human behavior. Aesthetic sensitivity, logical consistency, morality, freedom, scientific and historical understanding, religiosity, rationality, culture, democracy, education, and knowledge are some examples of ideals. People value their ideals and think of them as good. But they may be mistaken. For my purposes, what is essential to ideals is that they should be valued goals, not that the valuation be justified. The purpose of this chapter is to enlarge upon this understanding of ideals.

II. *A Description of Ideals*[2]

The subject-matters of perennial arguments are ideals themselves and not the forms in which they are exemplified. Perennial arguments are about the nature of morality, freedom, or democracy and not about the morality of an act, the freedom of a society, or about whether a particular institution is democratic. Nevertheless, the form in which ideals occur in inseparable from the conduct of perenial argumentation, for even though the arguments concern the ideals themselves, the ideals must be exemplified in some form or another.

For those who accept an ideal, its exemplifications count as models, paradigms, or paragons. The exemplification may be the behavior of a real or fictional person; or it may be the historical or imaginative reconstruction of a society, of an approach or a way of looking at things; or the ideal may be exemplified in signal artistic or intellectual achievements. Scientific understanding, for instance, is exemplified in the great works of Galileo, Newton, Darwin, and Crick and Watson; democracy by the form of government in Periclean Athens and by the conduct of a New England town meeting; rationality by Robinson Crusoe's behavior after he reached his island and by Spinoza's behavior almost always.

Perennial arguments, however, do not concern the merits of these cases as such, but their merits only insofar as they render the ideals represented by them public, concrete, discussible. So ideals in my sense are not transcendental entities, but human goals whose concrete expressions may be more or less satisfactory. There is nothing arcane, metaphysical, or platonic about ideals. They are readily inspectible in the form of actual, symbolic, or historical representations. Given my usage, nothing qualifies as an ideal which lacks this feature. Thus universal love, mystical union with the absolute, redemption, and grace may be valued human goals, but they are not ideals in my sense.

An additional feature that must be possessed by something to qualify as an ideal is that it must be significant. An ideal is significant if it is a possible solution of an enduring problem and if it is publicly recognized as such. What this requirement conveys is that the ideals which form the subject-matter of perennial arguments are not trivial, personal, or idiosyncratic; they are important in that they represent available options among which people in a given intellectual epoch must choose. The necessity of choice is dictated by the pressing enduring problems which require the adoption of a policy for coping with them. The significance of ideals consists in the generally shared knowledge that the cluster of prevalent ideals represents a range of possible goals toward which the contemplated policies must aim.

The stock of significant ideals changes from context to context. A developing or disintegrating society is characterized by many external perennial arguments about ideals. These debates are about the choice of ideals which should guide policies for solving enduring problems. This, of course, indicates a lack of fundamental agreement about the most basic assumptions. A newly formed nation may debate in this way the form of government it should adopt. Or an intellectual discipline of uncertain orientation may be beset by doubts about the direction of its development. For instance, it is a fundamental problem for psychoanalysis whether it should be guided by the objective, rigorous scientific ideal of search for knowledge or by the therapeutic moral one of helping the afflicted.

On the other hand, homogeneous and robust societies are often preoccupied with internal perennial arguments about mutually shared ideals. Their debates concern the question of how to interpret the ideals which are generally accepted. Thus in a democratic society there may be a debate about the extent to which democracy requires the liberty as opposed to the equality of its citizens. Or in an established discipline, like history, practitioners might agree in their search for knowledge as their ideal and be deeply divided over the question of whether their inquiries should be guided by scientific precision requiring quantitative statistical analysis or by a humanistic aspiration requiring a narrative technique.

As I read Hayek in the motto of this chapter, a society is characterized by the kinds of fundamental debates it has and also by the ones it does not have. That certain ideals are unquestioned is just as important to understanding the climate of thought as the fact that some are passionately debated.

The point I want to stress about the notion of ideal I am developing is that ideals are generally shared because they are in the public domain and because they represent solutions to enduring problems that are generally recognized at least as problems. This requirement excludes a large number of valued goals from the ranks of ideals. It certainly excludes private aspirations. Thus someone wishing to become the same sort of person as his grandfather was is not pursuing an ideal in my sense. Nor are generally recognized good ends ideals unless they represent possible solutions to enduring problems. Winning the Rose Bowl Game, breaking the world record in the 1-mile run, building the tallest structure in the world, participating in an immortal musical performance may all be ideals in some sense of the word, but not in mine. For though these are worthy aspirations, they are not solutions of enduring problems.

But it is not enough for ideals to be possible solutions of enduring problems: the problems must also be generally recognized at the very least as problems. Now general recognition is an imprecise notion. I do not mean by it that everybody must share the recognition; nor do I mean that it is sufficient if only members of a small group think of an ideal this way. In most societies there is an enlightened public opinion, it is formed by the opinions of the moderately learned, literate, and thoughtful members. By general recognition I mean recognition by this group.

Some illustrations of what I mean by debates about ideals are the current internal perennial arguments about the importance of sex to morality, the claims of freedom as opposed to equality in interpreting the ideal of democracy; and the external perennial arguments about whether religiosity is an ideal capable of solving any enduring problems, or the question of whether the ideal represented by the law should or can take precedence over the ideal of morality.

If something is generally recognized as a possible solution of an enduring problem, then it is significant; significance is a necessary condition of being an ideal. It has, however, little to do with truth. Tyranny and democracy, racial superiority and equality, scientific understanding and religiosity may all function as ideals, for they may be generally thought to represent possible solutions to enduring problems. It is not part of being an ideal that people who accept it should be right.

The next requirement is that the exemplifications of ideals must be internally complex. By this I mean that the exemplifications must consist of many elements some of which play an essential role in exemplifying the ideal. An element contributes to internal complexity if without it the particular exemplification would fail to exemplify. So internal complexity is due to necessary and not merely to accidental elements.

As an illustration, consider behavior exemplifying rationality. Some necessary elements of such behavior are that the agent should believe that he is not acting on false beliefs; that he should expect the activity to lead to the goal whose achievement is the aim of the performance; that the behavior should be consistent in that part of the performance should not make the performance of other parts impossible or futile; that the agent should have some ground for the belief that the activity will lead to its goal; and so on.

This is not yet a sufficiently precise account of internal complexity, because there are an untold number of elements necessarily involved in the performance of any activity. For instance, if the agent did not breathe, or if he did not have a head, or if the solar system did not exist, then the activity could not be performed. So additional restrictions are required on what is to count as an element contributing to internal complexity; these will be discussed shortly.

The normative character of the exemplifications of ideals is due to the totality of the relevant elements. These elements combine to form the exemplification of an ideal. Thus it is important not to confuse the recognition of the contribution made by an element with the judgment about the value of the exemplifications as a whole. Such confusion results in common errors like the equation of being logical with rationality, equality with democracy, or feelingfulness with aesthetic sensibility.

The importance of the elements in an internally complex exemplification is variously assessable. Participants in perennial arguments usually agree about what elements are necessary, their disagreements then concern the importance of particular elements to the pursuit of the ideal.

As an illustration, consider again rational behavior. Nobody is likely to deny that in normal circumstances attention to truth, success in action, conformity to logic, consideration of available evidence, are essential components of rational behavior. But it is by no means obvious that rational agents give equal weight to these elements. For instance, new evidence may indicate that what everybody has accepted for a long time is in fact dubious. In this sort of situation, some people may opt for revising their beliefs, while others may attempt to discredit the new evidence. When tradition and innovation, rules and practice, common sense and theory conflict, people genuinely devoted to rationality may assess the situation differently. Their different assessments are not properly attributable to ignorance of the competing views; they disagree because they prefer their own hierarchical ranking of the elements over the rankings of others.

The recognition of the internal complexity and various assessability of elements in ideals is a key to understanding perennial arguments. It will be recalled that in Chapter Two I argued that perennial arguments are neither verbal nor scientific, but arguments concerning interpretation. This left us with two questions: the first was about the nature of these supposed disputes of interpretation, and the second was about what makes them rational. The answer to the second question must still be postponed. Internal complexity and various assessability, however, make it possible to say a little more about this matter of arguments about interpretation.

The situation of participants in a perennial argument is that they face a problem with which they must cope. The problem is persistent; it is not open to a solution which would make it cease to be a problem; it stems from the unalterable facts of life; and unless it is solved all participants will suffer. Some typical problems of this kind are what form of government a society should have, how the environment should be treated, what written and unwritten rules should guide people's relation with each other, and what attitude people should have toward themselves. Solving these problems consists in developing a policy for coping with them. And the policy chosen should reflect the ideals people have about government, law and morality, nature, and the pursuit of happiness. But these ideals are internally complex, because they are composed of many elements, and the respective contributions made by different necessary elements are variously assessable. Perennial arguments concern themselves with the assessment of the contribution made by these many elements, and in this way concern the interpretation of ideals.

Thus if the perennial argument is internal it might be about the question of whether liberty or equality is more important to a democratic society; or it might deal with the problem of whether the impartial application of rules, altruism, or self-improvement is the dominant feature of morality; or it might center on having to decide whether a thorough liberal education, spontaneity, or a sterling character is the primary requirement of personal happiness. And if the perennial argument is external and indicates disagreement about the worth of the ideal itself, then understanding the nature of the ideal is no less important.

It is in this way that the requirements of the internal complexity and the various assessability of ideals explain why perennial arguments occur, how they are about interpetation, and why they are important.

Another noteworthy feature of ideals which follows from their various assessability is their openness. To illustrate the importance of openness, consider an activity, such as tasting, which is not internally complex, but simple: there are not many ways of doing it. It can be done only by bringing the stuff in contact with one's tongue. There are many ways of being rational or moral, but the ways in which a person can skip a stream, clap his hands, or scratch his nose are severely limited. The result is that the chances of adjusting a simple activity, object, or institution to changing situations are very much poorer than the chances of modifying an internally complex one.

Modification becomes possible when the various elements can be ranked in different hierarchies. Internal complexity and various assessability of the elements guarantee the openness of the relevant ideals, and their openness makes them modifiable. The value of modifiability is that if one fails to achieve the ideal in one way, then he can try again in another. Part of the importance of perennial arguments is that they concern this question of how the pursuit of ideals should be modified to fit changing circumstances.

Stressing the openness and modifiability of ideals goes against a certain philosophical outlook. One assumption underlying it is that philosophy views the scheme of things *sub specie aeternitatis*: under the aspect of eternity. Disciplines with more temporal or empirical aspiration may and should try to understand things as they are affected by causes and as they cause effects. But there is an ultimate, eternal, unchanging aspect to things, be that ontological or conceptual, and it is the task of philosophy to concentrate on it. A modifiable ideal, from this point of view, does not deserve philosophical attention, for this very feature indicates its shallowness and superficiality.

The first response to this criticism should be to identify it for what it is: Platonism, that is, a particular philosophical outlook. Philosophers frequently succumb to the temptation of equating philosophy with their particular outlooks. This longstanding rhetorical device enables its practitioners to escape fundamental criticism. For if one's outlook *is* what philosophy is, then criticisms from other points of view can be safely disregarded as non-philosophical and hence philosophically irrelevant.

But one's view of philosophy should be sufficiently liberal to include the history of the subject. And the conception of ideals as open and modifiable—the eudaimonistic one stemming from Protagoras and Aristotle—has as good a pedigree as the opposing Platonic conception. So I am justified in continuing to concentrate on ideals in my sense. I am not offering an account of philosophy which excludes anything from the subject on *a priori* grounds. My strategy is to concentrate on one, albeit central, kind of philosophical argument, try to describe it, show how it can be rationally settled, and explain why it is important. Naturally, this enterprise is compatible with the existence of other kinds of philosophical arguments.

Ideals, in my sense, are vague and general descriptions of desirable goals. These may be exemplified in societies, institutions, practices, mental states, or conditions of life. What makes them desirable is that they are seen by their champions as the goals to which available solutions of enduring problems should aim. The solutions are policies and the policies must fit the changing circumstances as well as the protean forms in which enduring problems manifest themselves.

For instance, the acceptance of the ideal of freedom does not provide one with any particular policy of action. One can be committed to maximizing freedom, but this comes to different things in different contexts. Freedom may be to be free from slavery, feudal bonds, exploitation, censorship, moral restraints, or social convention; or it may be to be free to cause harm to oneself, to sell the land one owns, to outrage one's neighbors, or to worship strange gods or none at all. If freedom were not an internally complex, variously assessable, open, and modifiable ideal, it could not be adapted to changing circumstances. If it did not include the elements of negative and positive freedom, of freedom from and freedom to, of freedom of conscience, expression, movement, or personal and political freedom, if freedom were defined as one rigid, specific thing, then the admittedly vague and general ideal of placing as few restraints on a person as possible would be destroyed. It is the vagueness and the generality of the ideal which makes its survival possible. And it is the removal of vagueness and generality in particular situations which is the unending task of perennial arguments. Making the ideal precise and developing a policy for applying it to particular situations is possible, however, only if the different elements can be given different weight. In wartime, freedom of conscience may be more important than freedom of movement; in a feudal society, the importance of freedom of movement outweighs freedom of speech; in a liberal society freedom from slavery need not be stressed, but the freedom to harm oneself may have to be. The features of openness and modifiability are the part of my account of ideals which allow for these possibilities.[3]

III. *Ideals and Presuppositions*

We have seen that some elements are essential to the various assessment of internally complex ideals. The present discussion will concentrate on these elements, and I shall call them presuppositions. Presuppositions are fundamental theoretical assumptions intrinsic to ideals.

By a presupposition being fundamental I mean that to abandon it would be tantamount to the abandonment of the ideal. For instance, it is fundamental to the rationality of believing that something is so that a person should not think that his belief is false. While it is not fundamental that the belief should be experimentally verifiable. A fundamental feature of the morality of an action is that no matter who performs it, the appraisal of the action should not change. But that an agent performs an action with the hope of benefiting mankind is not fundamental to its morality.

Another part of what I mean by the fundamentality of presuppositions is that they cannot be justified with reference to the ideal in which they are involved. Presuppositions are fundamental in that they are intrinsic and not instrumental to the ideal. For example, in normal circumstances, logical consistency is fundamental to the rationality of a belief. If someone were to demand a justification for logical consistency, it would not be a proper rejoinder that one should be logically consistent because that leads to rationality. Logical consistency is intrinsic to rationality and not a device for bringing it about. The justification of logical consistency may be self-interest or the incoherence of its supposed unjustifiability. But one cannot appeal here to rationality for justification, if question-begging is to be avoided.

Thus a presupposition is fundamental if it must be justified independently of the ideal to which it is intrinsic, and if abandoning it would require abandoning the ideal along with it.

Presuppositions are not only fundamental but also theoretical assumptions implicit in the ideal. They are theoretical in contrast with psychological, sociological, or political assumptions which may also be implicit in ideals. Logical consistency, truth-directedness, consideration of available evidence are theoretical presuppositions of rationality. That one should consider beliefs calmly and not in anger, if he wants to be rational, is a psychological assumption; that nonauthoritarian social institutions and the disappearance of religious belief are likely to favor rationality are sociological assumptions; that the spread of rationality is coextensive with the spread of democracy is a political assumption. Non-theoretical assumptions implicit in ideals change with people, societies, and political ideologies. Theoretical assumptions, however, constitute the hard core which, if changed, would radically alter the ideal. The justification of the changing nontheoretical assumptions implicit in ideals is pragmatic: if you accept, for instance, the ideal of rationality, then be calm and ready to question authority, and support democratic institutions. The justification of theoretical assumptions, on the other hand, must be independent of the ideal. What such justification could be I shall discuss in the next part of the book.

To say that these presuppositions are fundamental and theoretical is to say something about their form; but what about their content? What sorts of things are fundamentally and theoretically assumed by ideals? Such assumptions, of course, vary with ideals, but a classification of at least some of them is possible. One kind of assumption has to do with the method that is to be followed if the ideal is to be achieved. Thus it is intrinsic to rationality that logical rules be observed; it is constitutive of scientific understanding that theories be subjected to observational testing; it is essential to democracy that there be a mechanism through which people can express their opinions. Another kind of assumption concerns the fundamental distinctions implicit in ideals. These distinctions help to stake out the domain within which the ideal can be employed and they help also to chart the internal outlines of its employment. The distinctions between fact and value, act and agent, rule and goal, motive and consequence are basic to morality, the distinctions between premise and conclusion, axiom and inference, conjunction and negation are constitutive of logical consistency; while the distinctions between confirmation and falsification, certainty and doubt, necessity and contingency are fundamental to knowledge. Yet a third kind of assumption concerns the values implicit in ideals: for logical consistency, it is the valid-invalid distinction; for knowledge, it is the contrast between truth and falsehood; for morality it concerns good and bad or right and wrong; for rationality it is the reasonable and warranted *versus* the unreasonable and dubious. The last kind of assumption I shall mention concerns the existence of the kinds of things to which the ideal applies. Thus the ideal of knowledge assumes the existence of facts, scientific understanding of the world, rationality of people, beliefs, and actions, aesthetic sensibility of some medium of experience. What is assumed is not that these things exist but only that the exemplifications of the relevant ideals is possible only if they exist.

These four kinds of assumptions—methodological, classificatory, axiological, and existential—which I claim are implicit in ideals are not supposed to comprise a complete list. Nor do I claim that each ideal has implicit in it all possible kinds of assumptions. I present the assumptions only to elucidate further the notion of presuppositions.

In the discussion of various assessability I noted that perennial arguments are about the hierarchical ranking of necessary elements in an internally complex exemplification of an ideal. As it was observed, however, perennial arguments do not concern all the necessary elements. It is for instance a necessary element in perennial arguments about morality that there be moral agents, but perennial arguments about morality are never about the existence of moral agents. In the light of the foregoing discussion about presuppositions, I can now distinguish between the necessary elements which are subject to perennial argumentation and those which are not. The perennially debated necessary elements are presuppositions. The importance of these arguments is that the realization of the ideal depends partly upon their outcome. In a typical internal perennial argument the participants share the ideal, they agree about its presuppositions, but they disagree about the stress that should be placed upon the various presuppositions in attempting to achieve the ideal. External perennial arguments, on the other hand, may concern the identity of the presuppositions supposedly intrinsic to ideals.[4]

IV. *Conclusion*

In this chapter the connection between enduring problems, policies for solving them, and the ideals prescribing particular policies has been further elucidated. The importance of understanding these connections is that they explain the nature of perennial arguments.

My concern in this chapter was with ideals. The requirements which must be met by ideals are that they must be goals valued by those who accept them; ideals must be public, and they are rendered so through their exemplifications; they must be significant, that is, be possible solutions of enduring problems and be generally recognized as such; they must be internally complex, variously assessable, open, and modifiable; and lastly, the essential elements whose internal complexity renders them variously assessable and modifiable are presuppositions; presuppositions are fundamental theoretical assumptions intrinsic to ideals.

This characterization describes ideals. The discussion, however, is not complete until the question of how ideals can be justified is also answered. For the rationality of perennial arguments is intimately tied to the justifiability of ideals. Ideals, after all, prescribe the selection of policies for solving enduring problems. The rationality of these solutions depends on the possibility of justifying the prescriptions which prompted them. I shall turn to this task in the next part of the book.

IDEALS 57

NOTES

1. Friedrich A. Hayek, *The Counter-Revolution of Science* (Glencoe: Free Press, 1952), 191.

2. My discussion of ideals and their relation to perennial arguments is fundamentally influenced by William B. Gallie's discovery and discussion of essentially contested concepts. See his *Philosophy and the Historical Understanding* (London: Chatto and Windus, 1964), Chapter Eight. In my own "Essentially Contested Concepts: A Reconsideration," *Philosophy and Rhetoric*, 10 (1977), 71–89, I try to say why I think that Gallie's treatment is faulty. In any case, my ideals are very close to essentially contested concepts. The main difference between them is that I identify the internally complex elements of ideals with presuppositions and argue, although only in Chapter Eight, that through presuppositions ideals can be rationally justified. Gallie, it seems to me, cannot avoid relativism. My ideals are also related to open concepts, see Morris Weitz, *The Opening Mind* (Chicago: University of Chicago Press, 1977). I differ from Weitz because he thinks open concepts need not be normative, while my ideals necessarily are; he is interested in the way open concepts are used, I am interested in the rational evaluation of arguments, especially of perennial arguments, about them; he thinks that it is concepts which are open, I think that, while ideals are variously assessable, it is perennial arguments that are open. Yet our concerns are quite similar, even to the point of terminology: Weitz, for instance, discusses the perennial flexibility and perennial debatability of open concepts.

3. The view I here advocate is in some ways similar to what has been called Fictionalism. The origin of it is traceable to Kant's *Critique of Pure Reason*, especially to the "Appendix to the Transcendental Dialectic" and to the "Transcendental Doctrine of Elements." The ideas implicit in Kant have been developed by Friedrich A. Lange, *History of Materialism and Critique of Its Present Significance* (London: Macmillan, 1879), tr. E. C. Thomas, and by Hans Vaihinger, *The Philosophy of 'As If'* (London: Routledge, 1924), tr. C. K. Ogden. Traces of it can also be found in Bentham's theory of fictions, see Clifford K. Ogden, *Bentham's Theory of Fiction* (New York: Harcourt, 1932). What I call ideals resemble what in this tradition are called fictions. The resemblance, however, is only partial, for fictions are known to be false and have only heuristic significance. Ideals, on the other hand, incorporate factual assumptions whose truth is necessary for their justification; I shall discuss this in Chapter Eight.

4. My discussion of presuppositions is indebted to Robin G. Collingwood's *An Essay on Metaphysics* (Oxford: Clarendon, 1962); in my *A Justification of Rationality* (Albany: State University of New York Press, 1976), Chapter Thirteen, I explain both my indebtedness to and criticisms of Collingwood's theory. It will suffice to say here that I reject the relativism implicit in Collingwood's theory. The central idea in my discussion of how ideals can be rationally justified through their presuppositions has been very suggestively explored by James R. Flynn, "The Realm of the Moral," *American Philosophical Quarterly*, 13 (1976), 273–86.

Chapter Five

Worldviews and Wisdom

"There is a certain job which the philosophical teacher is paid to do, a certain sort of intellectual good which he is paid to provide for those who need it. If you want a name for it, I do not think there is a better one than 'wisdom'. And it is alleged that ... he did not provide it; it is even alleged sometimes that he made no serious effort to do so ... The majority of critics are ... persons who look at philosophy from the point of view of the consumer, if I may put it so, rather than the point of view of the producer. ... What the consumer mainly needs, I think, is a Weltanschauung, a unified outlook of the world. This is what he is asking for when he asks the philosopher for wisdom or guidance, or a clue to 'the meaning of the Universe'; and this is what the ... philosophers are failing to give him."

HENRY H. PRICE[1]

I. *Worldviews*

The purpose of this chapter is to explain what I mean by a worldview, how its possession can lead to wisdom, and how perennial arguments, problems, and ideals are related to world-views.

Philosophical theories may be as limited in scope as, for instance, an account of the nature of historical explanation, or an analysis of duty, knowledge, or rationality. Or they may include within their scope a comprehensive view of reality, such as Plato's, Spinoza's, or Hegel's. So far, I have been talking about philosophical theories in the narrow sense. The theories that interested me had the purpose of defending a particular ideal. Worldviews, however, include many ideals, as well as problems, theories, and arguments. Worldviews are sometimes called philosophical theories, philosophies, ideologies, metaphysical systems, or *Weltanschauungen*. I shall refer to them as worldviews and reserve the term: philosophical theory, for application only in its narrow sense.

What I mean by a worldview is "a set of common values that give meaning and purpose to ... life, that can be symbolically expressed, that fit with the situation of the time, as well as being linked to the historical past, and that do not outrage men's reason and at the same time appeal to their emotion."[2] A worldview is systematic. That is, the values are coherent and consistent, so that the pursuit of one does not undermine the pursuit of others. The sort of thing I have in mind can be illustrated by Platonism. If access to the truth is limited to an intellectual elite, then the political ideal cohering with it is likely to be aristocratic and not democratic, the artistic ideal will tend not to be unbridled creativity, but the presentation of truth in aesthetically pleasing form, the moral ideal will discourage the separation of goodness and knowledge, and the noblest life will be thought to be the one devoted to the pursuit of truth.

Some examples of worldviews are the philosophies of Plato, Spinoza, and Hegel; the theology of Christianity; the pragmatism of Dewey; the ideology of Marxism; the existentialism of Sartre; the liberal utilitarianism of J. S. Mill; the positivism of Comte, Spencer, and the Vienna Circle.

I shall say that something qualifies as a worldview only if it has the following five components:[3] a theory of the nature of reality or a *metaphysics*; an account of the human significance of the nature of reality of an *anthropology*; a system of ideals or a *culture*; an explanation of the discrepancy between the ideal and the actual state of affairs or a *diagnosis*; and a program for overcoming or minimizing the discrepancy or a *policy*.

The metaphysical component provides an explanation in terms of which all known facts can be accommodated. It is an overall interpretive scheme whose purpose is to defend a particular ordering of the facts. The questions it aims to answer are, for instance, what is the ultimate nature of reality? Is it material, spirtual, both, or some third thing? What is irreducibly basic and what is derivative? What things are appearances and what things are real? Can all real things be experienced? If there are things beyond experience, how can they be known?

There is an intimate connection between the metaphysics of a worldview and science. For clearly science is beyond comparison the most successful device for ascertaining what the facts are. Indeed, the progress of science and the establishment of closer and closer connection between science and metaphysics are two ways of referring to the same process. Yet the identification of science and metaphysics is an error for two reasons. The first is that the question of whether all reality if knowable through science is one that can be answered, if at all, by metaphysics and not by science.

Hence there are metaphysical problems which are not scientific problems. The second is that even if one accepts the view that what can be known about reality can be known scientifically, the supposed knowledge, that the limits of science and the limits of the knowable coincide, could not be a piece of scientific knowledge.

Nevertheless, philosophers who stress the continuity between science and metaphysics are right. The facts and theories of science are the best guide to what there is. Yet what should be stressed is just the *continuity*, and not the identity, of science and metaphysics. However, even if the reasons for denying this identity were insufficient, it would still be an error to identify science with a worldview. For there is much more to a worldview beside its metaphysical outlook. Science does not even make a pretence at providing ideals, examining their significance, and offering diagnoses and policies.

The second component of worldviews is an account of the human significance of the interpretation provided by metaphysics. I have called this an anthropology not because I think that this component is the social science going by that name, but because I found no better term for referring to accounts about the place of man in reality. In separating anthropology from metaphysics I do not mean to imply that man is not part of reality. A metaphysical theory is about reality, about everything there is, and one of the existing things is man. So human beings are a proper concern of a theory of reality. But the distinction between anthropology and metaphysics is warranted by the existence of a uniquely human perspective. A metaphysical theory attempts to offer an explanation of how everything is in itself. Of course, it is human beings who construct metaphysical theories. But the authorship of such theories is irrelevant to their content. The metaphysical perspective is upon things *sub specie aeternitatis*; if angels, Martians, or dolphins had metaphysical theories, they would attempt to portray human beings the same way as human metaphysical theories do.

The scheme of things is what it is independently of the existence, wishes, fears, and cognitive endeavors of human beings. But what we, human beings, take the scheme of things to be has a very special human significance. For even though the facts are what they are, not all facts are equally interesting and important from the human point of view. What establishes, in the first instance, the importance of some facts and what guides our interest in them is their relevance to the problems we encounter and the ideals we hold. I do not mean to suggest that we are interested only in problem-solving. But it does seem to me that we can be interested in things for their own sake only if our problems have been solved. We would have no opportunity for pursuing non-pragmatic interests if the enduring problems of life and reflection were to remain unsolved—for, then, we would all be dead.

The anthropological component of worldviews thus introduces a necessary specifically human perspective. Its concern is with viewing things *sub specie humanitatis*. The difference between the metaphysical and anthropological components, I want to emphasize, is not factual. The metaphysical task includes ascertaining, with the help of science and other endeavors, what the facts are. The human perspective cannot and should not try to change that. The difference is one of interpretation; a difference that arises because we, human beings, the constructors of metaphysical theories, have a special interest in what the facts are. For we must cope with them.

Thus a satisfactory worldview must not only contain an account of the nature of reality, it must also provide an account of the significance reality has for human beings. The former is metaphysics, the latter is anthropology.

The product of metaphysics is an interpretation of reality, a metaphysical theory. The product of anthropology is wisdom. I shall explain later in detail what I mean by it. The short explanation, however, is that wisdom is an attitude which enables those who have it to live harmoniously and knowledgeably. Wisdom, as I shall argue, is not just a cognitive attitude, but also one that engages one's feelings and imagination.

The third component of worldviews is a system of ideals which I have called culture. These ideals represent desirable solutions to enduring problems. They are political, moral, scientific, aesthetic, literary, religious, and other. They represent the aspirations of a society and they are formulated by novelists, artists, composers, dramatists, prophets, politicians, judges, and critics. They may, of course, be also formulated by philosophers. But what makes the ideals of concern to philosophy is not the matter of who formulated them but the need to justify them.

The justification of ideals is one of the prime philosophical tasks, as I see it, and this is the rationale for the conduct of perennial arguments. Because ideals are composed of presuppositions, their justification is the justification of their presuppositions. And because these arise in the culture of a society, philosophers cannot afford to be professionally unconcerned with the cultural endeavors surrounding them, for these produce or formulate the ideals that they are supposed to criticize or justify.

The development of an understanding of ideals in the surrounding culture is the development of sensibility. Sensibility is not merely a cognitive awareness of prevalent ideals. Ideals are valued and the experience of valuing them is not just cognitive but also emotional and imaginative. Understanding an ideal requires understanding its emotional and imaginative appeal. I do not, of course, mean that understanding an ideal in this sense is possible only by someone who accepts it. Sensibility requires being able to enter imaginatively into other ways of life and other habits of thought and feeling and in this way coming to see the emotional and imaginative appeal of many ideals. It requires the kind of intellectual and emotional agility and adventures that makes it possible for a person to imagine himself to be someone else. Part of the importance of literature, drama, film, and other arts is that they enable a person to do this.

To possess sensibility is desirable, for it enriches a person by making options available to him that he otherwise would not have. A philosopher cannot discharge his task without it. For understanding an ideal is necessary to justifying it, and understanding depends on the possession of sensibility. Thus the third component of worldviews, culture, makes demands not only upon the intellect but also upon the feelings and imagination of a person who shares in or tries to understand the worldview. I shall return to this point.

The fourth component of worldviews is a diagnosis. This medical metaphor is warranted because life in a culture always falls short of the ideals to which the culture aspires. The diagnosis provides an explanation of why this is so. Assuming that the system of ideals comprising the culture is rationally defensible, the diagnosis can attribute the source of the culture's shortcomings either to some weakness in human beings, or to some adverse feature in the scheme of things, or to a combination of both.

Thus, for example, the Christian diagnosis is that human beings have a basic flaw, original sin, which accounts for the impossibility of attaining the Christian ideal without divine help; the Marxist diagnosis is that the present unsatisfactory state of affairs is due to the conflicts among human beings all of whom act as the representatives of their classes and as such are the unwitting agents of the inevitable process of history; the positivistic diagnosis attributes existing ills to the failure to organize society according to the dictates of science—a failure due either to insufficient progress in science, or to human attachment to unscientific procedures; the Platonic diagnosis is that the wrong people rule and if philosophers were kings, truth, justice, and goodness would prevail; the Stoic-Spinozistic diagnosis is that the ills we perceive come from our lack of understanding the scheme of things and from the human failure to submit passions to rational control.

The diagnosis may be utopian and thus optimistic, leading to the recommendation that we should exert ourselves in particular ways to overcome the discrepancy between the actual present and the attainable ideals. Or the diagnosis may be pessimistic, prompting resignation or the more sanguine attitude to do as well as we can in the face of the unattainability of the ideals. Whatever form the diagnosis takes, it leads to the formulation of a policy.

A policy for coping with or overcoming the discrepancy between the ideal and the actual is the fifth component of worldviews. If the diagnosis is optimistic, the policy will be a forward looking plan of action. If the diagnosis is pessimistic, the aim of the policy will be adjustment, small-scale amelioration, doing as well as we can with what we have.

The Christian policy is to live so as to become worthy of grace; the Marxist plan is to hasten the disappearance of classes; the positivist urges the development and application of science; the Platonist recommends the kind of education that will produce the right rulers; and the Stoic-Spinozistic advice is to retire from active life, contemplate the scheme of things, and so obtain understanding and peace.

Some worldviews are old, others are new. The Platonic, Stoic-Spinozistic worldviews have been around for a very long time. The Marxist, positivist, liberal utilitarian, existentialist worldviews are more recent. The number of worldviews is small, but there is no reason to think that it is unchanging. Old ones may be rejected and new ones may be added. The magical-animistic worldview which prevailed before the hellenistic alternative had appeared and which still survives in some primitive societies is disappearing. The more recent worldviews named above have all been formulated during the last hundred years. There is no more important event in human history than the disappearance or the formulation of a worldview. For worldviews shape human lives; they provide whatever meaning and purpose we have.

Worldviews are characterized by both change and continuity. They have a central core that cannot be changed radically without abandoning the worldview. This core is formed by metaphysics and anthropology. It may happen, of course, that the facts out of which the metaphysics is formed undergo radical change due to scientific, historical, or other discoveries. In this case, the question is whether the changes can be reconciled with the traditional outlook of the metaphysics. If the reconciliation is possible, the metaphysics can continue with the appropriate alterations. If, however, the change is too radical for the traditional metaphysics to accommodate, then the reasonable attitude is to abandon it.

The changing outer layer of a worldview is composed of the diagnosis and the policy. For what these are may and perhaps should change with the changing historical situation in which the worldviews are held. Furthermore, it is perfectly possible to abandon a diagnosis and a policy which were found to be unsatisfactory and to replace them with more promising ones without thereby undermining the worldview. The Marxist policy of revolution may be abandoned in favor of parliamentary reform without damaging Marxism. The Christian policy of living monastically to please God may be replaced by the attempt to please God through good works without giving up Christianity. The positivistic view that the progress of science requires making the social sciences more like physics may well be changed to allow for the existence of different types of science and different types of progress without betraying the original view.

The position of the remaining component of worldviews, culture, is ambiguous with regard to change and continuity. The ideals to which a worldview is committed are as essential to it as the metaphysics and the anthropology. Yet, as we have seen, the ideals are internally complex and hence modifiable. They can be reinterpreted without changing them radically. The question about ideals is, therefore, whether the change they undergo is the kind of reinterpretation that internal perennial arguments bring about, or whether it amounts to the kind of replacement of one with another that follows from the resolution of an external perennial argument. In the former case, continuity is maintained and the worldview survives. In the latter case, change has occurred and the worldview must be given up.

The five components of worldviews are inseparably connected by their shared purpose of solving enduring problems; but the justification of worldviews must be piecemeal. Each component must be justified, but the consequences of failure are different for different components. If the diagnosis or policy fails, the worldview may still be defended by developing a more satisfactory replacement. If the metaphysics, anthropology, or culture fails, however, then the worldview itself must be abandoned.

The components of worldviews are expressed in terms of philosophical theories and the method of their justification will be discussed in the next part of the book.[4] The benefit bestowed upon a person for holding a justified worldview is the possibility of wisdom. This is what I shall now discuss.

II. *Wisdom*

There have been two themes struck repeatedly in the previous discussion which I want to unite now. The first is the lament that philosophy fails to provide guidance to the good life. The second is the hitherto insufficiently explained anthropological component of worldviews. The common element uniting these themes is the pursuit of wisdom. In taking note of the case against philosophy, I have argued that the failure consists in not providing a worldview and the reason why that matters is that it deprives man of its benefit: wisdom. But now, that I have finally reached the point of saying what a worldview is, I must show how immersion in it may lead to wisdom.

Wisdom is an interior state, a private possession. It is not inborn, nor is it bestowed on a person from the outside. Wisdom is cultivated and after very hard work it is sometimes achieved. Wisdom is an understanding of the scheme of things and the capacity to use that understanding for living harmoniously with nature, other people, and oneself. It is a combination of intellectual, emotional, and imaginative efforts. All three are essential to the possession of a worldview. But so far I have concentrated on the intellectual aspect. I now want to discuss the other two.

Possessing a worldview is more than having the facility to argue from a certain point of view. It is the possession also of an internal emotional and imaginative climate. Knowing how facts would be evaluated on the basis of having accepted a system of ideals is one thing. Evaluating facts that way is another. The difference is due partly to feeling that some facts are worthy, shocking, surprising, reassuring, obscene, or threatening. Another part of the difference is imagining how one would respond if certain facts obtained. Imagining possible feelings is no less important than having present ones, for that is to a great extent what guides one's actions. It strongly influences what states of affairs one wants to bring about or avoid; how hard one should work for or against them, how happy, miserable, offended, outraged, humiliated, or proud one would be if they happened.

The emotional and imaginative aspects of a worldview may be characterized as visionary. "When I say 'vision' I mean it: I do not want to romanticize. ... It is the piercing of that dead crust of tradition and convention, the breaking of those fetters which bind us to inherited preconceptions, so as to attain a new and broader way of looking at things ... every great philosopher was led by vision: without it no one could have given a new direction to human thought ... What is decisive is a new way of seeing things and what goes with it, the will to transform the whole intellectual scene."[5]

Imagination has a major role in vision. There are at least three different but related areas of human experience that are labelled imaginative. The first is in which imagination is intimately connected with memory. The conjuring up of images is the attempt to see with the mind's eye what is no longer in front of the actual eyes. This task of the imagination is to reproduce what happened in the past. In its second role, imagination is related to error. If a person is described as imagining that something is so, it is frequently implied that he is deceived; he takes as real what is not. The third role of imagination has to do with invention, creativity, ingenuity. One who is imaginative in this sense goes beyond the reproductive aspect and produces something new. These three aspects of imagination are closely connected. For my purposes, however, it is the third that is important.

The vision involved in a worldview is the work of the creative imagination applied to the task of making sense out of reality. The product of this use of creative imagination is a new way of thinking about reality. A worldview is a particular vision surrounded by arguments whose aim is to show that reality can be understood in its terms. Vision without justification is poetry, religion, or art. A worldview without vision is a logical skeleton: bare, cold, awaiting to be enlivened and rendered vulnerable to criticism. But it is necessary to be more concrete; how does having a vision show? What difference does its possession make?

Consider the lives of a Christian and an atheist. Observation of their behavior may not make it possible to identify them, because behavior is not hallmarked as Christian or atheistic. Indeed, apart from a direct avowal of their convictions, it may not be possible to find any behavioral grounds upon which to judge their religious leanings. The difference between them does not come from what they do, but from how they think and feel about what they do: their inner lives differ. The Christian regards his life as a preamble to eternity, and he hopes to spend it in the proximity of God. His moral convictions receive their ultimate sanction from a transcendental authority. He fears, trusts, loves God and recognizes His universal jurisdiction. The feelings of the atheist are not invested in any transcendental authority; he believes that his present life is the only one he has. His moral convictions are determined by his judgment about what is likely to be beneficial for mankind. The Christian regards humanity, good and evil, the past, present, and the future of man as the observable, sometimes mysterious, sometimes understandable, unfolding of a divine plan. For the atheist there is no plan; there is only choice and chance, and there is no design behind the obstacle race that mankind is running.

Part of the difference between these two men is in their feelings about their lot and their relation to reality. I shall call these feelings metaphysical sentiments. They constitute a species of feeling one of whose chief characteristic is endurance through time; they are the emotive components of such attitudes as pessimism or optimism, resignation or pleasure-seeking, anxiety or trust, awe or irony, and the like. The other main feature of metaphysical sentiments is that the object toward which they are directed is reality. Thus the feelings are quite general in their direction. When they are expressed with reference to particular objects, the suitability of the object depends on it being perceived as an instance of something far more general. Anxiety, pessimism, or awe are metaphysical sentiments only if it is the scheme of things, and not particular objects, that make one anxious, pessimistic, or be filled with awe. Metaphysical sentiments frequently prompt and almost invariably color one's attitudes toward reality and the perception of one's relation to it. Such sentiments are partly in terms of which one answers what Kant regarded as one of the three main questions of philosophy: for what may I hope?

The worldviews of Christians and positivists, of Spinoza and John Stuart Mill, of Marxists and existentialists, to offer some obvious contrasts, differ not only because they would assign different importance and truth-value to the same propositions, but also because to accept one rather than the other is to feel one way rather than another about reality and man's place in it. This is the reason why thinking about a worldview is an intellectual matter, while understanding and accepting it is to such a great extent also an emotional issue. And this explains why we can appreciate, say, the austerity and nobility of Spinoza's worldview, while recognizing that it does not survive objections. It explains also why a Christian may refuse to abandon his beliefs even though he accepts the inadequacy of the arguments supporting his position. And it is why a person might say that the arguments for materialism are strong, but he would not like materialism to be true. The simple fact of the matter is that we hope for the success and correctness of some worldviews and fear and recoil from the implications of others.

Philosophers, however, are not disposed to take official cognizance of this commonplace. Like the rope in the hanged man's house, metaphysical sentiments are rarely mentioned in philosophical arguments. What possibly underlies this widespread aversion is the suspicion of philosophers that these feelings are no more than large-scale prejudices. Intellectual integrity requires that one be on guard against what he wishes to be true and to pursue the argument even if it leads to conclusions that are judged to be deplorable. However, in striving to avoid wishful thinking all too many philosophers have come to ignore this important aspect of worldviews.

It might be said in reply that metaphysical sentiments ought to be ignored. Worldviews after all purport to be rational, they aim to tell the truth, and metaphysical sentiments are neither true nor false.

Indeed, feelings, metaphysical or otherwise, have no truth-value; but they may still be appropriate or inappropriate. Furthermore, a person may be justifiably concerned with rationally appraising the appropriateness of his feelings, and he may be prepared to curtail or inhibit them if they are judged to be inappropriate.

Consider, for instance, an atheist who is also a positivist. Suppose that over a period of time he meets one misfortune after another through no fault of his own. People he loves die, he is seriously injured in an accident that he was not responsible for, lightning destroys his house, he is falsely and unjustly accused of a crime, and so on. He may well develop a feeling of resentment against the scheme of things. His previous feeling of nature's neutrality turns into anger mixed with fear; he resents the unfairness of it all. These feelings, of course, are inappropriate, given that he is a positivist. Nature cannot be both impersonal and unfair, nonsentient and a proper object of anger and resentment.

One can understand how he came to feel in these ways, nevertheless it is unreasonable both to have these feelings and to accept positivism. The recognition of the inappropriateness of his feelings will not make the feelings disappear, but it may be the first step toward controlling them.

It is one thing to say that metaphysical sentiments may or may not be appropriate and quite another to give an account of how their appropriateness is to be rationally appraised. My view is that the rational appraisal of metaphysical sentiments depends upon the correctness of the worldview to which the owner of the feelings is committed and in terms of which these sentiments are expressible. Metaphysical sentiments are part of the anthropological component of worldviews. It is partly in their terms that the human significance of the facts interpreted by the metaphysical component is appraised. If it is a reasonable belief that reality is impersonal, morally neutral, devoid of design, then resenting it for what happens is inappropriate. If it is reasonable to believe in the God of the Bible, then it is proper to stand in awe of Him.

The rational appraisal of metaphysical sentiments may proceed in terms of two questions: first, what would reality have to be like for this metaphysical sentiment to be appropriate? and second, is there good reason for thinking that reality is like that? The second question amounts to asking how philosophical theories can be justified. The answer to it will be given in the next part of the book.

The consideration of the first question leads back to vision and imagination. The vision which informs a worldview moulds together the interpretation of the facts provided by metaphysics, the judgment of their human significance supplied by the anthropology, and the ideals systematized by culture. The imaginative effort required for the development of vision is necessary in order to reconcile the facts of metaphysics, the metaphysical sentiments of anthropology, and the ideals of the culture. For these frequently conflict and the conflict makes a coherent attitude toward solving enduring problems impossible. The positivist whose life is beset by ill-luck, the Christian who encounters genuine evil, the moral agent who becomes impressed by the inexorability of the laws of nature, are each in need of a coherent worldview, of a reconciling and integrating vision. In each case, the metaphysical interpretations of the facts pull in one direction, while the metaphysical sentiments and ideals pull in the other. The imaginatively created vision aims to remove these conflicts and form a consistent, coherent, conflict-free worldview. One benefit gained from its possession is an overall strategy for solving the enduring problem, a benefit without which life cannot go on.

Another benefit is wisdom. Wisdom is a quality that infuses the life, character, and actions of a person who has a rationally justified worldview. His beliefs and feelings about reality, his attitudes to nature, other people, and himself, the ideals which guide his actions all harmoniously coexist and form a coherent whole. He is a man who has come to terms with the scheme of things. He understands what is possible and he has emotionally accepted what he understands. He has developed policies for coping with enduring problems and he does as well as possible given the limitations imposed upon him by his circumstances.

Philosophers cannot make people wise. But they can and should try to develop worldviews in terms of which wisdom can be attained. Worldviews provide the frameworks within which people can, if they are willing to make the great effort, work for the good life. Public or private calamities and limitations may make the effort fruitless; the good life may recede from the grasp of even a wise man. There is no guarantee of success. On the other hand, in the absence of rationally justified worldviews and the exertion for the achievement of wisdom there is guarantee of failure. For without them the good life is impossible.

III. *The Autonomy of Philosophy*

The autonomy of philosophy consists in the possession of a clearly defined domain: worldviews. The task of the philosopher is their rational defence. Within this domain philosophy has sovereign authority.

I do not, of course, hold the view that only people called philosophers can do philosophy. My position is that the rational defence of worldviews is the paradigmatic philosophical task. Whoever does it is doing philosophy. It can be done well and badly. Trained philosophers are more likely to do it well than people without training. But regardless of who does it, the results must be judged by the same rigorous standards. I join critics of philosophy in regretting that most philosophers do it neither well nor badly. But the backsliding of experts is no excuse for relaxing the standards.

Nor is it my view that the autonomy of philosophy prohibits other endeavors from considering matters within the domain of philosophy. On the contrary, it is an important feature of philosophy that its facts, enduring problems, and ideals arise outside of it. There are no uniquely philosophical facts, enduring problems, or ideals. What guarantees the autonomy of philosophy is what it does with the elements it shares with other endeavors. And that is to attempt to construct a worldview in terms of which problems can be solved in accordance with ideals on the basis of facts.

Some religions, many works of literature, and a few ideologies are as interested in enduring problems as philosophy. But they are not interested in rationally justifying their solutions. Science and history insist upon the rational justification of their theories. Their task, however, does not include the solution of enduring problems in accordance with ideals. Mysticism and cosmological theories offer nearly as comprehensive worldviews as does philosophy. Yet the rational defence of ideals is not among their concerns. Philosophy is autonomous because it alone combines metaphysics, anthropology, and culture, with a diagnosis and policy to form a worldview for solving enduring problems and thus making wisdom attainable.

The difference between the senses in which philosophy and other endeavors are autonomous is that philosophy does not possess a set of facts which can be labelled philosophical and be distinguished from scientific, historical, or social facts. For the domain of philosophy is reality and so no fact can be excluded *prima facie* as having no possible relevance. This, of course, is not to say that all facts are relevant. The decision of relevance is based on the problems and ideals that are constitutive of the worldview. However, since philosophy does not supply its own facts, it is always possible to criticize a philosophical theory on the basis of having erred about the nature of facts it attempts to interpret. Such criticisms, however, do not undermine the autonomy of philosophy. For philosophical theories are interpretive and not descriptive, as we have seen previously. The autonomy of interpretive theories rests on the authority and independence of their interpretations and not on their views of what the facts are. The autonomy of philosophy thus consists in the independence of philosophical interpretations of nonphilosophical considerations and being the final authority in rationally justifying the interpretations which form worldviews. Philosophy is not independent and it has no authority over the facts upon which its interpretations are based. Indeed, it is partly through these facts that it is possible to exercise rational control over philosophical interpretations.

THE STATE OF THE ARGUMENT

The human condition requires us to cope with problems. The problems occur because achieving what we want is frustrated by our physical environment, by the facts of social life, and by our own abilities and limitations. Some of these problems are removable, but others are not. The solution of these latter, enduring, problems is the task of philosophy.

The solution consists in developing a policy for coping with the problems. However, there are many policies available for coping with each enduring problem. Naturally, we want to adopt the best policy. Which policy is the best is determined by the ideal in accordance with which we want to solve the problem. But just as there are many policies, so also there are many ideals and many interpretations of each ideal.

Perennial arguments are about the ideals in accordance with which particular policies are developed for solving enduring problems. They may be external, if they concern the conflict between different ideals; or they may be internal, if they concern conflicting interpretations of the same ideal.

Perennial arguments are recurrent and endless, because the forms in which enduring problems present themselves change from age to age and because the ideals and their interpretations also change. Consequently, the policies, which depend on these changing ideals and problems, also change.

The enduring problems which perennial arguments aim to solve may be either theoretical problems of reflection or problems of life occurring independently of theories. Problems of reflection arise because problems of life have competing solutions and it is necessary to decide between them. Problems of life, however, occur regardless of what beliefs or theories are held; their sources are the inevitable conflicts between human wants and their satisfaction. Genuine problems of reflection are always traceable to problems of life. Thus the test of the solution of enduring problems is whether the relevant problems of reflection, and ultimately, the problems of life, are solved. The existence of this test is one key to the rational evaluation of perennial arguments.

The ideals in accordance with which enduring problems can be solved are goals valued by people who accept them. These ideals are exemplified and publicly available. They are significant, because they are generally recognized as possible ideals for solving enduring problems. What makes them suitable for this purpose is their internal complexity and various assessability. They are composed of many necessary elements: their presuppositions; and it is their complex composition which renders them open and modifiable, and thus capable of being adjusted to the changing forms of enduring problems.

Scientific and historical understanding, freedom, rationality, morality, knowledge, democracy, religiosity, culture, education, and aesthetic sensibility are some of the ideals I have in mind.

A philosophical theory aims to justify a particular ideal for solving an enduring problem as it occurs in a given problem-situation. The disputants in a perennial argument champion competing philosophical theories. The resolution of a perennial argument is thus the selection of a particular philosophical theory. The selection is based on the success of the theory's justification of the ideal or of the interpretation of the ideal in accordance with which the enduring problem is to be solved.

The task of philosophy is to solve enduring problems. This is accomplished by having a system of philosophical theories. Such a system is a worldview. What a worldview aims to do, therefore, is to embody a cluster of policies for solving all the enduring problems of a particular society in accordance with a rationally justified system of ideals. The benefit a person gains from participation in such a worldview is not just the pragmatic one of having a device for solving his problems, but also of having a system of ideals which makes these solutions worthwhile, thus giving meaning and purpose to his life.

In this second part of the book I have shown what perennial arguments are, how and why they are conducted, and what good we can get out of them. But I have not shown how perennial arguments can be rationally resolved. This is what I aim to do in the next part.

NOTES

1. Henry H. Price, "Clarity Is Not Enough," *Clarity Is Not Enough,* ed. H. D. Lewis (London: Allen and Unwin, 1963), 16 and 35.

2. Clyde Kluckhohn, "Culture and Behaviour," *Collected Essays of Clyde Kluckhohn,* ed. R. Kluckhohn (New York: Free Press, 1962), 297–8.

3. This discussion of worldviews is indebted to Leslie Stevenson's *Seven Theories of Human Nature* (Oxford: Clarendon, 1974), Part One.

4. W. T. Jones, "Philosophical Disagreements and World Views," *Proceedings*

and *Addresses of the American Philosophical Association*, 43 (1969–70), 24–42, puts forward a view about the connection between philosophy and worldviews which is very close to my own. The main difference between our views is that he denies and I assert that worldviews can be rationally justified.

5. Friedrich Waismann, "How I See Philosophy," *Contemporary British Philosophy*, Third Series, ed. H. D. Lewis (London: Allen and Unwin, 1966), 32.

PART THREE

PHILOSOPHICAL
JUSTIFICATION

Chapter Six

The Domain of Justification

"A philosophical problem can be resolved only when it is set and dealt with in relation to the events which have made it arise, and which have to be understood in order to understand it. Otherwise the philosophical problem remains abstract and gives rise to those inconclusive and interminable arguments which are so frequent with professional philosophers that they seem to have become a natural element in their lives, where they come and go ... in vain, always agitated here and there and everywhere, but always at the same stage of development. If philosophy has been, and is, the subject of a special mockery which has never been aimed at either mathematics, physics, natural science, or historiography, that mockery must have a special motive which is the one we have described."

BENEDETTO CROCE[1]

I. *Introduction*

In this part of the book I shall discuss the nature of philosophical justification. I shall begin by asking what sort of considerations are relevant to justification in philosophy. This question is intimately connected with the nature of philosophy. For what is being asked is what sort of arguments play a role in philosophy, what sort of arguments are philosophical. In answering these questions I shall leave the mainstream of contemporary Anglo-American philosophy. There is widespread agreement in that tradition that psychological, sociological, moral, religious, historical, or political influences do not and cannot have a bearing on the justification of ideals. In my view this is an error; some combination of these influences must be taken into account.

I shall refer collectively to the considerations whose relevance to justification is contested as cultural influences. I mean by them the intellectual climate, the existing learned consensus about what is traditional and what is novel; the prevailing judgments about what is problematic, worrisome, or disturbing in current affairs; the general agreement about what sort of questions are fundamental as opposed to being secondary questions of detail. Cultural influences shape the intelligent view about what inquiries are respectable and disreputable, about what is groundbreaking and banal. Cultural

79

influences make a person use language in certain ways, they result in people regarding some images and metaphors as particularly compelling and others as cliches; they form the connotations and help establish the emotional force of words and phrases. Such cultural influences incline a person to find some things interesting, exciting, provocative, or shocking, and other things as irrelevant and boring. When the mind of a person is described as the product of his age, culture, or milieu, what is meant is that his thought and sensibility bear the identifiable imprints of the cultural influences of the worldview prevailing in his society.

My contention is that cultural influences must be taken into account in philosophical justification. Many of those who deny this fear that the admission of cultural influences will undermine the autonomy of philosophy and corrupt the first philosophical virtue of searching for truth regardless of what it may be. I shall show that these fears are groundless.

II. *The Distinction Between Discovery and Justification*

Plato has Socrates rebuke the young Phaedrus by saying: "The men of old ... deemed that if they heard the truth even from 'oak or rock', it was enough to them; whereas you seem to consider not whether a thing is true or is not true, but who the speaker is and from what country the tale comes."[2] Implicit in Plato's words is a distinction between the question of whether something is true or false and the question about the origin of the proposition whose truth is one's concern. It is implied by the rebuke that considerations of origin are irrelevant to the question of whether the proposition is true. Thus what is supposed to matter is whether what is said is true and not who the speaker is or where he comes from.

This has come to be known as the distinction between the context of discovery and the context of justification.[3] Into the context of discovery belong the cultural influences upon a person in his development and statement of a proposition. Whereas the context of justification comprises attempts to determine the truth of the proposition. The view that the cultural influences within the context of discovery have any bearing on the context of justification has been called the genetic fallacy. The context of justification is the domain of epistemology, while the context of discovery is the domain of social sciences and history. One aim of epistemology is to analyze and clarify the notions of truth, proof, evidence, justification, theory, rationality, and other similar ones involved in the attempt to find out whether the proposition is true.[4]

The distinction between discovery and justification represents a philosophical ideal whose credentials are first rate. The ideal is that philosophy is a search for truth and whether a proposition is true depends on its correspondence with facts. Justification is the process of ascertaining whether this correspondence obtains. The confusion of discovery with justification is supposed to be a fallacy because whatever has influenced a person in developing or stating a proposition is said to have no bearing on the correspondence of the proposition to facts.

The genetic fallacy, however, is thought to be more than just an epistemological mistake: it is also a threat to intellectual integrity. For if it becomes permissible to consider such matters as the character, social standing, religious preferences, or historical roots of the person whose theory is being judged, then prejudice, taste, and ideology will intrude and pervert one's judgment. The disinterested search for truth is a difficult ideal to live up to in any case. The genetic fallacy makes it even more difficult and thus plays into the hands of religious dogmatists, political ideologues, and other fanatics.

In arguing against the distinction between discovery and justification, I do not want to weaken the ideal which the distinction aims to protect. On the contrary, I intend to defend the ideal by offering stronger arguments for it than what can be summoned in defence of this ill-conceived distinction. But first we must see what arguments there are supporting the distinction.[5]

III. *The First Argument: The Autonomy of Philosophy*

One argument in favor of the distinction between discovery and justification rests on a view of the nature of philosophy. According to this view, philosophy has a special subject-matter. It is the authority on matters which fall within its domain and it is uniquely qualified to justify claims made under its jurisdiction.

The special subject-matter of philosophy, on this view, is the "massive central core of human thinking which has no history ... there are categories and concepts which, in their most fundamental character, change not at all. ... They are the ... indispensable core of the conceptual equipment."[6] The philosopher's concern is with this fundamental central core: "[T]he problems that confront the philosopher here are not the specific ones of whether any particular claims made by a scientist, an historian, or a specialist within any other discipline deserve the name of knowledge. ... [A]ny claim to knowledge presupposes, if it is to be a valid claim, the satisfaction of conditions concerning grounds, truth, meaning, and perhaps other things. To investigate these conditions is a philosophical task. To establish these general conditions ... is a prime task of the philosopher."[7]

Since philosophers are interested in the most general concepts or categories which are presupposed by all particular inquiries, the findings of these particular inquiries can, then, have no bearing on the justification of philosophical claims. "No theory of knowledge that makes use of the results of experimental science can withstand criticism, for it is impossible to inquire into the validity or non-validity of knowledge if we presuppose the validity of specific results achieved with the help of the very criteria that are in question."[8]

The argument in support of the distinction between discovery and justification rests on the combination of the view that philosophy is autonomous and the view that the appeal to cultural influences in the attempt to justify philosophical propositions is circular.[9] The autonomy and the circularity arguments have two important assumptions in common: one correct, the other not. The correct assumption is that philosophy deals with fundamental questions and answers to these questions are presupposed by less fundamental inquiries. The incorrect assumption is that the authority of philosophy to examine and justify fundamental presuppositions rests on the correctness of a particular analysis of these presuppositions. According to this analysis, they are not factual, for they cannot be verified or falsified by observation. Yet they are not logical either for their denial is not self-contradictory. Presuppositions can be justified neither by scientific, historical, or other empirical inquiries, nor by appeal to logic. If they are to be justified at all, it must be done philosophically. Philosophy is autonomous because it alone is capable of performing what has come to be called conceptual inquiries. Presuppositions are conceptual truths and their identification, analysis, and justification result from successfully performed conceptual inquiries.

What are conceptual inquiries? According to the best account known to me "there is a class of truths that might be called 'conceptual truths.' If all necessary truths depend on the concepts we have ... then conceptual truths are all the necessary truths that there are. Analytic truths constitute a subclass of conceptual truths. ... The complexity of the possible relationships between concepts ... may be considerable; to sort out these matters is one of philosophy's major tasks. Thus a philosophical investigation of the concepts within any particular domain or sphere should result, if successful, in the acceptance of certain conceptual truths, certain statements that have a claim to being necessarily true. To make assertions of this kind is not to lay claim to the ability to arrive at necessary truths about the world by the exercise of thought alone; it is, however, to lay claim to the ability to arrive at an understanding of how certain things must be understood. ... We know of their truth without further reference to experience when we understand them, but that understanding itself is relative to the form of life or sensibility we have."[10]

Conceptual truths express what has been called conditional necessities.[11] Conditional necessities are based on the fact that whether or not certain necessities obtain depends on contingent states of affairs. Conditional necessities are not true in all possible worlds, but only in a world in which a relevant set of facts holds. But provided that these facts exist, it is necessarily the case that certain things follow. Thus, for instance, it is supposed to be a conceptual truth that in our way of thinking persons and bodies are irreducible primitives.[12] The supposition is not that this is a necessary feature of the world, but that given the world as we know it, it is a necessary feature. The necessity is conditional upon the world being what we think it is. A similar claim is that given the language we have, it is a necessary truth that it must be public. This conceptual truth is necessary in that its denial leads to absurdity. But it is also conditional for it is a contingent fact that we have a language at all.[13]

The argument in favor of distinguishing discovery and justification, then, is that justification concerns the establishment of conceptual truths which are presupposed by all nonphilosophical inquiries. The justification of conceptual truths is a unique task of philosophy. This guarantees the autonomy of philosophy as well as the circularity of any appeal to the findings of nonphilosophical inquiries in attempting to justify conceptual truths. For nonphilosophical inquiries presuppose those conceptual truths whose justification is the unique task of philosophy.

IV. Criticism of the First Argument

The reason for the failure of this defence of the distinction between discovery and justification is that the notion of conceptual truth is faulty. The trouble with it is that conceptual truths do not form a unique class. All truths embody the mixture of factual and logical components that are supposed to be the hallmark of conceptual truths. If there is no unique class of conceptual truths, then, it follows from this mistaken view, philosophy is not autonomous, for it has no domain sharply distinguishable from the domains of other inquiries. Nor is it circular, then, to consider the findings of other inquiries in attempting to justify philosophical claims. For if all truths are conceptual, then no truths can enjoy the privileged status which this mistaken view claims for them.

The argument showing the defect in the notion of conceptual truth starts with the denial that propositions are exhaustively classifiable as either factual or logical. The truth or falsehood of logical propositions is supposed to be a purely logical matter, while the truth or falsehood of factual propositions is claimed to depend solely on facts and to be ascertainable by observation.

The argument against the factual-logical distinction is that neither of the key terms can be elucidated without reference to the other. Logical and factual truths are interdependent and inseparable. Factual truths are partially dependent on the language in which they are stated and logical truths partly depend on the extension of the terms used in stating them. The result is that logical and factual components are unavoidably involved in every proposition.[14]

I shall not follow the twists and turns of these well-known arguments. It will suffice to note for the present purposes that in my view the objections to the factual-logical distinction as an exhaustive classification of propositions are decisive. The important consequence is the emergence of a way of looking at the system formed by all propositions whose truth we accept. This system contains all and only mixed propositions, since each proposition in it has both logical and factual components. One difference among propositions is due to their centrality in the system. Some propositions are so central that if they were regarded as falsified, the whole system would have to be readjusted. Other propositions have only a marginal importance and a change in our thinking about their truth-value would require no basic alteration of the system. Centrally important propositions are mainly logical, while marginal propositions are mainly factual. But due to the interdependence of the notions of logical and factual, no proposition is purely one or the other.

The significance of this is twofold. First, no proposition is beyond revision. For, since each proposition contains a factual component, and since these are subject to change, every proposition is subject to change. There are thus no timeless nonhistorical truths. There are only propositions whose truth-value we are reluctant to change. If some propositions present evidence against these protected ones, we rather distrust the proposition bearing the counterevidence than the proposition against which they are supposed to count.

The second significant feature of the interdependence of the notions of logical and factual is that justification must be seen as a matter of coherence of the propositions within the system and not as having to do with the correspondence of the system and the facts depicted by it. The only way of establishing the supposed correspondence between propositions and facts is through observation. But if there are no purely factual propositions, then observation cannot be pure and must be dependent on the system in which it is made. Correspondence thus remains an impossible task to establish.[15]

Philosophers who accept that justification is a matter of coherence differ among themselves about the number of possible alternative systems within which coherence can be established. Some hold that in the last analysis there is only one system: science.[16] Others think that there are many systems each with its own standards of justification and it is not possible to choose between them rationally.[17] There is a third group occupying a middle ground between the previous two. They acknowledge science as the prominent system, but deny that it is possible to decide rationally between equally coherent alternatives within science.[18]

The common consequence of all these views is that justification is regarded as an internal matter. It occurs within a system that contains the propositions requiring to be justified and it dictates also the method of justification. Since correspondence as an ideal of justification is abandoned, and since the system contains psychological, sociological, historical, and other propositions as well, there is no way of excluding these propositions from having a bearing on justification. It seems, then, that if justification is a matter of coherence, discovery and justification cannot be distinguished, and thus the so-called genetic fallacy is not a fallacy at all. I do not think that defenders of the coherence theory of justification recognize this consequence of their position and I doubt that they either intend it, or would be happy with it.

For the consequence means that it is no longer possible to determine what is relevant and what is irrelevant to justification. If justification is a matter of coherence within a system, then it is arbitrary to select one set of propositions with which the proposition to be justified must cohere. If the truth-values of propositions expressing observations do not depend on the correspondence of the propositions to facts but on their coherence with each other and with the rest of the system, then the unique status of observation as a test of truth is abandoned. There is, then, no reason why justification should not be taken to require the coherence of a proposition with political, moral, religious, or social propositions. In other words, the ancient ideal of the integrity of the search for truth is watered down to such an extent that it amounts to a betrayal. What is accepted as true may still be said to depend on justification, but justification now may include not just observation but also cultural influences. As a result, a proposition cohering with propositions expressing observation-reports and failing to cohere with political, moral, religious, or other propositions may justifiably be rejected.

An attempt to avoid the force of this point is to allow that some considerations relevant to the origin or the acceptance of a proposition may have a bearing on its justification, and thus not constitute an instance of the genetic fallacy. "Items within the context of discovery can sometimes be correctly incorporated into the context of justification by showing that there is an objective connection between that aspect of the discovery and the truth or falsity of the conclusion. The argument then requires a premise stating this objective connection. The genetic fallacy, on the other hand, consists of citing a feature of the discovery without providing any such connection with justification."[19]

This reply, however, simply assumes what is contested, namely, that an objective connection can be established. If justification is a matter of coherence, then coherence is the criterion of objectivity. The question of how to decide with what other propositions a given proposition should cohere remains unanswered.

The problem faced by philosophers who accept that justification is a matter of coherence, and who are thus unwittingly committed to denying that the genetic fallacy is a fallacy, is to justify the system itself within which coherence is sought. The usual answer they give, and as far as I can see the only one open to them, is that the system can be justified pragmatically. Pragmatic justification of a system can take different forms. But in every form it is composed of an agent, the goal the agent has, and the system which is supposed to get the agent to his goal. The justification of the system is that it gets the agent to his goal.

The result of pragmatic justification is the naturalization of philosophy. I mean by that the identification of philosophical justification with some form of scientific justification. Thus, for instance, when the agent in a pragmatic justification is taken to be an individual human being, then his goal is the satisfaction of his self-interest. The justification of his system is that it serves that goal and it consists in a psychological account of its development and pursuit. Psychologists disagree whether the proper account should be introspective, behavioristic, or developmental, but they agree in thinking that if an account is possible, then the system is thereby justified.[20]

The agent, however, may be taken to be a species and the goal served by the system is survival. In this case, the justification of the system is biological.[21] If the agent is taken to be a class, then its goal is the domination of other classes and the justification of the system depends on how well this is accomplished. Philosophical justification is accordingly identified with sociological or historical description.[22] The agent, however, may be regarded as a culture and the goal is to serve whatever are the conventional goals of the culture. The justification of the system then is an anthropological account of the culture.[23]

Whatever form pragmatic justification takes and however philosophy is naturalized, the system as a whole cannot properly be justified in this manner. For a system can be said to be justified in terms of a goal only if the goal itself is justified. Individuals, species, classes, and cultures may pursue a wide variety of goals. But their activities are not self-justifying, they are warranted only if the goals have warrant.

That there is a logical difference between pragmatic success and justification can be brought out by noticing that pragmatic success may well depend on acting from ignorance or false propositions. Imagine, for instance, that given the moral immaturity of mankind, if we had reliable information about how to manipulate our gene-pool, we could cause irreparable harm to our species. Our ignorance or misinformation about the manipulation of the gene-pool thus may assure pragmatic success, but hardly can it be said to justify existing beliefs.

To sum up: the first argument for the distinction between discovery and justification fails because it rests on a mistaken conception of the domain of philosophy. The mistake is to think that the únique subject-matter of philosophy is the class of conceptual truths. But since the exhaustive classification of all propositions into logical and factual cannot be defended, the notion of conceptual truth and with it this attempt to establish the autonomy of philosophy collapse. The result is the realization of the worst fears of the defenders of the distinction between discovery and justification: the corruption of the disinterested pursuit of truth.

My own view is that philosophy is autonomous, but, as we have seen in Chapter Five, its autonomy does not rest on the distinction between discovery and justification, nor on there being conceptual truths.

V. *The Second Argument: Philosophy as Rational Reconstruction*

According to this view: "The main problem [of philosophy] concerns the rational reconstruction of the concepts of all fields of knowledge on the basis of concepts that refer to the immediately given. By rational reconstruction is here meant the searching out of new definitions for old concepts. The old concepts did not ordinarily originate by way of deliberate formulation, but in more or less unreflected and spontaneous development. The new definitions should be superior to the old in clarity and exactness, and, above all, should fit into a systematic structure of concepts. Such clarification of concepts ... seem to me one of the most important tasks of philosophy."[24] The systematic structure of concepts should be an axiomatized theory. "A theory is *axiomatized* when all statements of the theory are arranged in the form of a deductive system whose basis is formed by the axioms, and when all concepts of the theory are arranged in the form of a constructional system whose basis is formed by fundamental concepts."[25]

The relevance of this view of philosophy to the distinction between discovery and justification follows from the distinction between the unreflective and spontaneous old concepts and the reconstructed and axiomatized new concepts. The old concepts incorporate the cultural influences in combination with elements upon which rest the justification of propositions making use of these concepts. The new concepts, properly reconstructed and fitted into the axiomatized system, are free of all the elements which have no bearing on the truth-value of propositions in which the concepts are used. Thus, while it may be that the distinction between discovery and justification cannot be drawn in the case of old concepts, there is no difficulty in upholding it for new concepts. The elements eliminated from the new concepts are those which belong only to the context of discovery. "Epistemology does not regard the processes of thinking in their actual occurrence. ... What epistemology intends is to construct thinking processes in a way in which they ought to occur if they are to be ranged in a consistent system. ... Epistemology thus considers a logical substitute rather than real processes."[26]

The process of rational reconstruction is one of epistemological purification. A properly axiomatized system contains only basic concepts which denote the immediately given, concepts constructed out of more basic ones, and logical rules of syntax and semantics. The cultural influences upon the development of the unreconstructed concepts are excluded as reconstruction progresses. In an ideally axiomatized system the problem of distinguishing between elements relevant to discovery and to justification could not even arise. That the problem arises in contemporary philosophy is simply a symptom of failure in approximating the ideal.

VI. *Criticism of the Second Argument*

The first difficulty is that the notion of rational reconstruction presupposes the empiricist theory of concept formation.[27] This theory is meant to explain how it is that we acquire empirical concepts. The explanation is that we associate a particular symbol, such as the word red, with a feature of the world, namely the color red. When the word is used only on the appropriate occasions, then the user can be said to have acquired the concept of red. The trouble with this theory is that it is logically impossible for concepts to be acquired in this way, since the acquisition of any one concept is possible only if the person already possesses other concepts. The word red can be associated with the color red only if the person knows the difference between colors, shapes, sounds, and only if he can make judgments of identity and similarity. But knowing the difference and making such judgments requires the possession of general concepts, such as color, sound, shape, identity, and difference, and of particular concepts, such as green, yellow, round, square, loud, and high-pitched. If the person does not have these concepts, he cannot make the judgments of similarity and difference required for the formation of the concept of red. Hence he cannot acquire concepts one by one, they must be acquired wholesale.[28]

The empiricist theory of concept formation is presupposed by the idea of philosophy as rational reconstruction, because forming the association between a color and a word, for instance, is supposed to be necessary for the acquisition of the concepts which constitute the foundation of the axiomatized system. But if concepts are not acquired singly, and if the possession of one concept requires the possession of many others, then this presupposition of rational reconstruction collapses, and so does the view of philosophy which rests upon it.

It might be argued, however, that the idea of rational reconstruction can be held independently of the empiricist theory of concept formation. In an axiomatized system there will still be basic concepts, but they need not denote the immediately given. Concepts are basic only in the sense that in any system some concepts have to be more fundamental than others. Their being basic is dictated by the purposes of the system and not by any objective feature of the world. Given this modified conception of rational reconstruction, the distinction between discovery and justification can be maintained with as great plausibility as before. The key to the defence of the distinction is the axiomatization of the system: with its help all nontruth-functional elements can be excluded.

We must ask, however, what is the test of adequacy of the attempted reconstruction. The answer proposed is that the reconstruction "to be given is not arbitrary; it is bound to actual thinking by the postulate of correspondence. It is even, in a certain sense, a better way of thinking than actual thinking. In being set before the rational reconstruction, we have the feeling that only now do we understand what we think; and we admit that the rational reconstruction expresses what we mean, properly speaking. ... If a more convenient determination of this concept of rational reconstruction is wanted, we might say that it corresponds to the form in which thinking processes are communicated to other persons instead of the form in which they are subjectively performed."[29]

But this proposed test of adequacy will not do. The problem is to distinguish between adequate and inadequate reconstructions. It must be possible to draw this distinction, for the replacement of an unreconstructed concept by a reconstructed one which fits into an axiomatized system may be inadequate. The new concept may not be faithful to the old one. Clearly, the criterion proposed above, that the replacement is adequate if "we have the feeling that only now do we understand what we think," is hopelessly unreliable. What happens if feelings conflict? Why suppose that the feeling one has is appropriate? Nor does it help as a criterion that an adequate replacement takes the form "in which thinking processes are communicated to other persons." For the question is whether what is communicated to other persons is an adequate expression of what was previously uncommunicated.

A test of adequacy must be a test of the faithfulness of the reconstruction. This presents an unavoidable dilemma for any proposed reconstruction. The purpose of the reconstruction is to understand the old concepts better by replacing them with more precise new concepts. The replacement requires that a new concept be faithful to the old one. To judge that the reconstruction is faithful, one must be able to understand both the old and the new concepts. But if one already understands the old concepts, then the reconstruction, having that understanding as its aim, is unnecessary. On the other hand, if the faithfulness of the reconstruction cannot be judged because the old concept is not understood, then there is no way of judging the adequacy of the reconstruction. Thus reconstruction is either unnecessary or unreliable. As a result, either all elements of the old concept are built into the new one and then the elimination of cultural influences fails, or some elements are excluded and then the old concept is different from the new one.[30]

Defenders of rational reconstruction may argue against this criticism in two ways.[31] One is to admit that in reconstruction cultural influences are excluded and the new concept is not an exact replica of the old. They may claim however that the exclusion affects only elements which are truth-functionally irrelevant. This rejoinder is question-begging, for the very problem rational reconstruction was meant to solve is that of determining which elements are truth-functionally relevant. If someone thinks that cultural influences have a bearing on the justification of propositions, he will not be answered if he is presented with propositions from which cultural influences have been deliberately excluded.

The other defence of reconstruction is to deny the importance of faithfulness. A truly toughminded reconstructionist could argue that out of a quagmire of imprecision he crystallized an argument and he is interested in finding out whether it is true or false. But this rejoinder is also unsatisfactory. For it merely changes what it is to which the reconstruction should be faithful. Independently of this rejoinder, the faithfulness of the reconstruction depended upon the correspondence of new concepts to old concepts. In having repudiated this correspondence, the reconstructionist merely substitutes another correspondence as test of faithfulness, namely, between his own interpretation of the old concepts and the new ones. Nothing is gained by this substitution, and whatever authority the old concepts had is lost. I conclude therefore that the second argument in favor of the distinction between discovery and justification also fails.

VII. *Conclusion*

I have argued in this chapter that the distinction between the context of justification and the context of discovery cannot be sustained. For cultural influences mistakenly relegated to the context of discovery form a necessary condition of justification. The claim that upon this distinction rests the autonomy of philosophy and the ideal of disinterested search for truth is dubious. Neither depends on this distinction and both can be defended independently of it.

NOTES

1. Benedetto Croce, *History as the Story of Liberty*, tr. S. Sprigge (Chicago: Regnery, 1970), 147–8.

2. Plato, *Phaedrus*, 275b–c, *The Dialogues of Plato*, tr. B. Jowett (New York: Random House, 1937).

3. The distinction is ubiquitous, although it is not always labelled as I do here. See for instance Henry Sidgwick, *Philosophy, Its Scope and Relations* (London: Macmillan, 1902), 162–71; Hans Reichenbach, *Experience and Prediction* (Chicago: University of Chicago Press, 1938), 6–7; David Hamlyn, "The Logical and Psychological Aspects of Learning," *The Concept of Education*, ed. R. S. Peters (London: Routledge, 1967), 24–5; Karl R. Popper, "Epistemology Without a Knowing Subject," *Objective Knowledge* (Oxford: Clarendon, 1972); Israel Scheffler, *Science and Subjectivity* (Indianapolis: Bobbs-Merrill, 1967), 71–3; Wesley C. Salmon, *Logic* (Englewood Cliffs, N.J.: Prentice-Hall, 1963), 10–14.

4. For one statement of this position see David Hamlyn, *The Theory of Knowledge* (London: Macmillan, 1970), 4–5.

5. The following discussion is indebted to an excellent article by Susan Haack, "The Relevance of Psychology to Epistemology," *Metaphilosophy*, 6 (1975),

161–76. I disagree with her thesis, but I have been greatly helped by her references and her statement of the arguments.

6. Peter F. Strawson, *Individuals* (New York: Doubleday, 1963), xiv.

7. Hamlyn, *The Theory of Knowledge, op. cit.*, 4–5.

8. Leszek Kolakowski, *The Alienation of Reason,* tr. N. Guterman (New York: Doubleday, 1969), 114. Kolakowski here reports Husserl's criticisms of Avenarius and Mach.

9. The clearest statement of this position I know of is Peter Winch's *The Idea of a Social Science* (London: Routledge, 1958), Chapter I.

10. See Hamlyn, *The Theory of Knowledge, op. cit.*, Chapter 9; the quotation is from 272–5.

11. Conditional necessity has long historical roots. Aristotle's categories, Kant's synthetic a priori propositions, and Collingwood's absolute presuppositions are among its ancestors. More recent and closely related notions are Kuhn's paradigms, Korner's nonuniquely *a priori* statements, Watkins's haunted universe doctrines, Strawson's basic particulars, and Lakatos's research programs.

12. See Strawson's *Individuals, op. cit.*

13. This is Wittgenstein's private language argument. For the fullest account see John T. Saunders and Donald F. Henze, *The Private-Language Problem* (New York: Random House, 1967).

14. The argument for the circularity of analyticity is Willard V. Quine's in "Two Dogmas of Empiricism," *From a Logical Point of View* (Cambridge: Harvard University Press, 1953). There is a very large body of literature concerning this question; a good bibliography is in *Analyticity*, eds. J. F. Harris and R. H. Severens (Chicago: Quadrangle, 1970). The argument for the incoherence of the notion of synthetic is John W. N. Watkins's see "Between Analytic and Empirical," *Philosophy*, 32 (1957), 112–31, and "Confirmable and Influential Metaphysics," *Mind*, 67 (1958), 344–65, and "When Are Statements Empirical?", *British Journal for the Philosophy of Science*, 10 (1960), 287–309.

15. There is an immense literature on the impossibility of pure observation and on the theory-boundedness of all synthetic statements. The main works in this connection are three extremely influential collections of essays. Quine's *From a Logical Point of View*, op. cit., Karl R. Popper's *Conjectures and Refutations* (New York: Harper, 1963), and Wilfrid Sellars's *Science, Perception, and Reality* (London: Routledge, 1963).

16. Popper, Quine, and Sellars in the works cited in note 15 hold this view.

17. Paul K. Feyerabend, in *Against Method* (Atlantic Highlands: Humanities Press, 1975) and Peter Winch in *The Idea of a Social Science*, op. cit., and in "Understanding a Primitive Society," *American Philosophical Quarterly*, 1 (1964), 307–24, hold this view.

18. Thomas S. Kuhn in *The Structure of Scientific Revolutions* (Chicago: University of Chicago Press, 1962); Michael Polanyi in *Personal Knowledge* (London: Routledge, 1958); and Norwood R. Hanson in *Patterns of Discovery* (Cambridge: Cambridge University Press, 1958), represent this tendency.

19. Salmon, *Logic, op. cit.*, 12.

20. Classical empiricism held out for the introspective account; Willard V. Quine in "Epistemology Naturalized," *Proceedings of the XIVth International Congress of Philosophy* (Vienna: Herder, 1971), 83–102, argues for a behavioristic account; Jean Piaget in *Genetic Epistemology* (New York: Columbia University Press, 1970), argues for a developmental analysis.

21. Popper's *Objective Knowledge, op. cit.*, Stephen Toulmin's *Human Understanding* (Oxford: Clarendon, 1972), and Nicholas Rescher's *Methodological Pragmatism* (Oxford: Blackwell, 1977), represent this approach.

22. This is the rationale for the Hegelian and Marxist attempts to replace epistemology by the sociology of knowledge. The best discussions known to me are Karl R. Popper's *The Poverty of Historicism* (London: Routledge, 1957) and

Maurice Mandelbaum's "Historicism," in *History, Man, and Reason* (Baltimore: Johns Hopkins Press, 1971).

23. Winch in the works cited in note 17 represents this view.

24. Rudolf Carnap, *The Logical Structure of the World*, tr. R. A. George (London: Routledge, 1967), v.

25. Carnap, *The Logical Structure of the World, op. cit.*, 6–7.

26. Reichenbach, *Experience and Prediction, op. cit.*, 5.

27. An excellent and sympathetic account is Panayot Butchvarov's *Resemblance and Identity* (Bloomington: Indiana University Press, 1966).

28. The classical criticisms of the empiricist theory of concept formation are Ludwig Wittgenstein's in *Philosophical Investigations*, tr. G. E. M. Anscombe (Oxford: Blackwell, 1968), and Sellars's in "Empiricism and The Philosophy of Mind," *Science, Perception, and Reality, op. cit.*

29. Reichenbach, *Experience and Prediction, op. cit.*, 6.

30. The best statement of this criticism is Peter F. Strawson's in "Carnap's Views on Constructed Systems versus Natural Languages in Analytic Philosophy," *The Philosophy of Rudolf Carnap*, ed. P. A. Schilpp (La Salle, Ill.: Open Court, 1963), 503–18.

31. Willard V. Quine, *Word and Object* (Cambridge: MIT Press, 1960), par. 53.

Chapter Seven

Justification in Philosophy: The Context of Introduction

"New ideas, from science or from changing social experience, impinge upon the older inherited ideas and seem to be in logical conflict with them. These conflicts, when socially significant enough to affect a considerable part of society, or at least the intellectual class, present new and insistent problems of adjustment and assimilation. They challenge thinkers to explore the bearing of the new issues upon the old, throughout all the institutions of culture. This necessitates a careful intellectual clarification and criticism. Normally the process culminates in a reconstruction of both old and new. ... At his proudest the philosopher is the statesman of ideas, constructing in his novel synthesis a new constitutional framework within which men can henceforth conduct their altered lines of thinking. This is the more imaginative and creative function of the philosopher. ... [I]t leads to the erection of one of the great architectonic edifices of ideas that can give us perspective on all times and all eternity. But even such imaginative expressions of the wisdom of organized culture must be set upon the solid foundation of an adjustment or synthesis between old and new."

JOHN H. RANDALL[1]

I. *Introduction*

This chapter and the next contain my account of philosophical justification. The aim of philosophical justification is the justification of a worldview. As we have seen, however, worldviews are composed of many elements. The justification of a worldview is thus the justification of the elements which compose it. The justification of these elements occurs through philosophical theories. A philosophical theory champions a particular ideal or a particular interpretation of an ideal which represents a desirable way of solving an enduring problem. And championing it means defending it against rival ideals or rival interpretations of the same ideal. External perennial arguments are about the claims of rival ideals; internal perennial arguments are about the claims of rival interpretations of the same ideal.

Justifying a philosophical theory thus amounts to justifying an

95

ideal or an interpretation of an ideal. Such a justification, however, involves the resolution of perennial arguments in particular problem-situations. So the aim of philosophical justification can be expressed either as the justification of a philosophical theory, or the justification of an ideal or of the interpretation of an ideal, or the resolution of an external or internal perennial argument, or finding the best solution of an enduring problem for a society. Enduring problems, ideals for solving them, philosophical theories defending particular solutions, and perennial arguments about them are thus inextricably connected. The complex question of the justification of a worldview can be approached by beginning with any one of the elements, for we shall be led to the others.

I shall state the question in terms of the justification of philosophical theories. A start has been made toward answering it, for I have shown in Chapter Six that the standard solution involving the distinction between discovery and justification fails. The distinction is faulty, but the intention behind it is sound. For clearly, there ought to be a way of excluding irrelevant considerations that pervert the search for truth. I propose to realize this intention by replacing the discovery-justification distinction with another: between the introduction and the acceptance of a philosophical theory. These occur in two different contexts against the background of two different problem-situations. Justification is relevant to both, but considerations that justify the introduction of a philosophical theory are different from considerations that justify its acceptance.

II. *The Background*

One focal point of arguments about philosophical justification in recent years has been the conflict between foundationalists[2] and coherentists.[3] They share the goal of providing an account of justification. In this, they present a common front against sceptics[4] who deny the possibility of justification. The conflict occurs because foundationalists and coherentists disagree about what kind of justification is possible. Part of my aim here is to shift the perspective in which this disagreement is viewed by showing that it rests on a mistaken assumption shared by both parties, as well as by sceptics.

The foundationalistic view of justification can be represented on the model of a hierarchy. The hierarchy is our worldview. At its base are privileged beliefs that either do not need justification or already have all the justification needed. Other beliefs in the hierarchy are justified with reference to privileged basic beliefs. There is disagreement among foundationalists about what these basic and privileged beliefs are, how much justification they need, and how much they have. But these matters will not concern us here.

The coherentist view of justification is that it occurs within a worldview comprising a system of mutually justifying beliefs. What justifies a belief is that it coheres with other beliefs in the system. If a belief fails to cohere, then either it or the beliefs inconsistent with it are rejected as unjustified. The question of which alternative to choose depends on the centrality of the conflicting beliefs to the worldview. The more central one tends to be retained, for its rejection would cause greater upheaval in the worldview. But no belief in the worldview, no matter how central, is immune to revision. Coherentists, too, disagree about what beliefs are central, about what counts as coherence, and how far revision should go. However, I shall ignore these conflicts as well.

Between the more extreme versions of foundationalism and coherentism there are a number of intermediate positions.[5] But these refinements are also irrelevant to my purposes. For my goal is to attack an assumption to which all shades of foundationalism and coherentism are committed.

In the argument between foundationalists and coherentists each side has a constructive and critical task. The critical task is excellently performed by both sides, while the constructive one falls far short of its goal. The critical task is to show what is wrong with the opponents' position; the constructive task is to defend one's position against criticism.

The central foundationalistic criticism of coherentism is that if justification is a matter of approximating truth, then justification must be more than the coherence of beliefs in a worldview, for false beliefs may also cohere. The coherentist has no rational way of choosing between equally coherent worldviews. If it is recognized that examples of competing worldviews are not the rather shopworn conflicts between the Ptolemaic and Copernican cosmologies, or between the Newtonian and Einsteinian ones, but between our worldview and such ghastly alternatives as the mysticism of Indian fakirs, the religiosity of some fanatical sect like the Flagellants, the morally indifferent aestheticism of people like Huysmans or Baudelaire, or the political ideology of Stalin or of Nazism, then the coherentist failure to make rational choice possible will perhaps be taken to count more seriously against that position. The really important choices are between worldviews whose problems, ideals, and presuppositions are radically different from one's own. A person accepting one worldview frequently belittles the problems, abominates the ideals, and refuses to accept the presuppositions of alternative worldviews. Surely, philosophy ought to be able to offer some ground for justification and criticism in such situations. If it cannot, the most unpalatable form of scepticism prevails.

The key coherentist criticism of foundationalism, on the other hand, is no less devastating. It is that the basic beliefs required by foundationalism turn out to be no more privileged and have no better justification than many other beliefs. This can be expressed either by saying that all candidates for privileged basic beliefs have been accepted as such arbitrarily, without rational justification, or that there is no privileged class of beliefs whose members have all the justification they need to have. The Cartesian clear and distinct ideas, self-evidence, the "given" of empiricism, the phenomenological intuition of "essence", the protocol sentences of early logical positivism, the sense data of phenomenalism, the incorrigible avowals of Wittgenstein, all lack the joint qualification of requiring no further justification and of other beliefs being justified with reference to them. Nor is there any method, standard, or rule which, if adhered to, would endow basic beliefs with the required justification. Induction, deduction, the verifiability principle, falsifiability, translatability into an empiricist language, all certify beliefs which, for different reasons, fall short of the kind of justification foundationalists require for privileged basic beliefs.

Clearly, in any worldview, some beliefs are basic. But being basic is not a privileged but a conventional, contingent, variable status. It is not based on the rational justification whose possibility foundationalism offers. Thus foundationalism is in the same epistemological predicament as coherentism: there are alternative worldviews with different beliefs forming the foundation or the core, and since there is no external justification available for these beliefs, the choice of worldviews must be unjustifiable. That this is so is the claim of the sceptic.

I am persuaded both by the foundationalistic criticism of coherentism and by the coherentist criticism of foundationalism. Yet I am unwilling to accept scepticism. What is the way out of this situation?

III. *The Two Contexts of Justification*

A clue is provided by Ramsey's maxim: "In such cases it is a heuristic maxim that truth lies not in one of the two disputed views but in some third possibility which has not yet been thought of, which we can only discover by rejecting something assumed as obvious by both the disputants."[6] The common assumption of foundationalism and coherentism that I propose to reject is that justification consists in increasing the likelihood of truth or decreasing the likelihood of falsehood.

What is the third possibility to which the rejection of this assumption leads? It is that justification depends on two equally important standards: one is the sole standard recognized by foundationalists and coherentists, the other is problem-solving. The two standards are so related that the question of truth cannot arise until the other standard, problem-solving, is met. Thus my criticism of the two views I reject is not that their assumption is mistaken because it is false, but that it is mistaken because it is incomplete. It leaves out the first half of justification.

Part of the significance of this third possibility is that it distinguishes between two considerations which the first two views have mistakenly treated as one. Foundationalists and coherentists assume that the correspondence between theories and the world is what provides, if anything, an external standard of justification. This is the reason why foundationalists think that giving up correspondence means giving up the possibility of justification. And this is why coherentists, having rejected the possibility of establishing correspondence, aim to interpret justification in terms internal to theories. In contrast, I think that justification does have external standards, and it is not only correspondence, but also problem-solving.

The central idea of my thesis is that there are these two contexts of justification, not merely one as foundationalists and coherentists suppose. Each context has a standard of justification. In one context, the standard is problem-solving. It is a standard external to any theory. Yet conformity to it or deviation from it is independent of the question of truth. In the other context, the standard is truth-directedness. The dispute between foundationalists and coherentists occurs in that context.

My concern here is not with settling this dispute. It is rather to show that the dispute is less important than it is commonly supposed. For we can answer the questions of whether worldviews can be justified, whether there is an external standard of justification, whether scepticism can be refuted, whether we can distinguish between theories we ought to consider seriously and theories we can dismiss, without engaging in this hoary debate.

My view is that the purpose of the justification of philosophical theories is to find the successful solution of an enduring problem in accordance with an ideal. The justification of these theories occurs on two levels. The first involves the distinction between theories that could be successful solutions and theories that could not be. The result of justification on this level is a number of candidates for being successful solutions. The second level of justification requires drawing the distinction between a theory that is a successful solution and theories that are unsuccessful solutions. This yields a theory which in fact solves an enduring problem in accordance with an ideal.

The problem of drawing the distinction between theories that could and could not be successful solutions is the problem of justifying the *introduction* of a theory. It is justified to introduce a theory if it is reasonable to suppose that it could be a successful solution. When it is reasonable to suppose this is the problem of justification on the first level. I shall discuss it here.

The problem of distinguishing between successful and unsuccessful theories is the problem of justifying the *acceptance* of a theory. Accepting a theory is justified if it is reasonable to suppose that it is a successful solution. The problem of justification on the second level is to decide when it is reasonable to suppose that a theory is a successful solution. I shall discuss that problem in the next chapter.

The considerations that justify the introduction of a theory are different from the considerations that justify its acceptance. For what could make it reasonable to suppose that a theory *may be* successful is different from what could make it reasonable to suppose that it *is* successful.

This difference is partly due to the dissimilarity of the problem-situation in which a theory is introduced as opposed to the one in which a theory is accepted. The problem in the context of introduction is finding some way of solving an enduring problem. The problem in the context of acceptance is choosing the best solution among many competitors.

The dissimilarity between the context of introduction and the context of acceptance, however, should not be overemphasized. There is an important similarity as well. They share the ultimate purpose of introducing and accepting a theory: to find the best available solution to an enduring problem in accordance with an ideal. In an ideal case, only one theory is introduced and the same theory is accepted. In that case, even though the problem-situations are still different, the two levels of justification come to the same thing. For if the one theory introduced is also the best one available, then it is that theory which should be accepted.

The ideal case, however, rarely occurs. Choosing solutions for enduring problems is a far too complex matter not to require the kind of critical probing and sustained challenging that engagement in a perennial argument provides. So while both the similarity and the dissimilarity between the contexts of introduction and acceptance must be recognized, in practice, which falls short of the ideal, the dissimilarities count and the similarities do not.

One difficulty with the discovery-justification distinction is that it fails to take account of the two contexts of justification. As a result, justification is restricted to finding the best solution. This has the unfortunate consequence that the selection of candidates for being the best solution cannot be justified. For the process of selection is relegated to the supposedly nonrational context of discovery.

The distinction between introduction and acceptance avoids this flaw by recognizing two levels of justification: one proper to the context of introduction and one to that of acceptance. Thus both the selection of possible solutions and the selection of the best available solution are brought under rational control.

Corresponding to the two levels are two standards of justification. One is *problem-solving* and the other is *truth-directedness*. My view is that the justification of a theory involves both standards. A theory is justified if it is a possible solution of an enduring problem in accordance with an ideal and if it is the best available solution; where the best is the closest approximation of the truth.

These two standards, however, do not play an equal role in the two contexts. In the context of introduction problem-solving is primary and truth-directedness is secondary. In the context of acceptance truth-directedness is primary and problem-solving is secondary. The reason for this is that what justifies the introduction of a theory is mainly that it is a possible solution of an enduring problem in accordance with an ideal. While the justification of the acceptance of a theory is largely that it is the closest approximation of the truth among several possible solutions.[7]

In the context of introduction cultural influences are essential to justification. For the primary emphasis there is on the problems and the ideals. Since problems and ideals can be understood only by taking cultural influences into consideration, justification and cultural influences are intimately connected in that context. On the other hand, the primary emphasis in the context of acceptance is upon truth-directedness. This being a matter of correspondence between propositions and facts, cultural influences have a lesser role. Thus cultural influences are directly relevant to justification by problem-solving and indirectly relevant to justification by truth-directedness.

This, then, is the outline of my account of the justification of philosophical theories. The next step is to consider the two levels of justification and the two contexts in which they occur.

IV. *Justification and the Context of Introduction*

By the introduction of a theory I do not merely mean that someone offers one. It is necessary also that the theory should enter the public domain and be recognized at least by some thinking people. Thus a theory is introduced if it is being publicly considered as an option. So the introduction of a theory is a constellation of at least two factors. One is the psychological process of creativity. The other is the sociological phenomenon of the receptivity of a society to new ideas. I am not competent to discuss these psychological and sociological matters, nor do I have to beyond noting one obvious feature of the situation. A theory is likely to be introduced, that is, be offered and considered, if there is a need for it. It is on this element of need that I shall concentrate.

In typical situations theories are introduced against the background of a worldview. The worldview is the conventional outlook of the society. The need for the introduction of a theory arises if there is doubt that the traditional way of handling problems is satisfactory. The doubt is occasioned by a conflict.

The conflict may be between the tradition and novelty. New scientific, social, political, demographic, economical, technological, or other developments may have to be dealt with. This requires that they be incorporated into the worldview by being brought within the tradition. Frequently there are no ready ways of doing this and so new ones have to be developed. The new theory is needed to function as a bridge between tradition and novelty. Its task is to develop the worldview in a way which is faithful to the old and yet capable of accommodating the new developments.

Another source of conflict may be internal tensions within the worldview. The particular forms these tensions take change from worldview to worldview. There are, however, some discernible patterns. One type of internal conflict may be between conclusions prompted by the best theories in a society and the personal experience of its members. In our society, for instance, science seems increasingly to support determinism, yet we all experience the act of choosing. Another internal conflict is between realism and supernaturalism. That is, between the tendency to look for the explanation of recalcitrant data to the unknown parts of nature and the tendency to seek it in a supernatural realm. The conflict between the scientific outlook and the appeal to occultism, mysticism, and religion is of this kind. The pattern of conflict may be the tension between viewing things *sub specie aeternitatis* as opposed to *sub specie humanitatis*: from the impersonal position of an ideally objective observer in contrast with the anthropocentric focus dictated by human interest. Yet a different pattern is the opposition between scepticism and conservatism; between the disposition to challenge, probe, and criticize the presuppositions and achievements of the worldview and the contrary disposition to value and cherish them for allowing us to cope with problems.

Whatever forms these conflicts take, the health of the society requires both that they should continue in general and that they be resolved in particular cases. For unless they are resolved, they prevent the development of ways of coping with enduring problems. This, then, is another task calling for the introduction of new theories: the resolution of conflicts within a worldview. The need for introducing new theories thus arises both to reconcile the worldview with novelty and to resolve tensions within the world-view.[8]

The justification for the introduction of theories is that they offer these reconciliations and so they become candidates for solving the problems of a society in conformity with the prevalent ideals. The theories I am discussing are philosophical and so their purpose is to solve enduring problems.

But just how is it decided whether a theory is a possible, as opposed to a successful, solution? The question of what makes a solution successful belongs to the context of acceptance and it will be discussed in the next chapter. The question of what counts as a possible solution normally has to do with its logical possibility.

There may be situations, however, in which the question of the logical possibility of a solution does not arise. If the problem-situation is such that there is an urgent problem of life, there is only one solution available, and people in the situation are aware of no reason for not acting on the only solution they have available, then acting on it is justified even if its theoretical formulation turns out to be logically inconsistent later on. I shall return to this point in the next chapter.

In most situations, however, there are very many possible theories, some plausible, others not. It should, therefore be possible to make the justified introduction of theories stricter and thereby exclude logically possible but implausible theories. This can be done by the further criterion of making the initial plausibility of a theory dependent, in addition to its logical possibility, on its capacity to conform to the worldview which forms its background. For the initial plausibility of a theory is determined by how well it is capable of resolving a conflict in familiar terms.

Let us now illustrate this by considering two examples. The first is an internal perennial argument about the ideal of religiosity. I am assuming that the enduring problem which the ideal aims to solve is the meaning of life and that the worldview forming the background is Christianity. The immediate conflict is the apparent failure of all the arguments for the existence of God. The internal perennial argument, I assume further, occurs between Christian traditionalists and reformers. Their task is to deal with the problem presented by there being no acceptable argument for the existence of God. This they attempt to do by introducing a theory. The theory introduced by the traditionalist emphasizes the importance of religious experience. His intention is not to offer yet another argument for the existence of God, but to show the importance of direct experience as a substitute. The reformist, in contrast, introduces a theory which emphasizes the metaphorical, inspirational, and moral elements of Christianity and claims that the failure of the arguments for the existence of God leaves these elements unaffected. Thus both the traditionalist and the reformist introduce theories which reinterpret the worldview in order to meet the challenge presented by the absence of arguments. They disagree with each other about what is the better way of defending the tradition which represents the ideal they both accept. Their answers are not only logically possible, they each also have initial plausibility. This is derived from their attempt to reconcile the worldview with their inability to defend one of its presuppositions, namely, that God exists.

Consider, however, some arguments that would lack this initial plausibility. The reformist may simply concede that there is no reason for believing in God and attempt to maintain the worldview without it. The traditionalist, on the other hand, may reject the importance of arguments and thus minimize the importance of there not being an acceptable one for God. These heroic devices lack initial plausibility, for they conflict with the worldview and are in fact destructive of it. If God did not exist or if arguments did not matter, the Christian worldview would be fatally weakened. For God's existence and conformity to reason are presuppositions of the ideal of religiosity represented by Christianity.

It may happen that the initially plausible theories fail in that they are not ultimately acceptable. In that case, the ideal is threatened. The farther afield the defenders have to stray from the worldview, the more the worldview is altered. It is hard to say when a worldview has changed so much that it no longer deserves to be called by the same name. But clearly, if it was thought that God did not exist and if arguments and thus theology were excluded, the Christian worldview would be abandoned.

The other illustration is of an external perennial argument about the conflicting political ideals of freedom and equality. The enduring problem to which these ideals offer solutions is the position of the individual in relation to other individuals in society. I assume that the worldview is the prevailing one in Western democracies and the conflict concerns the question of how wealth should be distributed. I shall call the defenders of freedom libertarians and the champions of equality egalitarians. The problem presented by the unequal distribution of wealth is that it is inconsistent with equality and it diminishes the freedom of those who have very little of it. Thus both libertarians and egalitarians have to introduce a theory to solve the problem in accordance with their different ideals.

Suppose that the egalitarian theory recommends the equalization of wealth by increased government control through graduated income tax and high inheritance tax. The libertarian, on the other hand, recommends a social arrangement that encourages achievement by financial incentives and discourages financial gains without achievement. Both these theories fit in with the prevailing worldview of Western democracies and they both offer solutions to the problem presented by the unequal distribution of wealth.

But now consider whether it would be a plausible libertarian solution to abolish all control and a plausible egalitarian solution to guarantee equal income for everyone. The answer, of course, is that these extreme solutions have very little in their favor, given the Western democratic worldview. For both solutions are inconsistent with presuppositions of the worldview whose problems they were designed to solve. To abolish all control would be to abolish authority, and to have guaranteed equal pay would be to withhold reward from those who deserve it and thereby undermine individual initiative, and promote injustice. Authority, individual initiative, and justice are presuppositions of the Western democratic ideal. The implausibility of the introduction of theories championing these solutions is due to their self-defeating nature. For they would jeopardize the worldview they were supposed to defend. Revolutionary solutions, overturning a worldview, may of course be called for, but only in circumstances in which the worldview has been shown to be incapable of solving its enduring problems in accordance with justified ideals.

One last remark in connection with this example: the resolution of the external perennial argument between libertarians and egalitarians depends on the critical examination of the presuppositions involved in the ideals of freedom and equality. The examination concerns the question of whether it is reasonable to believe that the presuppositions are true. How to answer that question will be the concern of the next chapter.

It should be noted nevertheless that it is at this point that truth-directedness as a secondary standard of the justification of the introduction of theories enters. For what makes a theory initially plausible is that it seems to have a good chance of being true. This chance is established through the theory's connection with the worldview. The closer the newly introduced theory is to the worldview, the better chance it has of being true. The reason for this is that the worldview is the conventional way of the society to solve its problems, because it has been successful. And what has made it successful is that the metaphysics, culture, and anthropology implicit in the worldview are likely to have much truth to them. Success is *prima facie* evidence for being right. Successful problem-solving and truth-directedness are thus connected. Still, in the context of introduction one's primary interest is in having as many possible solutions as possible; their plausibility and truth are of secondary importance. On the other hand, in the context of acceptance one's primary interest is in finding the best solution and so truth becomes the dominant consideration; while problem-solving is secondary, for it is possessed by all theories.

V. *Conclusion*

The point of discussing these two examples is to illustrate how the introduction of philosophical theories can be rationally justified. The justification depends, in the first instance, on a theory being a logically possible solution of an enduring problem in accordance with an ideal. Logical possibility, however, is too permissive a standard, for both plausible and implausible theories may be logically possible. Justification of the introduction of theories can be refined by adhering to the additional standard requiring conformity to the existing worldview as a sign of initial plausibility. Initial plausibility is an important but not a decisive consideration. It is important because it helps to select those among introduced theories which are most likely to reconcile the worldview with whatever conflict it confronts. But it is not decisive because new theories always depart from the existing worldview, so conformity is a matter of degree and its evaluation depends on fallible judgment, not on the application of tight criteria. Furthermore, conformity to a worldview is a good thing only if the worldview is viable. Given a viable worldview confronted by a conflict, the introduction of a theory is justified if the theory provides a logically possible and initially plausible reconciliation of the conflict, a reconciliation which provides a possible solution of an enduring problem in accordance with an ideal.

Problem-solving is an external standard of justification. The enduring problems whose solution is the task of philosophy may be problems of reflection or problems of life. But since genuine examples of the former presuppose the latter, enduring problems are ultimately problems of life. And this is what guarantees the externality of the standard of justification based upon solving enduring problems. For problems of life arise because of the demands of nature and because coping with these demands depends on successful interaction with the world. Problems of life are not produced by our theories; on the contrary, our theories are produced to solve problems of life.

This view partially agrees and partially disagrees with both foundationalism and coherentism. In agreement with foundationalism and disagreement with coherentism, it is committed to there being an external standard of justification. In agreement with coherentism and disagreement with foundationalism, it denies that correspondence between one's theories and the world is *the* external standard. And in disagreement with both, it denies that conformity to the primary standard of justification in the context of introduction brings one closer to truth. Problem-solving is not truth-directed.

It would be a radical misunderstanding of my view, however, to suppose it to be a version of pragmatism. This supposition would be just if problem-solving had been put forward as the only standard of justification. But this is not so. There are two equally important standards of justification: problem-solving and truth-directedness. Each is necessary and jointly they are sufficient for justification in philosophy. Problem-solving justifies the introduction of candidates as possible solutions; truth-directedness justifies the acceptance of candidates as the best solution. For the best solution is the true solution and the best explanation of why a philosophical theory has been successful in solving an enduring problem is that it is a true theory.

This account of problem-solving makes it possible to answer a number of questions which appeared to be unanswerable when raised in the context of the controversy between foundationalists and coherentists.

One such question is about the existence of an external standard of justification. We can now say that problem-solving is such a standard. But we can also see why foundationalists failed to find it and why coherentists were right in their criticism of the foundationalistic attempts. The reason is that they supposed that the external standard must guarantee the truth-directedness of theories. The distinction between the two contexts of justification makes it possible to separate the question of the possibility of an external standard of justification and the question of truth.

A second difficulty can also be removed. This is meeting the sceptical challenge. The sceptic required a justification for accepting one worldview over another. The justification could not be provided by foundationalists, because they failed in their search for a standard external to worldviews. Nor could coherentists refute the sceptic, for they denied that there were external standards. In problem-solving, however, we found the required standard. The justification for preferring one worldview to another is based on the comparative problem-solving capacity of competing worldviews. The problems solved, in the last analysis, are problems of life, and as such shared by all human beings, including the sceptic.

Yet another problem disposed of is the demarcation of theories which are worthy of our attention from those which are not. Theories offering possible solutions to specified problems are worthwhile, theories failing to do so are not. Problem-solving thus makes it possible to establish a pool of candidates from which the acceptable solution will be chosen. Problem-solving does not tell us which theory is true, it tells us which theories are those whose truth we ought to try to determine. Problem-solving thus functions as the censor of theories.

On this view of the introduction and justification of philosophical theories, the inseparability of philosophy and cultural influences becomes obvious. For the problems and the ideals are cultural and the attempt to solve the former in accordance with the latter is philosophical. The problems are produced by human beings having to live in the world. The ideals exemplified by particular cases of morality, politics, aesthetic sensibility, religiosity, or scientific understanding represent ways of doing this. Philosophy contributes the analysis, criticism, and justification of the ideals, as well as the philosohical theories by which problems could be solved in accordance with the ideals. These tasks are essential—a society cannot do without someone performing them, if it is to survive.

NOTES

1. John H. Randall, Jr., *How Philosophy Uses Its Past* (New York: Columbia University Press, 1963), 26–7.

2. Foundationalism is defended among others by Roderick Chisholm, *Perceiving* (Ithaca: Cornell University Press, 1957), and *Theory of Knowledge* (Englewood Cliffs, N. J.: Prentice-Hall, 1966); David M. Armstrong, *Belief, Truth and Knowledge* (London: Routledge, 1973); John L. Pollock, *Knowledge and Justification* (Princeton: Princeton University Press, 1974).

3. Coherentism is defended among others by Willard V. Quine, *From a Logical Point of View* (Cambridge: Harvard University Press, 1953), and *Word and Object* (Cambridge: MIT Press, 1960); by Wilfrid Sellars, *Science, Perception and Reality* (London: Routledge, 1963); Keith Lehrer, *Knowledge* (Oxford: Clarendon, 1974); Gilbert Harman, *Thought* (Princeton: Princeton University Press, 1973); Nicholas Rescher, *The Coherence Theory of Truth* (Oxford: Clarendon, 1973); Peter Winch, *The Idea of a Social Science* (London: Routledge, 1958).

4. Scepticism is defended among others by Peter Unger, *Ignorance* (Oxford: Clarendon, 1973); Paul K. Feyerabend, *Against Method* (London: New Left Books, 1973).

5. These are well described by James W. Cornman, "Foundational versus Nonfoundational Theories of Empirical Justification," *American Philosophical*

Quarterly, 14 (1977), 287–97, and by Laurence Bonjour, "Can Empirical Knowledge Have a Foundation?", *American Philosophical Quarterly*, 15 (1978), 1–13.

6. Frank P. Ramsey, *The Foundations of Mathematics* (London: Allen & Unwin, 1931), 115–16.

7. The distinction proposed here between different contexts of justification is related to some similar attempts. The best known is Peirce's theory of abduction. Cf. Kim T. Fann, *Peirce's Theory of Abduction* (Hague: Nijhoff, 1970). The main difference between my account and Peirce's is that he justifies the introduction of a theory with reference to its truth-directedness, while I do so on the basis of its problem-solving capacity. Charles A. Hooker's "Critical Notice of *Minnesota Studies in Philosophy of Science, Vol. IV,*" *Canadian Journal of Philosophy*, 1 (1972), 489–509, distinguishes between retrospective and prospective methodology. He restricts their uses to the philosophy of science and it is unclear what role, if any, problem-solving plays in these methodologies. Larry Laudan's *Progress and Its Problems* (Berkeley: University of California Press, 1977), 108–14, contains a distinction between two contexts of justification: acceptance and pursuit. My distinction is very close to his; the crucial difference is that he considers problem-solving to be the standard in both contexts, while I do not.

8. The interaction between the need and the introduction of a new theory is splendidly illustrated by several works. The classical application of this general theme to philosophy is John H. Randall, Jr., *The Career of Philosophy*, Vols. I–II (New York: Columbia University Press, 1962); in art it is Ernst H. Gombrich, *Art and Illusion* (Princeton: Princeton University Press, 1960); in science it is Joseph Agassi, "The Nature of Scientific Problems and Their Roots in Metaphysics," *The Critical Approach*, ed. M. Bunge (New York: Macmillan, 1964) and *Towards a Historiography of Science, History and Theory*, Beiheft 2 (1963); in the theory of liberal education it is Sheldon Rothblatt, *Tradition and Change in English Liberal Education* (London: Faber, 1976); in ethics it is Alasdair MacIntyre, *A Short History of Ethics* (London: Routledge, 1967).

Chapter Eight

Justification in Philosophy: The Context of Acceptance

"The gods did not reveal from the beginning,
All things to us; but in the course of time,
Through seeking, men find that which is the better ...

These things are, we conjecture, like the truth.

But as for certain truth, no man has known it,
Nor will he know it; neither of the gods,
Nor yet of all the things of which I speak.
And even if by chance he were to utter
The final truth, he would himself not know it."

XENOPHANES[1]

I. *Introduction*

The context of acceptance is composed of the philosophical theories whose introduction has been justified. Thus all theories considered in this context are logically possible solutions of enduring problems in accordance with ideals and they are made initially plausible by their conformity to the worldview which forms their background. The problem of justifying the acceptance of a theory is to decide which of the justifiably introduced theories should be accepted.

The selection can be made by appealing to the second standard of justification: truth-directedness. This dictates that of the justifiably introduced theories that one should be accepted which has the best chance of being true. The determination of which this is depends on comparing rival theories on the basis of their logical consistency, adequacy of interpretation, and capacity to withstand criticism. I shall now discuss these notions.

II. *The Three Tests of Truth-Directedness*

An acceptable theory must be logically consistent. It must not happen that a conclusion entailed by a central part of the theory formally contradicts a conclusion that follows from another central part of the same theory. Consistency requires that the logical consequences of a theory should harmoniously coexist and should not exclude each other.

The reason why a theory should be logically consistent is that it is an attempt to provide a possible way of thinking about a segment of reality and inconsistency demonstrates that reality cannot be that way. A logically inconsistent theory is self-defeating. For the purpose of the theory, the formulation of a possible way of thinking, is rendered unattainable by the theory itself if it results in an impossible way of thinking.

There is, however, a difficulty here presented by the existence of alternative logical systems. It might be accepted that a theory must be logically consistent, but if what counts as logical consistency depends upon the logical system one happens to accept, then this test is trivialized.

The supposed existence of alternative logical systems can be interpreted in at least two ways. The system we have is concerned with establishing the formal relations among propositions. There may be alternatives to it in that logical systems could be constructed whose aims are different; for instance, dialectical logic is an alternative in this sense. These two systems, however, are not rivals, for consistency can be treated as a purely formal relation within mathematical logic.

The more acute form of the difficulty is that there may be alternative logical systems where each presents a rival account of the formal relations among propositions. If the competing logical systems yield identical propositions as consistent and differ only in their *modus operandi*, then once again this presents no challenge to the requirement of consistency.

But what if the two systems give conflicting analyses of consistency? What if some of the things that are logically possible in one system are logically impossible in the other? The resolution in that case must be practical. If there are no detectable errors in either system, then it must be ascertained whether what each claims to be logically impossible is indeed so. That can be done by comparing the problem-solving capacity of the contested propositions.[2]

There is much resistance, however, to this suggestion. For it is generally supposed that logical consistency cannot be subordinated to such practical considerations as problem-solving. But this resistance is misplaced. It is based on the mistaken assumption that the distinction between logical consistency and inconsistency enables one to demarcate the domain of statements which could possibly be true from the domain of statements which are not even candidates for truth. I shall express this by saying that the distinction corresponds to the *truth-possible* and *truth-impossible* distinction. A statement is truth-possible if it is possibly true and it is truth-impossible if it is impossible for it to be true.

The question we need to ask here is: why is it that consistency, that is, conformity to logical rules, can demarcate truth-possible and truth-impossible statements? Or, to put it differently, what gives logical rules the authority they seem to have. The authority of logical rules does not come from logicians. They do indeed formulate the rules, but they do not invent and impose them: logical rules are already there awaiting discovery. Well, how are they discovered?

Logical rules are the rules which guide successful practice. They are crystallizations of methodological principles that have proved successful in the past. Logical rules are implicit in practices we wish to perpetuate and their discovery consists in making explicit and codifying what has been implicit before.

Of course, not all logical rules are derived from successful practice: some are derived from other logical rules. Logical rules have consequences which are frequently difficult to discern. Discerning them is part of what is meant by research in logic. So this answer is not committed to the quite mistaken view that the task of logic is to scrutinize practice for the purpose of extracting rules from it. The rules have already been extracted. One of logic's concerns is to make explicit what has been implicit before.

Logical rules can be used for the identification of truth-possible statements because they embody in a pure form the method employed in successful practice. These rules are not meant to characterize the method of all successful practice. Their role is only to exhibit the method of arguing successfully from premises to conclusion. Logical rules are extracted from successful practice of this sort. But what practice counts as successful?

A practice is successful if it accomplishes its goals. This involves solving whatever problems prompt the practice in accordance with whatever goals the agent accepts. If the agent is mistaken about the nature of the problem he believes himself to have, or if the goal in accordance with which he aims to solve it is unjustifiable, then no matter how well-suited the practice is to the solution of the misidentified problem and to the pursuit of the unjustified goal, it cannot be said to be successful in any straightforward sense.

There is no need to be dogmatic about this. We can distinguish between weak and strong senses of success. A practice may be weakly successful if it leads to the solution of a misidentified problem in accordance with an unjustified goal. While the strong sense implies a genuine problem and a justified goal. The point I want to make concerns the strong sense of success.

In that sense, the correct identification of the problem and the justifiability of the goal are necessary conditions of a practice being successful. Since logical rules are extracted from successful practice, the authority of logical rules depends on the correct identification of problems and the justification of the goals involved in the practice. And this means that we cannot appeal to the authority of logical rules in identifying all problems and judging the justifiability of all goals. Therefore, there is a kind of argument which necessarily precedes the extraction of logical rules, namely the one involved in judging some of the problems and goals.

This point should not be taken to imply that the argument involved in the identification of problems and the justification of goals proceeds independently of logical rules. Of course logical rules are involved, for such rules are extracted from successful practice and at least sometimes the argument involved in the identification of problems and the justification of goals is successful. What the argument implies is that logical rules cannot be appealed to in distinguishing between successful and unsuccessful practice. The precedence of the problem-identifying goal-justifying argument over logic is not in their temporal order, but in the order of their justification.

The basic reason why the identification of the logically consistent with the truth-possible fails is that the practice from which the logical rules are extracted must be successful. However, to judge whether the practice is successful we must employ argument. This argument is either truth-possible or not. If it is truth-possible, then the truth-possible and the logically consistent do not coincide. If it is not truth-possible, then the authority of logical rules derived from it is undermined, for the practice from which it is extracted has not been shown to be successful.

There is a last point that needs to be made. Assume that the objection made above fails and the logically consistent coincides with the truth-possible. It still does not follow that the truth-possible coincides with the logically consistent. For that to follow it would have to be shown that there could not be a successful practice yielding a not yet discovered logical rule. I think that this cannot be shown since the number of such possible practices is unknown. Consequently, if a practice is deemed logically inconsistent, this may be because the logical rule demonstrating its truth-possibility has not yet been discovered. Thus, the failure to be logically consistent does not amount to truth-impossibility. So even if the logically consistent coincides with the truth-possible, the logically inconsistent need not coincide with the truth-impossible.

The conclusion I am drawing from this is that while logical consistency is a test of justification, it is not the most fundamental one. Problem-solving is prior, because practice is prior to the justification of practice.

This should be seen as reinforcing my distinction between the two contexts of justification. In the context of introduction, where the problem is to find *a* solution, logical consistency plays a subordinate role. In the context of acceptance, where the problem is to find the *best* solution, logical consistency is fundamental. But since the latter depends on the former, there must be cases in which logical consistency and justification do not coincide. If this argument is seen as supporting the primacy of practical over theoretical reason, I shall not complain.

The second way of testing the truth-directedness of a theory is through the adequacy of the interpretation it offers. As we have seen, an acceptable theory must offer a logically possible and initially plausible solution to the enduring problem that prompted it. The solution is an interpretation which provides a possible way of thinking about a segment of reality. Interpretations can be thought of as issuing a conditional: if you think of reality in this way and act accordingly, then what was previously problematic will no longer be so.

The obvious difficulty is that in each problem-situation there are many logically possible interpretations. Rival interpretations therefore have to be evaluated. This can be done by determining whether all the relevant facts have been accounted for and by seeing how the theories fare under criticism. The difficulty in deciding whether an interpretation accounts for all the relevant facts is that it is not clear what is to count as fact.

The distinction between facts provided by pure observation and interpretation provided by theory cannot be maintained. There is no pure observation. Cultural influences inevitably affect whether something is observed and the manner in which it is observed. One's worldview crucially influences the judgment of whether something is seen as a discrete unit or as part of a whole, whether it functions as evidence or as part of the problem to be explained, and whether it is important, noteworthy, or relevant.

Thus the problem is that, while part of the justification for accepting a theory is that it accounts for all the relevant facts, what counts as a fact depends on the theory. As a result, two or more rival theories might each legitimately claim to provide an interpretation of all the relevant facts and yet be explaining different sets of facts. It is unclear, therefore, how the truth-directedness of rival theories can be adjudicated on the basis of the conflicting interpretations they offer.

As a first step toward meeting this difficulty consider the strange and abnormal behavior described during the late medieval witchcraze as possession by the Devil. Nowadays the same behavior is described as a form of psychopathology. The descriptions come from different theoretical backgrounds. If what counts as fact were totally determined by particular theories, then there could not be a shared factual ground between late medieval demonology and contemporary medicine. Actually there is common ground, as there is, for instance, also between Marxist and Toynbean philosophies of history, between Nazi and democratic political theories about the authority a state should have, and between aesthetic and scientific explanations of color-effects, etc. The truth is that interpretations offered from the vantage point of rival theories are recognizably interpretations of the same facts. Rival theories typically agree about a common body of facts and they are rivals because they offer conflicting interpretations of them.

This state of affairs is made possible by the primacy of problems of life. At that fundamental level it is not a theoretical option what facts have to be considered and what problems must be dealt with. Being human means that we have to contend with some problems and facts. And the common ground between theories is guaranteed by this common starting point. (This will be further discussed in Chapter Nine.) Consequently it is possible to compare and evaluate theories by considering the respective merits of the interpretations they provide. This comparison and evaluation can be performed by subjecting rival theories to criticism. And this brings us to the third test of truth-directedness.[3]

The fundamental idea here is that the justification for accepting a theory depends, in addition to the considerations already discussed, upon its openness to criticism and capacity successfully to meet it. By openness to criticism I mean the logical possibility of specifying what sort of consideration would show that a theory is mistaken. The point, of course, is not that the acceptability of a theory demands that it should be mistaken. The requirement is rather that the formulation of a theory should permit the possibility of it being mistaken, the examination of whether that possibility obtains, and that the theory should survive that examination. Thus a theory is acceptable, on this score, if it is clear what would make it mistaken, if we try to show that it is mistaken, and if we fail in our attempted criticism.

This test follows from the nature of theories. A theory is an interpretation of some set of facts. The interpretation it offers is incompatible with other possible interpretations. The absence of anything that could be incompatible with an interpretation is conclusive evidence of its inadequacy. For an interpretation is a commitment to a particular view of some set of facts. A commitment always entails the denial of countless other options. Each of the denied options is a potential criticism of the theory in question. If the denial of nothing is entailed by the acceptance of a theory, then the commitment must be empty and the interpretation useless. Therefore, the possibility of criticism is a necessary condition of the adequacy of an interpretation.

The requirement of openness to and survival of criticism grows out of the inadequacy of the view that the justification of a theory depends on there being evidence for it. The mere existence of evidence for a theory contributes very little to its justified acceptability. For any theory, even one known to be unjustified, can have evidence in its favor. Astrological predictions are sometimes verified, people occasionally recover after the ministrations of faith healers, palmists sometimes correctly foretell the future, and some criminals and geniuses have just the sort of bumps on their skulls that phrenologists say they should have. Evidence for a theory may enhance the initial plausibility of the interpretation by showing that it applies to some cases. But one counterinstance is far more important than any number of verifications. For verifications can show only that some things are as the theory suggests; they can not establish that all things are that way. A single counterinstance, however, is sufficient to create a presumption that not everything is as the theory asserts.

Criticizability restricts the interpretation offered by theories in two ways. First, it prescribes the limits within which a justifiable interpetation falls: it must exclude many states of affairs. The more a theory excludes, the more criticizable it is. A high degree of criticizability indicates that the theory offers a great deal of precision and specificity, and conversely, the relative absence of vagueness and generality. Thus the more criticizable a theory is the better is the potential of the interpretation it offers.

Second, criticizability makes it possible to justify the acceptance of one of several rival theories which meet the previous requirements. The decision rests not merely upon noting that the competing theories are criticizable, but upon actually criticizing them. Severe and ingenious criticism is bound to weed out the weaklings. The criticism proceeds by attempting to show that what the theory excluded does, in fact, obtain. Thus the interpretation offered by the theory is shown to be mistaken.

The surviving theory becomes the solution of the problem. A criticizable theory that survives serious criticism, wins out against its competitors, and passes the other tests, is one that it is justifiable to accept. The conclusion warranted by critical attention to an acceptable theory is that what it is committed to excluding stays excluded, that what it says is reasonable to believe.

III. *Justification and the Context of Acceptance*

There is a point that should be noted about the justification of the acceptance of philosophical theories in general. Logical consistency and openness to criticism are tests that can be applied to a theory purely in its own terms. We need to know no more than the theory itself to be able to answer questions of whether it is free of internal contradictions and whether it is possible to specify the circumstances in which it would be shown to be mistaken.

However, for the application of the tests of adequacy of interpretation and the capacity to withstand criticism, it is necessary to look beyond the confines of the theory. The adequacy of an interpretation depends on the theory's capacity to reconcile the worldview in which it is formulated with whatever anomaly has presented itself. The achievement of this reconciliation depends on whether all the facts relevant to the conflict between the worldview and the anomaly can be accommodated by the theory. And this can be judged only if one is familiar with the worldview.

Similarly, whether a theory survives criticism requires looking beyond the theory. For the facts that the theory interpets and the facts that might count as criticisms of it both originate outside of the theory. In order to explain this in greater detail I need to discuss again the distinction introduced in Chapter Two between an account of what the facts are and an attempt to interpret the facts. There is no sharp distinction between these two concerns. The difference between them is largely a matter of emphasis. Nevertheless, the question of where the emphasis is placed is important for my purposes.

I have called accounts primarily concerned with what the facts are descriptive theories and those interested mainly in the interpretation of facts interpretive theories. Descriptive theories are the products of such inquiries as who killed John F. Kennedy, why did Churchill advocate that the Allied invasion of Europe should take place in Greece, what is the relationship between cholesterol level in the blood and heart failure, is cancer caused by a virus, is speed greater than the speed of light possible, and does raising the prime rate of interest tend to diminish inflation.

Typical interpretive theories are prompted by attempts to decipher the symbolism of a poem, to understand the significance of rituals in the ceremonies of a primitive tribe, to judge which of several narratives of the same event best conveys the emotional climate of the participants, to decide whether there are patterns in history, to gauge whether a person is reliable, and to make up one's mind whether lying or telling the cruel truth is likely to cause less suffering in the long run.[4]

Interpretive theories tend to be more general, involve more evaluation, rely more on personal experience and judgment, and provide explanation and understanding which tend to be less exclusive of competing possibilities than do descriptive theories. Descriptive theories, on the other hand, tend to be more open to experimental testing, more likely to provide causal explanations, and more easily allow for the derivation of predictions than interpretive theories do.

Philosophical theories are typical interpretive theories. They differ from them in being even more general. The kind of middle and low range scientific theories which are the daily concern of working scientists are typically descriptive. There is no clear distinction between descriptive scientific and interpretive philosophical theories. They are continuous, but they occupy opposite ends of the continuum. This is important for my purposes because I think that the justification of the acceptance of philosophical theories depends to a considerable extent on their connections with the descriptive theories upon whose resources they draw.

On the basis of the distinction between descriptive and interpretive theories it is possible to enlarge upon the justification of philosophical theories. The facts philosophical theories interpret are provided by common sense and descriptive theories. Since descriptive theories change, because they are refuted, improved, enlarged, or incorporated into more adequate descriptive theories, the facts they make available for philosophical interpretation also change. Thus one way of criticizing philosophical theories is by showing that the facts they have interpreted are no longer as the theory took them to be. In this way, descriptive theories act as a check on interpretive philosophical theories.

The connection between descriptive and philosophical theories has a consequence that I want to emphasize. I have argued at length that cultural influences upon philosophical theories cannot be disregarded if we want to justify them. Descriptive theories are among cultural influences and it is descriptive theories which provide the facts for philosophical theories, the ground upon which they can be criticized, and if they survive criticism, justified. So here is an additional reason why cultural influences cannot be ignored by philosophers.

The primary standard of justification in the context of acceptance is truth-directedness, but it is not the only standard. If the sole aim of inquiries were the accumulation of likely truths, we would end up with an enormously large amount of trivial and useless information. It is probably true and certainly important that deontological, teleological, and self-realizationist moral theories seem to constitute the presently available options. It is probably also true but quite unimportant that the number of available moral options is odd, that it is smaller than the number of planets, but greater than the number of living Habsburg pretenders. The truths we aim at and would like to discover or approximate are selected. The selections are dictated by our interests. And what fundamentally influences our interest are the problems we have and need to solve. Thus problem-solving provides a focus for the truth-directedness of our inquiries. Important and interesting approximations of truth are those which are likely to help us develop theories for solving enduring problems in accordance with ideals. In the context of acceptance our aim is to decide which theory is most likely to be true. But the theories available as options have already been selected on the basis of their possible problem-solving capacity. This is why problem-solving is a relevant though subsidiary standard in the context of acceptance.

IV. *Justification and Truth*

Finding a theory acceptable does not mean that it is true. For an acceptable theory has merely survived the criticisms of which one could think. It has been proved victorious only over presently available rivals. A true theory would have to survive all possible criticisms and be preferable to all possible rivals. It is logically impossible to show what all possible criticisms and rivals are, and even if a putative list were available, it would be impossible to determine whether it was complete.

It is thus a consequence of this requirement that theories cannot be known to be true. However, once it is understood how little this limitation actually means, its harmlessness becomes patent. First of all, it does not affect the claim that some theories are eminently reasonable and should be accepted. For if a theory offers a solution to the problem it was supposed to solve, if it is logically consistent, provides a criticizable interpretation, survives criticism, and prevails over its rivals, then one has all the reasons for accepting it and no reason at all for doubting it. Secondly, to say that a theory cannot be known to be true is merely to recognize the facts that all the criticisms may not have been thought of and that better rival interpretations may yet be invented. Thirdly, truth is far from being an unambiguous notion. If one has a right to call something true only if the logical possibility of error has been excluded, then theories should not be said to be true. But it may be meant by a true theory that one has a right to accept it and there is no reason to doubt it. Furthermore, not even in the strict sense is truth unemployable, for one can say that I believe that it is true, or that there is no reason for doubting its truth. Only the dogmatic claim is proscribed.

A closely related but much less widely recognized consequence of this requirement is that theories cannot be known to be false either. A theory would be false if what it was committed to asserting was shown not to be so. But just as conclusive verification is impossible due to the impossibility of excluding potential rivals and criticisms, so also is conclusive criticism excluded. For how could it be determined that there could not be a legitimate way for the theory to handle criticism? And how could it be determined that the criticism itself could not be shown to be faulty? The best that can be done is to accept the criticism because as things are it cannot be met and to give up the theory because nobody can think of a legitimate way of defending it. There is a point beyond which a theory should be rejected, just as there is a point beyond which it should be accepted. But these points do not coincide with the truth and falsehood of the theory.

This gap between the truth and falsehood of theories and the justification for accepting or rejecting them is created by human fallibility. Truth and falsehood are ideal limits between which the justification of theories must fall. The ideal limits cannot be known to have been attained because there cannot be a demonstration that all possibility of error has been eliminated. But the implications of this cannot comfort irrationalists, for it does not follow that the acceptance or rejection of a theory cannot be supported by excellent reasons. Indubitability and conclusive evidence are indeed impossible. If it is realized, however, that philosophy does not deal with eternal truths but with enduring human problems and ideals, then these unreasonable expectations should be seen for what they are: unreasonable.

The recognition that there is a gap between truth and falsehood and their reasoned approximations makes it possible to explain a frequent and otherwise inexplicable occurrence in the history of ideas. There are many theories whose acceptance was justified at one time and were shown to be mistaken later. Other theories have sometimes been justifiably rejected only to be shown to be viable options later. The obvious thing to say about such cases is that a theory we have good reasons for regarding as false now was in fact acceptable in the past and a theory which is now reasonably thought to be true should have been rejected at another time. Truth and falsehood are timeless and unattainable. Justified acceptance and rejection vary with time, but they are within our grasp. If justified acceptance were possible only if the theory is true and justified rejection only if it is false, then the acceptance of all false theories would have to be declared irrational and it would be reasonable to accept only true theories. As a result, most of our predecessors would have to be suspected of irrationality and most of our contemporaries would become paragons of rationality. This is a disturbingly antihistorical attitude whose intolerance is matched only by its implausibility. The attitude comes from ignoring the worldview which forms the background of theories.

V. *Conclusion*

In this chapter I have concentrated on the second context of justification: the context of acceptance. The question to be answered in this context is: which of the justifiably introduced philosophical theories offers the best solution of the relevant enduring problem in accordance with a particular ideal.

As an illustration of how the justification of the acceptance of a theory can be debated I shall apply the three tests of truth-directedness to an internal perennial argument between the traditionalist and reformist attempts to reconcile the Christian tradition with what seems to be the failure of all the arguments for the existence of God. Each attempts to achieve the reconciliation by putting new emphasis upon the importance of a presupposition of the Christian ideal and by deemphasizing the role of arguments for the existence of God. Thus the traditionalist stresses the importance of religious experience, while the reformist gives pride of place to moral inspiration and metaphorical teaching. I shall assume for the sake of argument that the introduction of these interpretations of Christianity is justified. The present question is: how could one come to a rational decision regarding the justifiability of the acceptance of one of these interpretations? The point of raising the question is not to settle it but to illustrate how it could be debated.

If we apply the first test, logical consistency, both interpretations encounter serious difficulties. The traditionalist emphasizes religious experience at the expense of arguments. The problem he faces is that if this experience is of a supernatural being, then it is hard to see how a human being could have it. For human experiences seem to be restricted to the natural world. If the experience is of a natural embodiment or expression of the supernatural, such as the historical Jesus, then some argument is needed to establish the supposed connection between the supernatural and its embodiment. If the argument is given, the traditionalist interpretation fails, for its purpose was to stress religious experiences at the expense of the failed arguments. If the argument is not given, the interpretation fails again for it offers no justification for believing that the experience is of anything supernatural.

The reformist's position, however, also has its problems about logical consistency. If the stressed element is the moral vision expressed in the inspirational language of metaphor, then what happens to such factual claims of Christianity as the divinity of Jesus and the occurrence of miracles? In the past, the justification of the moral vision had been that it rested upon the truth of these factual claims. But the reformist interpretation no longer relies on them. This leaves the reformist without a justification for accepting his vision. Thus if the reformist offers a justification, his interpretation is indistinguishable from the standard one whose problems he was trying to solve. If he fails to offer a justification, then there is no reason for accepting his interpretation.

These difficulties carry over to the application of the second test of truth-directedness: adequacy of interpretation. The success of both the traditionalist and reformist theories depends on reconciling the ideal of Christianity with the apparent failure of the arguments for the existence of God. This requires that all the essential elements of the ideal, all its presuppositions, be accommodated in the new interpetation. For if they are not, then what is offered is not an interpretation of the ideal, but something else: a new ideal perhaps. Now it is perfectly in order to rearrange the importance of various presuppositions in offering a new interpretation; that in effect is what it is to have a new interpretation. It seems, however, that the traditionalist and the reformist actually reject some presuppositions of Christianity in order to come to terms with the conflict presented by the apparent refutation of all proofs for God's existence. The traditionalist appears to dismiss the theological element in Christianity; it thus removes its appeal to man's reason. The reformist eliminates the factual claims of Christianity; its vision and metaphors consequently become indistinguishable from fantasy and myth.

The third test of truth-directedness is openness to and capacity to withstand criticism. The discussion of logical consistency and adequacy of interpretation clearly show that both interpretations are open to criticism. The question is whether they also withstand it. I have indicated my doubts on this score. If the interpretations succumb to criticism, there are two possibilities. Either a better interpretation is offered and then the ideal overcomes the conflict between the tradition and the contemporary doubts about it, or, if no satisfactory interpretation is found, the ideal should be abandoned. For it will then have been shown to be a possible though unsuccessful solution to the enduring problem of giving meaning and purpose to human life.

The judgment of whether a philosophical theory is acceptable can be made on the basis of the three tests of truth-directedness. In an ideal situation, we start with a number of philosophical theories whose introduction has been justified. We apply the three tests to them and find that one passes and the others fail to do so. Thus we accept the survivor as the best solution of the enduring problem in accordance with the ideal.

Even in this ideal situation, however, there is no guarantee that the justified theory is true. For we may have made a mistake in applying the tests. The mistakes need not though may be due to carelessness. Their source is human ignorance: we may not know all the facts relevant to appraising a theory, we may not have thought of all the criticisms, we may not have discovered all possible rival theories, and theories we have criticized may be defended in ways we have yet to find. Thus justification does not provide grounds for certainty. What it does do is to entitle one to claim that if a theory is justified, then he has all the reasons he can then have for accepting it and no available reason at all for doubting it. Since the reasons may change, the justification of the theory may also change.

Actual situations fall short of the ideal. Usually, the tests are being applied and thus there is disagreement about the justification of particular philosophical theories. Such disagreements show that the testing has not gone as far as it should. For there is a true or false answer to the question of whether a theory is logically consistent, whether its interpretation accounts for all the relevant facts, and whether it has survived all available criticism. From there being a definite answer, it does not follow that it is easy to find it. The persistence of disagreements indicates just how difficult it is. These disagreements, however, are good things. For they concern questions upon whose correct answer depends the well-being of society. What is being debated are fundamental human problems and the ideals that should guide us in solving them. There is no reason for thinking that the debates have a simple resolution, nor is there ground for despair just because they do not.

THE STATE OF THE ARGUMENT

In this part of the book I have given an account of the structure of justification in philosophy. I have answered the question of how philosophical theories can be justified. I have not asked and certainly not answered the question of what particular philosophical theories are in fact justified. It is a method for justification, rather than justification itself that I have provided.

Having such a method, however, is important. For with it we can justify philosophical theories, and this means that we can justify the ideals or the interpretation of ideals for solving our enduring problems. In other words, we can conduct and resolve perennial arguments in particular problem-situations. And because we can do all this, we can construct and justify the worldview which is composed of the enduring problems, the ideals for solving them, the philosophical theories championing their merits, and the perennial arguments between rival philosophical theories. The benefit such a worldview provides is the possibility of living a meaningful and purposeful life by members of the society whose worldview it is. A justified worldview makes the good life possible.

The key idea of my account of philosophical justification is the distinction between the contexts of introduction and acceptance. The distinction aims to replace the mistaken distinction between the contexts of discovery and justification. There are two main differences between the proposed and the criticized distinctions. The first is that justification plays a role in both the contexts of introduction and acceptance. This contrasts with the context of discovery being nonrational. The advantage gained is that the question of what theories should be considered as candidates becomes rationally answerable. The second difference is that the relevance of cultural influences must be recognized both to the introduction and to the acceptance of theories. The earlier distinction sharply divided the context to which cultural influences are relevant and the context where rational justification is possible. The removal of this ill-conceived division makes it possible for philosophy to play the role it needs to and should play in society.

Justification is relevant to both the introduction and the acceptance of theories, but the kinds of justification required are different. The justification of the introduction of a theory is in terms of its problem-solving capacity. It is testable by determining whether the theory is a possible solution of the enduring problem that prompted it and if so whether it is initially plausible. Initial plausibility is judged by finding out whether the theory manages to offer a possible reconciliation of the conflict occurring in the worldview. The worldview is the embodiment of the conventional interpretations of the ideals in accordance with which the enduring problems are to be solved.

The justification of the acceptance of a theory depends on its truth-directedness. The three tests are logical consistency, adequacy of interpretation, and the capacity to withstand criticism. These tests are applied to determine which of several possible and plausible solutions of problems has the best chance of being true.

Problem-solving and truth-directedness are to be applied jointly. Problem-solving by itself is a purely pragmatic criterion. It alone is insufficient, for it affords no way of choosing between temporary fortuitous success and success due to having come close to the truth. Truth-directedness by itself leads to triviality. For it is easy and pointless to generate a vast amount of likely truths. Some putative truths are important and it is these we want our theories to be. Problem-solving provides the required principle for distinguishing between important and trivial candidates for truths. Thus the rational justification of philosophical theories depends on their conformity to the standards of problem-solving and truth-directedness.

NOTES

1. Xenophanes, *Fragments*, DK 18, 35, 34.

2. Nicholas Rescher in Chapters XIII and XIV of *Methodological Pragmatism* (Oxford: Blackwell, 1977), gives an account of how this is to be done. I accept his account.

3. The notion I appeal to here is substantially Popper's idea of criticism. Cf., Essays 1, 2, 3, 8, and 10 in *Objective Knowledge* (New York: Harper and Row, 1968).

4. Joel J. Kupperman in Chapter Eight of *Philosophy, The Fundamental Problems* (New York: St. Martin's Press, 1978), gives an excellent account of some of the crucial differences between these two types of theories.

PART FOUR

PHILOSOPHY AND SOME
OF
ITS RELATIONS

Chapter Nine

Philosophy and Common Sense

"This, after all, you know, really is a finger: there is no doubt
about it: I know it and you all know it. And I think we may
safely challenge any philosopher to bring forward any
argument in favour either of the proposition that we do not
know it, or of the proposition that it is not true, which does not
at some point, rest upon some premise which is, beyond
comparison, less certain than is the proposition which it is
designed to attack."

GEORGE E. MOORE[1]

I. *Introduction*

In this fourth part of the book I aim to clarify further the nature of
philosophy by exploring its relations to common sense, science, and
history. I shall argue that the construction and justification of
worldviews for our time and society requires increased emphasis
upon common sense and historical understanding and the lessening
of the prevailing philosophical emphasis upon science.

I have argued in Chapter Eight that philosophical theories can
be evaluated by comparing the adequacy of the respective
interpretations they offer, because there is a shared ground
between them. I shall now argue that this shared ground is the
common sense view of the world. It is presupposed by all theories
about the world and this introduces an inevitable anthropocentric
element into worldviews. Anthropocentrism, however, is quite
compatible with the possibility of objective and rational justification, as we shall see in this chapter.

I shall start by defending the combination of three theses. The
first is that all of our beliefs about the nature of reality rest upon a
foundation. The second is that this foundation is the only one
possible for human beliefs. The third is that the foundation is what
I shall call the common sense view of the world (common sense,
from now on). The justification of any of our beliefs about the
nature of reality depends partly upon justifying the foundation
upon which they rest.

My view is that some beliefs are basic. These constitute the
foundation of all other beliefs about the nature of reality. Other

beliefs rest upon these basic beliefs in the sense that the truth-value of basic beliefs is independent of the truth-value of other beliefs, while the truth-value of other beliefs depends on the truth-value of basic beliefs. Any basic belief may be false. In that case, our system of beliefs would be irremediably faulty and the chances of human life continuing would be poor. Fortunately, there is no reason for thinking that basic beliefs are false and there are good reasons for thinking that they are true.

Basic beliefs are common sense beliefs. They constitute the foundation of all other beliefs about the nature of reality. They must do so because given human nature and the world, it cannot be otherwise.

This view can be attacked in at least two ways. The first is to deny that beliefs have an unavoidable foundation. According to this criticism, what beliefs are basic is a contingent matter decided by convention. The second attack is to concede that beliefs have an unavoidable foundation, but to deny that it is constituted of common sense.

I shall meet both objections by showing why common sense beliefs must be basic. Since other beliefs about the nature of reality presuppose common sense beliefs, they cannot constitute a foundation alternative to common sense.

My procedure is to give an account of basic beliefs, show why they must be common sense beliefs, consider the extent to which they can be justified, and indicate the consequence this has for philosophy.

II. *Basic Beliefs*[2]

Examples of basic beliefs are that I have a body with my limbs and head attached to it, that there exist other people and many familiar material objects, that I have existed for many years, and that the world existed before I was born, and that it will continue to exist after I die, that I perceive the world through my senses, that I experience colors, sounds, smells, tastes, shapes, textures, and sizes, that the vast majority of my perceptions are correct, that I occasionally misperceive. Furthermore, the kind of basic beliefs I have are the same as the kind other people have.[3]

A belief is basic if and only if it has four characteristics: it is universally held, unavoidable, a necessary condition of action, and the likelihood of its truth cannot and need not be increased by additional evidence.

The first defining characteristic of basic beliefs is that they are universal: every sane, normal, and healthy human being has them. For instance, everybody believes that he has a body. I do not mean that everybody has the fairly abstract concept of a human body. But that everybody believes that he has what we mean by a body: a head, a trunk, and several limbs. How people in different cultures and historical periods think or feel about their bodies differs of course. But they differ in their attitudes towards their bodies, not in their beliefs about having one.

A person may come to doubt momentarily that he has a body. After an accident perhaps someome may think that he is dead and his experiences occur in afterlife. But these are abnormal cases. Something very exceptional has to happen to put a person in that unusual frame of mind. The universality of basic beliefs applies only to normal cases. When a person doubts that he has a body, there is always some very special explanation for his doing so.

A person need not be conscious of a belief he holds. One can be said to hold a belief if he is commited to it: he thinks and acts as if the belief were true. If he is challenged, he may avow the belief. But commitment to basic beliefs is so fundamental and obvious that people usually go through life without needing or having an opportunity of expressing them. Why would one want to say that he has a head? Nor is it necessary that when a person has a basic belief he should be able to express it; he may not, because he has no words for it. If he had them, he would express them—provided there was a need for it.

The second defining characteristic of basic beliefs is that they are unavoidable. A person has no choice about holding them. The acquisition of basic beliefs does not depend on persuasion, on gathering evidence, on passing from a state of neutrality to a state of commitment. Willing to believe or not to believe plays no role in basic beliefs. Such beliefs as that one has a body, or that one has existed for many years, or that material objects continue to exist even when they are not perceived, or that one sees colors and hears sounds, are not beliefs that a person can or needs to make an effort to hold. In a sense, yet to be explained, basic beliefs are natural, as walking, breathing, and getting hungry or tired are natural.

Nor can one make a successful effort not to hold basic beliefs. A person can certainly say that he does not believe that he has existed for many years, or that he doubts that he has a body. But denying it does not amount to disbelieving it, for the person's actions betray his continued commitment to the belief he denies. And other things he says, to his physician, to the census taker, to the passport issuing officer, clearly contradict his denial. If a person did the impossible and succeeded in persuading himself not to hold some of his basic beliefs, his world would collapse. For the truth of basic beliefs is presupposed by nonbasic beliefs. For instance, if someone did not believe that he has existed for many years, he could not trust his memory, he would have to treat his own feelings about his family, friends, enemies, superiors, and subordinates as unreliable. As a result he could perform no action where the past is the guide to the present; and there are few such actions.

This leads to the third defining characteristic of basic beliefs. Holding basic beliefs is a necessary condition of action. In performing an action, a person intends to accomplish some goal. Obviously, he would not perform the action unless he believed that its performance would offer at least a chance of achieving the intended goal. Basic beliefs are necessary conditions of action because if they were false, action would become pointless or impossible. If one did not have a body, he could not act. If the world did not exist, there would be nothing to act towards. If perceptions were not generally reliable, actions, based upon their reliability, would be pointless.

It might be objected that the acknowledged falsehood of a basic belief, in the existence of other people, for instance, would not make all action pointless or impossible. Even if there were no other people, there may still be a point in action directed toward material objects.

This objection calls for an important qualification of the account of basic beliefs. Basic beliefs form a system. The understanding and acceptance of individual basic beliefs are indissolubly connected. My belief in the existence of other people depends on my ability to distinguish between people and material objects; my beliefs in my past existence and in the continued existence of the world when I do not perceive it depend on my ability to distinguish between myself and the world; and if I did not distinguish between different colors, sounds, and smells, I could not believe that I perceive the world in terms of colors, sounds, and smells. The understanding and acceptance of basic beliefs does not occur piecemeal, it must be comprehensive.

The fourth defining characteristic of basic beliefs is that additional evidence does not and need not increase the likelihood of their truth. Basic beliefs do not need additional evidence. Belief in the existence of material objects is not strengthened by the perception of further material objects, and doubts about their existence are not resolved by urging the doubter to observe the world. Whatever evidence there is in favor of basic beliefs is already in.

The explanation of this feature is that what is contested by those who doubt the truth of basic beliefs is not the quality or quantity of the supporting evidence, but its interpretation. Nobody doubts that human beings hold basic beliefs and do so on the basis of experience. What is doubted is that anyone is justified in holding basic beliefs.

The four defining characteristics of basic beliefs identify them. The identification does not amount to a justification. It is possible that everybody holds these basic beliefs and everybody is mistaken. Many defenders of common sense have resigned themselves to the unjustifiability of basic beliefs. Hume's remarks about pyrrhonian scepticism are typical in this respect: scepticism "can have no other tendency than to show the whimsical condition of mankind, who must *act and reason and believe*, though they are not able, by their most diligent enquiry, to satisfy themselves concerning the foundations of these operations or to remove the objections which may be raised against them."[4] We can do better.

III. *Basic Beliefs and Common Sense*[5]

The system of basic beliefs is the common sense view of the world. The reason why common sense and not some other kind of beliefs are basic has to do with human nature: common sense beliefs are natural. I use the term in contrast with cultivated. Common sense beliefs are natural in that they are nonreflective, physiologically based, and untaught.

The traditional defence of common sense has usually gone hand in hand with the empiricist distinction between beliefs based on pure observation and theoretical beliefs. Common sense beliefs were thought to be basic because they were supposed to be based on pure observation. I shall assume that the empiricist distinction in untenable, for there is no pure observation. Observation is unavoidably tainted by interpretation. Common sense beliefs, like all others, involve interpretation.

Yet the empiricists had a point. It may be that all observation involves interpretation, but some kinds of observation involve less interpretation than others, and some interpretations are not matters of conventional preference. In saying that common sense beliefs are nonreflective I mean to call attention to that one of their features which guarantees that the interpretations they involve are not arbitrary, conventional, or a matter of preference.

Believing that one has a body, that material objects exist, that the world will continue to exist after one dies, are not constructions one puts on experiences after thinking about them, subjecting them to criticism, and successfully verifying them. One holds them because no other interpretation of experiences seems possible; they are forced upon normal human beings. This is what I mean by saying that common sense beliefs are nonreflective. Thus, if common sense beliefs are false, the interpretation involved in them cannot be replaced by some other interpretation, for there are no alternatives to it.

But what about the sceptical hypotheses? What about Descartes' evil demon, the possibility of systematic deception by some powerful outside agency? These sceptical possibilities do not provide an alternative interpetation. For, as I shall shortly show, they either leave the nature of the supposed deceiving agency unspecified, in which case the hypothesis is simply the already admitted possibility that the common sense interpretation may be mistaken; or, the nature of the deceiving agency is specified, but the specification presupposes the truth of common sense, and so no genuine alternative have been presented. Of course, the sceptical demand that the system of basic beliefs be justified has to be met. My point here is simply that the sceptical objections do not prevent the identification of the system of basic beliefs with common sense.

The reason why common sense beliefs are nonreflective, and so no alternative interpretation of them is possible, is that they are physiologically based. This means that, apart from a very small minority with genetic or acquired abnormalities, people come to hold common sense beliefs, because this is the information their senses provide. It is simply a fact about human beings that they perceive the world in five sense modalities. So in the most innocuous sense possible, it is natural for human beings to believe what they see, hear, taste, touch, and smell.

This is not to deny that whatever is perceived is subject to interpretation. The interpretation reflects a conscious or unconscious theoretical bias, and this may change what is perceived. Perception is influenced by past experience, expectations, by the accepted categories of classification. These change from person to person and especially from culture to culture. But it does not follow that there is nothing that is naturally perceived.

Consider a case. Suppose that the perception in question is a Bach recording being heard by a musically knowledgeable person in this society. Interpretation would play an enormous role in his description of the event. But what would happen if the same piece of music was heard by a snake-charmer, a tone-deaf burglar, and a New Guinea headhunter? Their respective interpretations would be vastly different. But beyond their interpretations we find that they would all hear sounds. The sounds would be interpreted variously, but the raw material would be perceived by all.

Perhaps there is interpretation involved even in the experience of hearing sounds. Could it not be that the headhunter does not hear a continuous melody, but merely a series of discrete auditory stimuli? This too is possible. But it does not alter the fact that they all hear sounds. The fact that given a stimulus of a certain sort people will have auditory, visual, olefactory experiences establishes that common sense is physiologically based. Common sense is that part of human experience that a person cannot help having by dint of being human.

The physiological base does not guarantee the truth of common sense or free it from interpretation. For it may be that the human physiological apparatus consistently misinforms, and so, while our experiences are physiologically based, they are misleading. It is also possible and likely that an animal or an extraterrestrial being would perceive the same stimulus and interpret it differently. The point of arguing for a physiological base for common sense is not to render it immune to criticism, but to establish it as the base from which any human being must start. The fundamentality of common sense amounts to no more, and to no less, than the recognition that the point of departure for theories about the world is not arbitrary, but determined by the human physiological apparatus.

Not only are the modalities in which human beings perceive the world determined by our physiology, but the repertoire of possible responses is also bound by the capabilities of the human body. Consumption and elimination, pain and pleasure, sleep and wakefulness, rest and motion, maturing and aging, are some of the inescapable dimensions of being human. Of course there are immense individual, cultural, and historical differences between people. But these are due partly to the manner in which people at different times and in different social groups have coped with the limits imposed by their bodies. Common sense marks the outer limits of human possibility; variations and differences occur within these limits.

The fundamentality of common sense does not mean, however, that these limits cannot be overcome. Pain can be alleviated and pleasure produced by manipulating the brain; sleep may be induced and wakefulness artificially sustained; consumption can be replaced by intravenous injections and elimination drastically reduced. And, of course, scientific instruments can be used to supplement existing senses and thereby enormously increase the humanly perceivable parts of the world. However, none of this changes the fact that even the most sophisticated scientific instrument must be calibrated with reference to the human senses and the success and failure of all techniques designed to manipulate physiological functions must be judged by the criterion of human experience. X-rays, microscopes, or telescopes function well if we can actually see what is otherwise beyond our reach, and pain is alleviated only if the person suffering from it no longer *feels* it. Common sense is fundamental because it is the view with which normal human beings must start. Refinements and alterations and the acquisition of depth and breadth occur against the background of common sense.

Another reason for thinking of common sense beliefs as natural is that children need not be taught to believe that they have bodies, that the world exists, that they perceive colors, sounds, and tastes. As soon as they are old enough to understand what is involved in these beliefs, they accept them. It is immaterial whether common sense beliefs are untaught because they are innate or because people immediately come to hold them when their development reaches a certain stage. What is important is that, innate or acquired, there seem to be no choices involved in coming to hold common sense beliefs. A child cannot do well or badly in picking them up, although he may be precocious or retarded.

I have identified basic beliefs with common sense beliefs. The ground of this identification is that whatever beliefs turn out to be basic must rest on human nature, and be, in that sense, natural. Common sense beliefs are natural because they are nonreflective, physiologically based, and untaught.

IV. *The Justification of Common Sense*

A critic of common sense may admit that the world comes to us filtered through our physiology and deny that there is any justification for accepting the resultant beliefs. What a justification has to provide is some reason for trusting our method of acquiring information. The argument for common sense being basic does not provide such a justification. The existence of an unavoidable foundation is compatible with the unreliability of the foundation.

The required justification, however, lies close at hand. The justification is that the world seems to be as common sense depicts it and when one acts on the assumption that it really is that way—as we all do—then by and large the actions are successful. The explanation of this pattern of successful action is that the common sense beliefs upon which it is based are true.

This justification has its problems. The first has to do with what constitutes success in action. It may be objected that success is determined with reference to the achievement of ideals. But there are no ideals implicit in common sense, for no ideal meets the requirements of universality, unavoidability, being the necessary condition of all action, and not needing additional evidential support. Survival comes as close as any to being a common sense ideal. But heros, martyrs, and suicides put a lie to that. This being the case, the success of actions based on common sense beliefs cannot be judged.

My reply to this objection is to deny that success must be judged with reference to the achievement of ideals. Problem-solving is another way of gauging success, and in the context of common sense, it is the only way. To develop this point I have to turn back to the distinction between problems of life and problems of reflection drawn in Chapter Three.

In the context of common sense, success in action means solving problems of life. What is meant by success here is not any particular solution, but simply the fact of having one. Some solutions are preferable to others; but my concern at the moment is with having a solution as opposed to not having any. The context is the context of introduction and not the context of acceptance, as I have noted in Chapters Seven and Eight.

There is a clear connection between common sense and problems of life. They are both universally and unavoidably human. They are also both natural. For it requires no reflection to encounter problems of life. Furthermore, problems of life are physiologically based: people have them because they have their bodies with physiological and motor capacities, and that is the equipment they have for coping with challenges presented by the world. Nor does a person have to be taught to encounter problems of life; they occur to all people regardless of their learning.

The difference between problems of life and common sense comes in part from the different roles they play in action. Problems of life call for action on the part of the person who has them. Common sense suggests what action is to be taken. The justification of common sense is that the actions it prompts do solve problems of life: that constitutes success.

The truth is, however, that actions prompted by common sense are not always successful. Furthermore, there are situations in which common sense prompts no response at all, or even worse, it prompts a harmful one.

Common sense is adequate when everything is going as expected. But when the routine is upset and expectations are basically disappointed, when crises occur, then the picture of the world that common sense presents must be supplemented and made more sophisticated. Theories attempt to provide answers where common sense has proved inadequate. Part of the task of such efforts is to construct a picture of the world capable of accommodating anomalies which have proved too difficult for common sense. In so doing, theories may help solve problems of life by rendering events understandable.

But no matter how sophisticated the theoretical approach becomes, the fundamentality of common sense remains indisputable. For the ultimate test as well as the initial starting point of all theories must be the original problem-situation that is composed of common sense and some anomaly or another. The restriction is created by the physiological boundaries human beings inescapably have.

There are very many problems—problems of reflection—whose roots are other than the conflict between common sense and anomalous experience. They may occur because theories give contrary accounts of the same segment of the world; or because there is methodological disagreement about the kind of theory that is needed. Other problems concern the practical, political, or moral implications of various theories. All of these problems, however, are parasitic upon theories, and theories arise because common sense is thwarted.

This raises the second difficulty the justification of common sense may be said to have: the justification is too pragmatic. Success in coping with the vicissitudes of life is one thing, epistemological justification is another. This is true, but not a difficulty for my thesis.

Problem-solving is one standard of justification, truth-directedness is the other. Problem-solving is the dominant standard in the context of introduction, truth-directedness is the dominant standard in the context of acceptance. When we operate in the context of common sense and problems of life, problem-solving is the relevant standard. This is the context with which we must start and with reference to which success is ultimately judged. For this context is composed of the facts of physiology and the world imposing upon us the limits within which we must live.

As we have seen, however, common sense is not always adequate, and even when it is, there may be several equally commonsensical solutions to each problem of life, and we want to choose the best. The occasional inadequacy of common sense and the availability of competing solutions forces one to leave behind common sense and problems of life for theoretical solutions and problems of reflection. The passage is from the context of introduction to the context of acceptance. The corollary is that the dominant standard of justification changes from problem-solving to truth-directedness.

In this new context we no longer face the pragmatic problem of finding a solution. The problem becomes the epistemological one of choosing the best solution among many. The test of justification correspondingly changes from practical success to the approximation of truth. So while it is true that pragmatic justification plays an important role in the defence of common sense, it is also true that epistemological justification has a role as well, and one that is no less important.

A third possible difficulty is presented by the admission just made that actions based on common sense are not always successful. It may be objected that if this is so, then the justification of common sense is correspondingly weakened.

My reply is that the justification of common sense does not involve the claim that problems of life can successfully be solved by relying on common sense alone. The justification does not depend on common sense being sufficient, but only on being necessary for successful action. Indeed, no reasonable defender of common sense would deny that common sense must be supplemented by theories which go far beyond it. The advancement of knowledge consists in transcending common sense. However, the relation between theoretical sophistication and common sense is the relation between a structure and its foundation, and not the relation between learned truth and primitive error.

Thus my reply to the objection that action based on common sense may be unsuccessful is that failure is due either to erroneous beliefs other than common sense ones, or to the insufficiency of common sense beliefs by themselves. In neither case does failure imply the falsehood of common sense beliefs.

Another objection against the justification of common sense is that while there are actions whose success is explained by the truth of common sense beliefs, their success has explanations which compete with the one defenders of common sense favor. Thus to justify common sense, these other explanations must be eliminated. The reply to this objection has already been touched upon, but I shall elaborate it here.

The other explanations of successful actions are the numerous and ingenious sceptical hypotheses. They take the form of postulating some powerful agent who causes one to have *all* the experiences of the world he has. The veracity of experiences cannot be checked by predicting one's future experiences, because they too will be similarly caused. Nor can one appeal to other people's experiences, for both the supposed other people and the putative act of appeal depend on having accepted as reliable the experiences whose reliability is being called into question.

All these sceptical hypotheses, however, face a dilemma. It centers on the identity of the powerful manipulating agent. Either the description of this agent is so vague as to allow no further specification than that it causes in some mysterious way our experiences. If so, the substance of the sceptical hypothesis is that common sense may be mistaken. This has not been denied by defenders of common sense; on the contrary, we insist upon it. But to say that common sense may be mistaken is not to present an alternative to it. The possibility of error does not favor the hypothesis that an error has actually been made.

Or, to take the other lemma, the manipulating agent and his *modus operandi* are described. We are told who he is and how he does it.[6] But in giving this description very many of the basic common sense beliefs are presupposed. The description assumes, for instance, that a world external to the perceiver exists; that the nature of that world is independent of the perceiver; that other sentient beings exist who are either human or whose description presupposes knowledge of humans; that the world existed before the manipulation started; something needs to be said also about the mechanics of the manipulation and this can hardly avoid reference to material objects; and so on. The result is that in the course of giving an alternative to common sense, common sense is presupposed. Thus the attempt to give an alternative to it fails. And this is not unexpected. For if common sense is indeed basic, then all descriptions of the world presuppose it. So this objection to the justification of common sense also collapses.

The conclusion is that we have all the reason we can and need to have for believing that common sense beliefs are justified and no reason at all for doubting their justification. So that we can say that common sense is not only the foundation of our beliefs, but also that it is a reliable foundation.

V. *Common Sense and Worldviews*

It will be remembered that in the previous discussion of worldviews the anthropological component was identified as the source of human significance and perspective. The tendency to view reality anthropologically, from the human perspective, *sub specie humanitatis*, was contrasted with the tendency to view it metaphysically, from an impersonal perspective, *sub specie aeternitatis*. The importance of both was emphasized. For, while reality is what it is independently of human interest and concern, what reality happens to be has a great human significance.

But now we can go a step further. If common sense is basic, then the anthropological component of worldviews is primary and the metaphysical component is secondary. The first takes precedence over the second in the order of justification. For if common sense is basic and all other beliefs, including metaphysical ones, presuppose it, then the truth of all other beliefs is contingent upon the truth of common sense.

This is not a surprising conclusion if it is remembered that worldviews are developed by human beings who are bound by the limits of their nature.[7] It is just as much a matter of necessity that the human understanding of reality must start with and return to the human frame of reference as it is that whatever kind of being attempts to understand reality must do so in its own terms.

We are unavoidably attached to our bodies and so we must start with what our senses tell us and with what our motor capacities allow us to do. But our humanity is not only the starting point, it is also the touchstone with reference to which problems must be solved and comprehension achieved. For problems are human problems, solved by human beings, and the solutions enable human beings to do what they previously could not.

I hasten to add that I am not advocating the mistaken view that man is the measure of all things. Man, however, is the measurer of all things. Man is not the measure because the anthropological view must do justice to the facts: to what science and metaphysics tell us about the nature of reality. Man is the measurer, however, because he and only he can decide what significance the facts have. By themselves, all facts are brute, and equally so.

The implication of the epistemological primacy of the anthropological component of worldviews is that no scientific or metaphysical theory can contradict common sense and be consistent. For if there are basic beliefs, then scientific or metaphysical theories presuppose them. If there follows from a theory a conclusion whose truth is incompatible with the assumptions of the same theory, then the theory is inconsistent. And pointing that out is a sufficient criticism of the theory.

I hope that this will not be misunderstood. The point is not that the beliefs of common men should take epistemological precedence over the beliefs of experts. Rather, it is that if a belief is basic, then common men, experts, indeed all men, hold it and must do so. Basic beliefs are the foundation upon which all theories about reality are built. Thus no theory can consistently contradict them. Nor am I saying that a basic belief cannot be false: it can be. But its falsehood cannot be demonstrated by a theory which assumes its truth.

The fundamentality of common sense has another consequence for philosophical justification. I have argued previously that philosophical theories which aim to describe the world are justified by two criteria: problem-solving and truth-directedness. One test of truth-directedness is the adequacy of interpretation provided by these philosophical theories. A difficulty emerged, however, in trying to decide which of several theories offers the most adequate interpretation. For the adequacy of an interpretation depends on a theory providing a satisfactory account of all the relevant facts, and different theories may disagree about what facts are relevant. Thus each may claim to have offered an adequate interpretation and yet be accounting for different facts. This difficulty was resolved by arguing that there is a shared stock of facts which each theory must admit as relevant, and further discussion was promised.

The promise can now be redeemed by identifying the shared

stock of facts with facts vouchsafed for by common sense. The present suggestion is that whether a philosophical theory passes the test of offering an adequate interpretation of all the relevant facts depends, in part, on its success in accounting for the facts held to be such by basic beliefs. The dependence is only partial, because adequacy of interpretation involves more than giving a satisfactory account of the facts of common sense: there are other facts awaiting interpretation as well. And the justification of philosophical theories, as we have seen, must go further than passing the test of adequate interpretation.

The importance of this requirement is not just that a class of relevant facts that must be accounted for has been identified, but also that this class is relevant to the justification of all philosophical theories which aim to describe part or the whole of reality. For all philosophical theories presuppose the common sense beliefs in these facts. They differ from each other in many ways. But if two or more such philosophical theories attempt to solve the same problem, we can be sure that their assumptions at least partially coincide, for they all accept common sense. So it simply cannot happen that philosophical theories trying to solve the same problem are incommensurate. They must share at least some of the relevant facts, for they have them as their starting point.

The recognition that common sense is basic should have a most beneficial effect upon philosophy. For it imposes a necessary discipline upon the development of worldviews. Worldviews are constrained in their development by the enduring problems which they aim to solve and by the ideals in accordance with which the problems must be solved. The fundamentality of common sense adds to this the restriction that the solutions must presuppose and account for the facts licensed by common sense.

If my defence of common sense is right, there is a common starting point for all philosophical theories about reality and there are some facts that no philosopher can dismiss or dispute. If this is seen by philosophers, it will act as a curb on the more absurd flights of philosophical fancy. But it was not meant to and it will not curb the essential philosophical enterprise of developing worldviews by which men can live. Beginning with common sense is necessary, but going beyond it is equally so. For common sense is beset by problems which can be solved only by going beyond it. In this chapter I have emphasized the importance of common sense, but this should not be taken as a denial of the need to supercede it.

NOTES

1. George E. Moore, "Some Judgments of Perception," *Philosophical Studies* (London: Routledge, 1922), 228.

2. My conception of basic beliefs is very similar to Hume's theory of natural beliefs. For the best discussion see Ronald J. Butler, "Natural Belief and the Enigma of Hume," *Archiv für Geschichte der Philosophie*, 42 (1960), 73–100 and John C. Gaskin, "God, Hume and Natural Belief," *Philosophy*, 49 (1974), 281–94.

3. Nobody can give such a list without being acutely conscious of trying to imitate Moore's inimitable list in his "A Defence of Common Sense," *Philosophical Papers* (London: Allen & Unwin, 1969).

4. David Hume, *An Enquiry Concerning Human Understanding* (New York: Scribner, 1955), 168–9, ed. C. W. Hendel.

5. My argument for the fundamentality of common sense belongs to a philosophical tradition proceeding from Berkeley and Hume, through the Scottish philosophy of common sense developed by Reid and Stewart, the critical common-sensism of Peirce, Moore's almost contemporary defence of it, and Popper's quite recent work on the subject. See the articles on Hume referred to in (2) above; Gavin Ardley, "Common Sense," in *Berkeley's Renovation of Philosophy* (Hague: Nijhoff, 1968), 96–132; S. A. Grave, *The Scottish Philosophy of Common Sense* (Oxford: Clarendon, 1960); Charles S. Peirce, "Critical Commonsensim," *Philosophical Writings of Peirce* (New York: Dover, 1953), 290–301, ed. Justus Buchler; George E. Moore, "A Defence of Common Sense," and "Proof of an External World," *Philosophical Papers* (London: Allen & Unwin, 1969), 32–59 and 127–50; Karl R. Popper, "Two Faces of Common Sense," *Objective Knowledge* (Oxford: Clarendon, 1973), 32–105.

6. For a very entertaining account see Jonathan Harrison's "A Philosopher's Nightmare or The Ghost Not Laid," *Proceedings of the Aristotelian Society*, 68 (1967), 179–88.

7. Cf. "'Tis evident, that all the sciences have a relation, greater or less, to human nature; and that however wide any of them may seem to run from it, they still return back by one passage or another. Even *Mathematics, Natural Philosophy* ... are in some measure dependent on the science of *Man*; since they lie under the cognizance of men, and are judged by their powers and faculties." David Hume, *A Treatise of Human Nature, op. cit.*, xiv.

Chapter Ten

Philosophy and Science

"We feel that even when all *possible* scientific questions have been answered the problems of life remain completely untouched."

LUDWIG WITTGENSTEIN[1]

I. *Introduction*

One of the recurrent themes of this book is that the relation between philosophy and science has been misconceived. "Philosophers constantly see the method of science before their eyes, and are irresistibly tempted to ask and answer questions in the way science does. This tendency ... leads the philosopher into complete darkness."[2] Perhaps the darkness is not complete, but the philosophical illumination achieved by the imitation of science is meagre.

There can be no serious doubt about the immense importance and value of science. Science is the most successful human enterprise. But it is not the only one. Understanding nature and achieving a measure of control over our physical environment are necessary for solving some problems. However, not all problems are of this kind and only some are solvable in this way. The reason why the misconception of the relation between philosophy and science is a serious error is that it results in ignoring problems which are not amenable to scientific solutions. Yet these problems are no less urgent than scientifically solvable ones. Undue emphasis upon the success of science thus brings about failure in other areas.

Perhaps the most uncompromising expression of the misconception is Quine's: "The relation between philosophy and science is not best seen ... in terms of give and take. Philosophy ... is an aspect of science."[3] There is a perfectly innocuous interpretation of this dictum. If we take science to be the label for all successful human endeavors, then obviously philosophy is an aspect of science. But so—absurdly—is poetry, literary criticism, and jurisprudence. What advocates of this scientific imperialism have in mind, however, is not the harmless, though infelicitous, extension of the term to cover new territory. What they are after is the evaluation of human endeavors by criteria developed in science; where science refers to inquiries like physics, biology, and geology. Philosophy is an aspect of science because from science, with the help of logic, "a canonical idiom can be abstracted and then adhered to in the statement of one's scientific theory. The doctrine is that all traits of reality worthy of the name can be set down in an idiom of this austere form if in any idiom. ... It is a doctrine that limits what can be said of things. ... It delimits what counts as scientifically admissible construction, and declares that whatever is not thus constructible ... must either by conceded the status of one more irreducible given term or eschewed."[4]

This is the error I shall be arguing against. First, however, it will be useful to summarize what I have said up to now about the relation between philosophy and science. One answer to the case against philosophy presented in Chapter One has been to argue for the continuity of philosophy and science. I noted there that even if the continuity exists, it does nothing to meet the need for a rationally justified worldview whose construction is the traditional task of philosophy. The detailed explanation of why this is so had to be postponed until Chapter Five where the account of world-views was given. In that chapter, metaphysics—the theory of the nature of reality—was identified as one of the components of worldviews. The continuity between philosophy and science is due to the continuity between metaphysical and scientific theories of the nature of reality. Both are interested in accounting for the facts, yet they go about it in different ways. Metaphysical theories tend to be more general, comprehensive, and interpretive than scientific theories whose scope tends to be more restricted and whose descriptive component tends to outweigh the interpretive one.

Yet the continuity falls short of identity and even shorter of the subordination of philosophy to science. The first reason for this is that a worldview contains several elements which have only the most tenuous relation to science: the anthropological element is concerned with the human significance of the theory of reality provided by science and metaphysics; the culture comprises the ideals in accordance with which problems are solved; the diagnosis explains why the actual falls short of the ideal; while the policy offers a way of approximating the ideal.

The second reason is that the identification of science even with the metaphysical element, where the continuity does persist, is also an error. For part of the task of metaphysics is to determine whether the nature of reality is scientifically explicable. And even if the answer is affirmative, the question is about the limits of science and consequently not scientifically answerable. Hence there are metaphysical questions which are not scientific.

The third reason arises out of the discussion of different types of problems in Chapter Three. Both philosophy and science aim to solve problems, but the problems they aim to solve coincide only minimally. If the distinctions between different problem-areas, between problems of life and reflection, and between removable and enduring problems are borne in mind, then the superficial similarity of philosophy and science as problem-solving ventures disappears.

The fourth reason is that science itself is an ideal which embodies existential, methodological, classificatory, and axiological presuppositions, as described in Chapters Four and Eight. The justification of scientific theories of course depends on the justification of these presuppositions. But since the presuppositions must be justified philosophically, the attempted identification of philosophy and science, let alone the subordination of the former to the latter, would be destructive of science's rational aspirations. For it would render question-begging the justification of the presuppositions of science.

My aim in this chapter is to describe the proper relation between philosophy and science. This involves criticizing the currently fashionable inflated claims for science. But I want to emphasize that it is the inflation and not science I am criticizing: I oppose scientific imperialism.

II. *Problem-Solving and Science*

Scientific imperialism may be the harmless verbal maneuver to label scientific all intellectually respectable enterprises. There is nothing to be gained from either accepting or resisting this proposed convention. For if it is accepted, then we shall have to introduce a new set of distinctions—this time within science—to mark off the different kinds of pursuits which previously were distinguished by calling them nonscientific. Thus even if literary criticism, musicology, biography, and the history of ideas are now to be called scientific, they must still be recognized to be different from physics, biology, and geology. Nothing is gained by thus stretching the meaning of science, for whatever precision the word had before is now further weakened and the need for a new set of distinctions must be met. Nor is there much point in resisting the extension of the scientific label to new areas, for language pretty well goes its own way and conventions rarely avail themselves to conscious control. The best course of action is to distinguish between an exclusive and an inclusive sense of science. In the former sense, science includes the physical and life sciences and perhaps also some of the social sciences. In the latter sense, science refers to all intellectually respectable enterprises. Scientific imperialism is harmless if it is a praise for science in the inclusive sense. For who would be churlish enough to begrudge these achievements?

The form of scientific imperialism I want to resist is one which employs science in the exclusive sense and holds it up as an ideal of intellectual excellence. The implication being that intellectual enterprises are to be judged according to the degree to which they approximate the scientific ideal (exclusively interpreted from now on). Thus insofar as bibliography, history, jurisprudence, etc., are scientific, so far only they are praiseworthy.

The argument in favor of this view cannot be that science is to be cherished because it alone is capable of providing truth. For such nonscientific endeavors as classical studies, philological investigations, judgments of character, the identification of the ills of a society, the proposals of programs for remedying injustice can all yield true or false statements. The argument may be, however, that the scientific pursuit of truth is more likely to be rewarding than other pursuits and as a result it is the best way of solving our problems.

This view is in fact widely held. One representative statement is Popper's: "Science is one of the very few human activities—perhaps the only one—in which errors are systematically criticized and fairly often, in time corrected. This is why we can say that, in science, we often learn from our mistakes, and why we can speak clearly and sensibly about making progress there. In most fields of human endeavour there is change, but rarely progress ... for almost every gain is balanced, or more than balanced, by some loss. And in most fields we do not even know how to evaluate change."[5]

This view of science has been contested by Kuhn.[6] Central to Kuhn's thesis is the distinction between normal and revolutionary science. The distinction rests on the notion of paradigm. A paradigm performs three main functions. First, it is a scientific achievement that has come to be regarded as a model or ideal of scientific research by scientists in a given period. The work of Newton or Darwin, for instance, constitutes paradigms in this sense. Another aspect of the paradigm is that it determines the type of questions that scientists ask. If certain observations suggest problems, it is because they are at odds with expectations based upon the paradigm. So the paradigm acts as a regulative ideal, prompting some questions, judging others as irrelevant or uninteresting, prescribing methods of research that are likely to be successful. In its third role the paradigm functions as an educational tool for the training of future scientists. It is a showcase of good science.[7]

Normal science refers to a period of scientific research when there is an agreed-upon paradigm; revolutionary science occurs when scientists become dissatisfied with the existing paradigm and it is being replaced by another. Normal science is what science largely is. The overwhelming majority of scientists spend all their professional time pursuing normal science, that is, research more or less determined by a paradigm. Scientific revolutions, the replacement of one paradigm by another, are very rare. When they occur, they determine for generations to come what normal science is to be.

The paradigm, according to Kuhn, imposes something like a grid upon nature. The grid has large gaps and it is not clear how to fill them. The task of normal science is to fill the gaps, to transform the loose grid into a finely meshed one. Scientific problems are the difficulties encountered in the way of completing the task of normal science. Normal scientists are given the general answers, the rules by which the answers can be reached, and an excellent example of reaching the answer—they are given all this by the paradigm—and their problem is to reconcile a particular observation with the dictates of the paradigm. Their activity, Kuhn suggests, is better described as puzzle-solving, rather than problem-solving. The solution of a problem of normal science is not the discovery of some new truth about nature, it is a successful reconciliation of an observation with the expectations created by the paradigm.

If Kuhn's view is correct, then science is not distinguished from other areas of human endeavor by its capacity for progress. Progress is possible in any field that has a paradigm. If an historian accepts, say, dialectical materialism, his paradigm is provided by Marx and progress consists in explaining more and more historical events in dialectical terms. If a jurist accepts the codification of social behavior as the legal ideal, then progress will be recognized as the extension of the legal system to increasingly greater areas of social life. Paradigms breed progress, and scientific progress has no special place.

Popper and Kuhn disagree about the nature of science, but they do not disagree about science being the rational enterprise *par excellence.* Kuhn, in reply to the charge that he defends irrationality in science, writes: "To describe the argument as a defence of irrationality in science seems to me not only absurd but vaguely obscene. I would describe it ... as an attempt to show that existing theories of rationality are not quite right and that we must readjust or change them to explain why science works as it does. To suppose, instead, that we possess criteria of rationality which are independent of our understanding of the essentials of the scientific process is to open the door to cloud-cuckoo land."[8] This is the pure expression of the assumption that needs defending. Popper and Kuhn agree in making it and they are at one in failing to defend it. The point of my argument is that unless the assumption is defended, scientific imperialism fails. For a critic of it need not deny that there is progress in Kuhn's sense. It is sufficient for him to point out that the paradigm has not been rationally justified. Thus there is no substantive difference between completing a paradigm, scientific or otherwise, and completing a jigsaw puzzle.

The difficulty encountered by Popper's and Kuhn's defence of science as the paradigm of rationality is due to an oversimple view they have of problems. Let us begin by recalling the distinction between the three problem-areas discussed in Chapter Three. Problems arise in the course of each person having to have some way of coping with his physical environment or nature, other people or society, and his own past, present, future, capacities, limitations, hopes, fears, and aspirations.

One's relations with other people is the concern of morality, politics, law, and the customs, habits, rituals, and practices that compose social life. One's attitude to himself is shaped by literature, biography, art, the film, by the criticism, advice, example, or encouragement of other people, and by the simple observation or the more complicated imaginative understanding and reflective appraisal of other ways of life. The problems that arise in these areas are not scientific, and science is neither intended to nor is capable of solving them. This is not an adverse comment on science, rather it is a consequence of understanding its function.

On the other hand, science is of immense help in coping with problems that arise in people's relation with their immediate physical environment, and more remotely, with nature. The scientific method is the most successful evolutionary device we have for solving certain kinds of problems in a certain way. But success in one area does not permit the application of the method to which success is due to quite different areas. The other two problem-areas are not amenable to scientific treatment, if science is understood in its exclusive sense.

If we follow Popper, Kuhn, and many others in thinking that science is the paradigm of successful problem-solving, then problems not tractable by science will appear to be unsolvable. Thus it seems that questions about how one should live his life and what moral and political views he should hold are not open to rational appraisal. In this way, the admiration of science leads to lack of rationality in social and private life.

But matters are even worse. For the acceptance of science as a paradigm of rationality is also something that needs to be justified, especially in view of the fact that there are alternative ideals. Mysticism, religiosity, commitment to such ideologies as Stalinism or Nazism dictate that goals other than developing a satisfactory way of coping with the physical environment be formed. What can a scientific rationalist say to such challenges? What Popper says is that "The choice before us is not simply an intellectual affair, or a matter of taste. It is a moral decision. ... For the question whether we adopt some more or less radical form of irrationalism or ... 'critical rationalism', will deeply affect our whole attitude towards other men, and towards the problems of social life."[9] If science is the paradigm of rationality and if the acceptance of the scientific way of solving problems rests on a moral decision, then the inescapable conclusion is that the moral decision is not rational. For it is a presupposition of rational decision-making. Consequently, in addition to leading to the lack of rationality of social and private life, the acceptance of science as the rational ideal is itself a nonrational choice.

The oversimplification of problems by champions of scientific imperialism is due not merely to the failure to recognize the inapplicability of science to problem-solving in two out of three problem-areas, but also the failure to recognize two other sets of distinctions: between problems of life and reflection and between removable and enduring problems.

Problems of life, it will be recalled, are pretheoretical and they are due to having to solve problems which people have in virtue of being human. Problems of reflection arise when the choice has to be made between conflicting solutions to problems of life; they arise and are solved in theoretical contexts. In each of the problem-areas discussed above there are problems of life and reflection. We have seen that science is inapplicable to the solution of either kind of problem in areas including one's attitude to himself and to other people. But what about the third area? Is it true that science is rightly regarded as paramount in solving problems which arise because human beings must develop some attitude to their physical environment?

Here too the claims for science must be curtailed. For the problems science is so good at solving are problems of reflection, not problems of life. Problems of life are frequently urgent and must be solved soon after they arise. For very many people in the past and in the present too the choice is not between various ways of solving these problems, but between having a solution and not having one. The people I have in mind live close to the subsistence level. To hold out the scientific ideal of problem-solving for such people would be to doom them to having their problems unsolved, for they have no science. In such contexts, it would be ludicrous to postulate science as the paradigm of rationality.

On the other hand, the strongest case for science is in the context of solving problems of reflection which arise when one has the luxury of choosing between several alternative ways of coping with the environment. Typically, our situation is like this. So perhaps it can be claimed that given our life, science is the paradigmatically rational way of dealing with this kind of problem of reflection.

But even this must be qualified in the light of the distinction between removable and enduring problems. Removable problems cease to exist after they are solved. Enduring problems are permanent features of our lives and their solution consists in developing a policy for coping with them. Trucking in water may solve the removable problem of protecting one's crop against a spell of draught. But the problem of what to do with the yield of one's land is enduring and requires the development of a farsighted policy.

The solution of both enduring and removable problems aims at the achievement of certain goals. I have called these goals ideals. The rationality of any given solution depends on the rationality of the ideal at which the solution aims. For clearly, the successful pursuit of an irrational ideal does not qualify as rational. Consequently, the rationality of solving removable and enduring problems scientifically depends upon the rationality of the ideals thus aimed at. So even if science is the paradigmatically rational method for the achievement of certain ideals, its rationality is not paramount, for it depends on the prior justification of the relevant ideal. The justification of that ideal, if anything, is the paradigm of rationality.

Thus, I find that there are the following reasons for rejecting the view that science is or ought to be our ideal for problem-solving. First, it is irrelevant to two out of three problem-areas. Second, its employment is warranted only to solving problems of reflection which arise in our attempt to choose between various solutions to how we should cope with the physical environment. Third, the rationality of scientific problem-solving depends on the rationality of the ideals these solutions aim at.

III. *Metaphysics and Science*

The strongest case for the identification of philosophy with an aspect of science is based on an analysis of the relation between metaphysics and science. According to this analysis, both aim to describe reality from a neutral, nonanthropocentric perspective. Their shared ambition is to view reality *sub specie aeternitatis.* Perhaps metaphysical theories are more general, involve more interpretation, make a greater proportion of conceptual claims than scientific theories. But both occupy a continuum on which all theories have the same aim, are committed to the same type of methods, and have the same criteria of success and failure.

This view of the relation between metaphysics and science can fairly be described as the dominant one in contemporary philosophy. Russell, Quine, Sellars, and Popper endorse it and its historical credentials go back through Mill, Hume, Locke, and perhaps Hobbes, to Bacon. There is also considerable opposition to it, and that has equally respectable historical roots. Aristotle puts the matter succinctly: "[T]here will be no scientific knowledge of the primary premisses ... a result which follows ... from the fact that demonstration cannot be the originative source of demonstration, nor, consequently, scientific knowledge of scientific knowledge."[10]

I shall oppose the dominant view on the ground that since science rests upon metaphysical presuppositions, metaphysics is more fundamental than science. I do not wish to deny that in some sense science and metaphysics are continuous. But in some respects, I shall show, they are discontinuous. And certainly, the view that metaphysics is an aspect of science is erroneous.

Defenders of science as the paradigm of rationality may come to agree with my previous argument about science being able to solve only certain problems. But they might rally to their cause by pointing out that when scientific problem-solving is compared with other methods of solving problems in other areas, the superiority of science is evident. Thus the interpretation of science being the paradigm of rationality is not that science is best for solving any problem, but that science in its proper sphere is far more successsful than any other method of problem-solving in its proper sphere. Imperialistic claims for science are thus replaced by claims for science being the ideal problem-solver.

I think that this claim is true. But its truth should not obscure the fact that what enables science to be the ideal problem-solver is that the presuppositions upon which it rests have been justified. If there indeed are presuppositions underlying science, then these clearly cannot be scientifically justified, for that would be question-begging. Thus the claim that science is the paradigm of rationality rests upon the justification of the presuppositions of science. If the presuppositions can be rationally justified, then the enterprise of justifying them has a better claim to being the paradigm of rationality than science does. If the presuppositions cannot be justified, then even the much weaker claim that science is rational collapses. So provided only that science rests upon presuppositions, it can not be the paradigm of rationality, not even if science is the ideal problem-solver. But does science rest upon presuppositions?

In Chapter Four I have argued that presuppositions are fundamental theoretical assumptions intrinsic to the ideal of which they are essential elements. The ideal presently considered is science, and the question is whether there are fundamental theoretical assumptions intrinsic in it. An assumption is fundamental to an ideal if its abandonment is tantamount to abandoning the ideal. And it is theoretical if the truth of the assumption is a necessary condition of the acceptability of the ideal.

Science is committed to several presuppositions: that nature exists, that it has discoverable order, that it is uniform, are existential presuppositions of science; the distinctions between space and time, cause and effect, the observer and the observed, real and apparent, orderly and chaotic, are classificatory presuppositions; while intersubjective testability, quantifiability, the public availability of data, are methodological presuppositions; some axiological presuppositions are the honest reporting of results, the worthwhileness of getting facts right, and scrupulousness in avoiding observational or experimental error.

If any one of these presuppositions were abandoned, science, as we know it, could not be done. Yet the acceptance of the presuppositions cannot be a matter of course, for each has been challenged and alternatives are readily available. Consider as an example Goethe's theory of colors and Freud's interpretations of dreams. Goethe's theory is unquantifiable and Freud's interpretations are intersubjectively untestable, hence they contradict methodological presuppositions of science. What can we say about these cases?

Intolerantly, it may be said that since these cases contradict accepted methods of scientific inquiry, they are irrational. Guided by a more liberal spirit, they could be declared to be merely unscientific, and the possibility of a favorable judgment of their rationality with reference to some nonscientific standard may be allowed. But this is a very peculiar way of dealing with counterexamples. Clearly, both Goethe and Freud thought that they were doing science, and they were not unacquainted with scientific methods. They seem, however, to reject the methods most scientists accept. Those and indeed any presuppositions can thus be questioned, and consequently adherence to them requires justification. The justification cannot merely be that this is how scientists do things, because scientific imperialists are prepared to criticize practice that conflicts with the scientific. Is this criticism rational, or is it just a flaunting of prejudices?

The argument in favor of accepting such methodological requirements as intersubjective testability and quantifiability is that with their aid scientific problems can be solved and the ideals of science can be approximated. It would not do of course to identify scientific problems and ideals as those tractable or realizable by the application of scientific methods. For if this suggestion were accepted, the whole scientific enterprise would become self-guaranteeing, since problems and ideals not amenable to scientific treatment would not be considered, and *simpliciter*, would not be considered unsuccessfully, consequently science could not fail.

The scientific way of solving problems and working for the achievement of certain ideals is *one* way: there are others. To judge other, nonscientific, approaches by applying to them yardsticks proper to science is of course question-begging. A successful argument for science being the paradigm of rationality must be based on the demonstration that the presuppositions of science are preferable to other presuppositions. That demonstration requires showing that science, relying on these presuppositions, is better at solving some problems and achieving some ideals than its competitors. But showing that cannot be the task of science. It is, in fact, one task of philosophy. Thus the enterprise of justifying the presuppositions of science by showing that with their help science is the best way of solving certain problems and achieving some ideals is a necessary precondition of the justification of science. Hence philosophy, and not science, is a stronger candidate for being the paradigm of rationality.

The fact is, however, that this competition for being the paradigm of rationality is misconceived. Rationality is closely connected with problem-solving and, as we have seen, there are many different problems. The expectation that there is an ideal way of solving all of them is unreasonable, if the diversity of problems is borne in mind.

What should be recognized, nevertheless, is that the enterprise of justifying presuppositions—that is, philosophy—is epistemologically prior to the justification of the inquiries of which these are presuppositions. Thus philosophy is more fundamental than other inquiries. It is misleading to express this by saying that philosophy is the paradigm of rationality; but it is less misleading than the claim that science is.

IV. *Worldviews and Science*

Metaphysics is one component of worldviews; the others are: anthropology, culture, diagnosis, and policy. I have been criticizing the idea that philosophy is an aspect of or identical with science. I shall continue to do this here by showing how extremely tenuous is the connection between science and the remaining four components of worldviews.

Let us begin with culture. At their best, science and metaphysics describe the world as it is. Culture, on the other hand, embodies the aspirations of a society about trying to transform at least parts of the world as it ought to be. Consequently, scientific and cultural pursuits are quite different. But there is also a connection: science, at least in our culture, is one of the ideals. We do aspire to understand the world.

Ideals are subject to perennial argumentation. Perennial arguments about science may be internal and concern the inter-pretation of the ideal. Or they may be external and concern the justification of its pursuit. There can be no serious external argument about the worthwhileness of science. For science, provided it is employed in its proper sphere, is the best way of solving problems of a certain kind. External perennial arguments, however, concern not just the justification of ideals but also the relative importance attributed to the pursuit of one ideal in comparison with other ideals. And on this score there is plenty of challenge to science.

The general point is that of the ideals which comprise a culture some are held to be more important and others less so. The challenge to science may take the form of arguing that its importance has been overemphasized. It is not, of course, that we ought not to try to understand reality as a precondition of solving many problems. Rather, the argument may be that since our resources are scarce and science has been so very successful, its pursuit ought to slow down and we should concentrate our resources on other kinds of problems. On the realization of social values or on the enrichment of the inner lives of individuals, for instance. In support of this point, it might be said that there have been highly successful societies—the pre-nineteenth century Chinese, for example—in whose culture science was quite an unimportant ideal. Thus the pre-eminence of the scientific ideal is not a necessary condition of having a successful society.

I am sympathetic to this point, but my concern is not with defending it. I raise the consideration in order to show that there can be serious questions about science in relation to other ideals and these are philosophical questions. The idea that philosophy is an aspect of science comes from being blind to the possibility of the kind of questions I here ask. How could it be sensibly denied that since there are philosophical questions about science, science and philosophy cannot be identified?

The importance of this consideration, in the context of our society, spreads to the discussion of the diagnostic and policy-making components of worldviews. For many people would argue that one reason why our society is not as it ought to be is that the value of science has been stressed at the expense of such values as morality, justice, or liberty. Once again, my concern is not with endorsing this diagnosis and the policy that it suggests, but with pointing at them as raising legitimate philosophical questions. And what follows from raising them is not that science should be taken down a peg, but that here is yet another fundamental and philosophical question which could not arise if philosophy were identical with or an aspect of science.

In turning to the anthropological component of worldviews I shall begin by a remark of Schlick, the leading light of the Vienna Circle, who cannot be accused of an antiscientific bias. He says: "I assure you most emphatically that I should *not* call the system of science true if I found its consequences incompatible with my own observations of nature, and the fact that it is adopted by the whole of mankind and taught in all the universities would make no impression on me. If all the scientists in the world told me that under certain experimental conditions I must see three black spots, and if under these conditions I saw only one spot, no power in the universe could make me think that the statement 'there is now only one black spot in the field of vision' is false."[11]

The significance of Schlick's convincing observation is twofold. First, it reminds us that the scientific perspective of the world is not the only one. For there is also the prior perspective provided by the unaided human senses: the common sense view of the world. Second, if the two perspectives conflict, common sense should take precedence. I would express Schlick's point by saying that the anthropological view, including common sense, provides an alternative interpretation of reality in the sense that the anthropological interpretation is basic and the scientific one is derivative. I have argued for these claims in Chapters Five and Nine.

Metaphysics, with the help of science, provides an interpretation of the nature of reality. The interpretation aims to be of the facts as they are independently of the interests, values, purposes, hopes, and fears of human beings who, of course, provide the interpretation. The ideal of objectivity to which metaphysics hopes to conform is to interpret the facts as an omniscient perfectly neutral observer would. So that the fact that metaphysics is done by human beings would be of no relevance.

Anthropology also provides an interpretation, but it does not aim to be neutral. On the contrary, its purpose is to understand the human significance of the facts discovered by metaphysics and science. There need be no factual difference between metaphysics and anthropology; the difference is due to the different interpretations of the importance, significance, or relevance of the same set of facts. Metaphysical interpretations aspire to be objective, they are given *sub specie aeternitatis*. Anthropological interpretations are anthropocentric, they are given *sub specie humanitatis.*

The existence of these two ways of looking at the world would be sufficient to establish in yet another way the impoverishment that would result from the identification of philosophy and science. For their identity would deprive us from the benefits of philosophical reflection upon the human significance of the facts. We would then know what the facts are, but not why they matter.

However, not only does anthropology provide an alternative to metaphysics, it is also presupposed by metaphysics. And one important consequence of that is that the metaphysical ideal of objectivity is unattainable. The reason for this is that common sense is basic, and all theories about the nature of reality presuppose it.

The point has been put by James: "our fundamental ways of thinking about things are discoveries of exceedingly remote ancestors, which have been able to preserve themselves throughout the experience of all subsequent time. They form one great equilibrium in the mind's development, the stage of *common sense.* Other stages have grafted themselves upon this stage, but have never succeeded in displacing it."[12] My only dispute with James is that I should want to emphasize that the discovery of common sense is not something that our remote ancestors could have failed to make. For if common sense beliefs are indeed natural in the sense of being nonreflective, physiologically based, and untaught, then a human being cannot help holding them.

The primacy of the anthropological interpretation is due to common sense being basic. Common sense is the foundation and all other beliefs must be grafted upon it, because common sense is simply part of being human. It comes from having the body, sense organs, and motor capacities that human beings inescapably have. Whatever information is provided by whatever theory, it must ultimately be tested against the human sense organs. For theories are refinements of common sense and scientific instruments are extensions of human sense organs and must be calibrated with reference to them.

Just as the justification of metaphysical presuppositions of science is a necessary condition of the rationality of science, so also is the justification of common sense another necessary condition.

Both kinds of justifications are philosophical tasks. If philosophy is identified with science, the first casualty is the rationality of science. For philosophy offers the only hope of justifying the foundation upon which science rests. So the conclusion I offer is that it is primarily in the interest of science that scientific imperialists should abandon the ill-conceived and, in any case, doomed, attempt to identify philosophy and science, or to subordinate the former to the latter.

V. *Conclusion*

In concluding, I want to emphasize again that the purpose of this chapter has been to argue for a certain conception of the relation between philosophy and science. This conception assigns a much more modest role to science, in its partnership with philosophy, than what is common. But my arguments have not been aimed at science; they have been aimed at false and exaggerated claims made on behalf of science. Science, in its place, is the greatest human accomplishment. It is the most reasonable ground for being optimistic about the future of humanity. For science demonstrates that we can solve some of our problems. Scientific imperialism is the product of the erroneous belief that problems are alike and consequently methods for solving them can be generalized. As we have seen, this is not so.

The task of philosophy is to develop and rationally justify a worldview. Science contributes to this task by being an incomparable way of discovering and interpreting the facts. But science rests upon presuppositions which must be justified, if science is to be a rational enterprise, and the justification is philosophical. Furthermore, we do not just want to show what the facts are, we also want to appreciate their implications for humanity; we are interested in learning about the facts, because we need to solve our problems, and solve them not just in any way, but in a way that is rendered desirable by our ideals about what private and public life ought to be. These philosophical tasks transcend the limitations of science. The attempt to draw the boundaries of philosophy no wider than the boundaries of science, impoverishes philosophy, dooms us to leaving personal and social problems without reasoned solutions, and undermines the justifiability of science. These are the undesirable consequences of scientific imperialism that I hope to avoid by offering an alternative conception of the relation between philosophy and science.

NOTES

1. Ludwig Wittgenstein, *Tractatus Logico-Philosophicus*, tr. D. F. Pears and B. F. McGuinness (London: Routledge, 1961), 6.52.

2. Ludwig Wittgenstein, *The Blue and Brown Books* (Oxford: Blackwell, 1969), 18.

3. Willard V. Quine, "Philosophical Progress in Language Theory," *Metaphilosophy*, 1 (1970), 2.

4. Willard V. Quine, *Word and Object* (Cambridge: MIT Press, 1960), 228–9.

5. Karl R. Popper, "Truth, Rationality, and the Growth of Scientific Knowledge," *Conjectures and Refutations* (New York: Harper & Row, 1968), 215 and 216–17.

6. Thomas S. Kuhn, *The Structure of Scientific Revolutions* (Chicago: University of Chicago Press, 1962).

7. This elucidation of the notion of the paradigm is Margaret Masterman's "The Nature of a Paradigm," in *Criticism and the Growth of Knowledge*, eds. I. Lakatos and A. Musgrave (Cambridge: Cambridge University Press, 1970).

8. Thomas S. Kuhn, "Reflections on My Critics," in *Criticism and the Growth of Knowledge, op. cit.*, 264.

9. Karl R. Popper, *The Open Society and Its Enemies* (London: Routledge, 1962), 4th rev. ed., Vol. II, 232.

10. Aristotle, *Posterior Analytics*, Book II, Chapter 19, 100b, 10., tr. G. R. G. Mure.

11. Moritz Schlick, "Facts and Propositions," *Analysis*, 2 (1935), 70.

12. William James, *Pragmatism* (New York: Longmans, Green, 1908), 170.

Chapter Eleven

Philosophy and History

> "To fail to learn to use the past of philosophy is to repeat the errors and the follies of that past. To use history is the only alternative to remaining its slave. To escape the continuing bondage to the past, we must understand the past. ... The past is what we must work with. It is what has given us our ideas, our categories, our assumptions, our methods, our techniques, the procedures available to bring to bear on our problems. Our entire stock of intellectual resources is inescapably a heritage from the past."
>
> JOHN H. RANDALL, JR.[1]

I. *Introduction*

The purpose of this chapter is to argue for the importance of historical understanding to the construction and justification of worldviews. We need a worldview to fill the void created by the weakening hold religion and political ideologies have on us, to cope with the immense technological, demographic, social, and moral changes which surround us, and to present a rational alternative to the many flourishing brands of unreason. Historical understanding is essential to all these. That this is so is itself an historical thesis. It is based on the arguable, but, it seems to me, the nevertheless correct judgment that we need to develop a rationally justified worldview to transform the one crumbling around us.

I have argued that philosophical justification depends on conformity to two standards: problem-solving and truth-directedness. Historical understanding is a necessary condition of judging whether a philosophical theory conforms to the first standard. For to know whether a philosophical theory does indeed serve as the bridge between problems and ideals requires historical knowledge of the problems and ideals.

So my claim is that history is relevant to understanding a philosophical theory and that it is both directly and indirectly relevant to justifying a philosophical theory. It is indirectly relevant, because unless a theory is understood, it cannot be justified. And it is directly relevant, because the judgment of

164

whether one standard of justification, problem-solving, has been met can be made only on the basis of historical knowledge.[2]

This thesis is rejected by very many contemporary philosophers on two different but indefensible grounds. The first is some version of the distinction between discovery and justification. The argument being that the justification of a theory is independent of the historical question of how the theory came to be formulated. However, I have shown in Chapter Six that this distinction is untenable.

The second ground for rejecting my thesis is the misplaced emphasis upon one of the two standards of justification. My critics stress truth-directedness as the standard by which philosophical theories must be judged, and they overlook the other standard: problem-solving. It is true that in the context of acceptance, that is, in the context where the question is which of several solutions one should accept, historical considerations do not play an important role. But the question my critics concentrate on can be asked only because the prior question of what counts as a solution has been asked and answered. That question is considered in the context of introduction and it is answered in terms of the problem-solving capacity of theories. In that context, however, historical considerations play an essential role. So historical questions do not frequently arise in that context, but only because they have been considered in a prior context.

I shall argue for the relevance of historical considerations to three different matters: to philosophical justification, to the improvement of worldviews, and to the formation of sensibility. All three are essential to the development and justification of worldviews. In the last analysis, it is the present need we have of a justified worldview which forces historical considerations upon us.

II. *Historical Understanding and Philosophical Justification*

I shall begin by proposing a rule for deciding what cultural influences are relevant to the understanding and justification of a philosophical theory. The rule is: in the event of there being conflicting and fundamentally different interpretations of a philosophical work, consider all and only those cultural influences which have a demonstrable bearing on the resolution of the conflict. I note that no major work in philosophy escapes such conflicting interpretations.

Proposing this rule is one thing, applying it is another. For the application requires familiarity with cultural influences that could have a bearing on the interpretation of the philosophical work in question. That familiarity is the product of historical knowledge. History, historical knowledge, historical understanding, however, are terms more suggestive than clear. I shall attempt to clarify them by drawing a number of distinctions.[3]

Let us begin by distinguishing between history and history of ideas. History, of course, is not synonymous with the past. Anything in the past may become a subject for history. But a necessary condition of this is that it be remembered. The fact is that most of the past is forgotten. History, then, deals with the remembered past.[4] However the domain of history does not include even all of the remembered past, for many trivialities are remembered. What is and what is not trivial from an historical point of view is a controversial question. There is, however, no controversy about some things being trivial. History is concerned with the nontrivial part of the remembered past: with wars, not usually with family tiffs; with changes of government, but normally not with changes of linen; with discoveries of what nobody knew, and only exceptionally with a person's recognition of his own ignorance. The history of ideas is part of history. Its domain comprises nontrivial ideas. Other parts of history are, for instance, economic and military history, the history of technology, diplomacy, navigation. Some ideas have exercised a formative influence upon people whose actions, in turn, had a significant effect upon events. These are the subject-matter of the history of ideas.

The history of ideas, however, needs to be distinguished from intellectual history. The history of ideas is the history of nontrivial ideas. Intellectual history, as I shall use the term, is the history of cognitive ideas. That is, ideas whose primary uses are to say something true or false. Thus the history of art, literature, or sexual mores, the history of changing conceptions of the relation between popular and high culture, or of the relation between style and production, are part of the history of ideas, but not of intellectual history. While the history of science, or, indeed, the history of history are within the domain of intellectual history. And if I am right in the view of philosophical justification I have been defending, then the history of philosophy is part of intellectual history as well.

Intellectual history may be general or special. General

intellectual history deals with all cognitive ideas, while special intellectual history is concerned with cognitive ideas within some subject. Thus what was believed to be true or false about reality during the Italian renaissance is a question for general intellectual history. The Victorian view of the rise and fall of the Roman Empire is a matter dealt with by special intellectual history; namely, by one devoted to the Victorian historiography of Rome. The history of philosophy is special intellectual history. The historian of philosophy is not interested in ideas *per se*, but in ideas that belong to the philosophical tradition. That tradition dictates the kind of questions, the identity of the people, and the nature of the methods which come under his scrutiny.

Special intellectual history may be external or internal. If the history of philosophy is considered externally, then the important question is the influence particular philosophical ideas had outside of philosophy. From that point of view, Dewey is more important than Peirce, Voltaire than Berkeley, Schopenhauer than Frege. From the internal point of view the reverse is the case. For that view concentrates on the importance of philosophical ideas to philosophy itself.

The disagreements occasioned by the different foci of internal and external histories tend to be acrimonious. For the practitioners in a field normally think that external history of their subject falsifies it by preferring the popular to the true. While intellectual historians, looking at the subject from the outside, wonder why they should be blamed for ignoring obscure specialists whose work has influenced no more than a handful of experts. As long as there is a discrepancy between highly regarded ideas in a field and influential ideas, this controversy will persist. Its existence, however, goes some way toward explaining the hostility of experts to history.

The case I want to make for the importance of history to philosophy interprets the relevant kind of history, in the first instance, as special, internal, intellectual history. It should not be thought, however, that the distinctions I am relying on are sharp or clearcut. They represent no more than tendencies of thought, preoccupations with some questions at the expense of others, a channelling of interests rather than rigidly separated spheres of inquiry. But if I can make out a convincing case for the philosophical relevance of special, internal, intellectual history, then, precisely because the distinctions are soft and muddy, the relevance of other kinds of history will follow.

My claim is that the history of cognitive philosophical ideas, considered from a philosophical point of view, which concentrates on the importance of these ideas to philosophy itself, is relevant to the justification of philosophical theories. But I cannot make good this claim until we distinguish between three approaches to doing this kind of history of philosophy: the descriptive, polemical, and problematic.[5]

The descriptive approach to the history of philosophy consists in giving a straightforward account of the thought of a philosopher. Its main task is exegesis. Nobody can work his way through the writings of all the philosophers. Descriptive histories serve as simplified substitutes. They help to introduce the student to the kind of thing a philosopher has said, and they help the philosopher to decide whether he should go to the original text itself.

But the descriptive approach leaves many philosophers dissatisfied. Creative philosophers would sympathize with Kant's lament that "There are scholarly men to whom the history of philosophy ... is philosophy itself ... nothing can be said which, in their opinion, has not been said before ... for ... it is hardly to be expected that we should not be able to discover analogies for every idea among the old sayings of past ages."[6] The complaint is about the abuse of the descriptive history of philosophy. It can stifle philosophical thought by an arid cataloguing of who said what, when, and then use the accumulated research to trace similarities between past and present thought.

Bearing this deadening attitude in mind, one can see the point of Wittgenstein's exaggerated exclamation: "What has history to do with me? Mine is the first and only world."[7] This rejection of history is the reaction of a creative philosopher who does not want to be shackled to the preconceptions of the past and who wants to "consider as undone all that has been done."[8] But the past cannot be undone, and the understandable passion notwithstanding, Wittgenstein's is not the first world. The choice, however, does not have to be between slavish adherence to the past and its rejection. There is a more reasonable middle course. We can learn from the history of philosophy.

One way of doing so is to use the writings of past philosophers as substitutes for the living disputing presence of the philosopher. This is polemical history of philosophy. Its purpose and rationale is "that the best preparation for original work on any philosophical problem is to study the solutions which have been proposed for it by men of genius whose views differ from each other as much as possible. The clash of their opinions may strike a light which will enable us to avoid the mistakes into which they have fallen; and by noticing the strong and weak points of each theory we may discover the direction in which further progress can be made."[9]

Polemical history of philosophy goes beyond descriptive history. What enables this progression to occur is that the latter has done its job, so the former can decide which philosophers are men of genius and what views are sufficiently different to present a useful contrast. Descriptive history of philosophy does not deserve scorn, but it must be kept in its place. Thus the use of polemical history is that it lets us learn from past mistakes, it enables contemporary philosophers to test their ideas against past ideas, and it makes it possible to achieve the second best to listening to and arguing with the greats.

The polemical approach, however, assumes that the preoccupations of philosophers in different ages were the same. Only if this is so can contemporary philosophers turn with benefit to historical figures for illumination. This assumption has been questioned. "You cannot find out what a man means by simply studying his spoken or written statements, even though he has spoken and written with perfect command of language and perfectly truthful intention. In order to find out his meaning you must also know what the question was ... to which the thing he said or written was meant as an answer."[10] Thus the polemical approach is likely to yield the benefits claimed for it if the assumption of historical continuity to which it is committed can be justified.

For the justification of this assumption one must turn to problematic history of philosophy. It is needed because one cannot understand what a philosopher is saying unless he understands the problem the philosopher is trying to solve. And what the problem is is frequently not obvious from the text. Philosophers write for their contemporaries and they usually take for granted their acquaintance with the problem-situation. The establishment of historical continuity, upon which polemical history rests, requires therefore the identification of problems philosophers are trying to solve. Thus polemical history depends upon problematic history.

"For the problematic historian ... the philosopher is essentially a puzzled man. The first question the problematic historian will ask himself is this: 'What problem was he trying to solve?' And then he will go on to ask himself such further questions as: 'How did this problem arise for him?', 'What methods of tackling it did he use?'"[11]

Problematic history of philosophy resolves the tension between the creative philosopher who regards himself as pursuing truth and the historian who is struck by the recurrence of the Kantian dream of philosophers to "consider as undone all that has been done." For problems connect the pursuit of truth with the history of that pursuit. "Truth has no history, but the discussion of problems has a history."[12] What guarantees the historical continuity of philosophy is that philosophers are concerned with the same problems.

The supposed continuity of problems, however, has been denied. "The problems of one age are ultimately irrelevant to those of another. ... What bond is there between the aims and problems of an Athenian poet, like Plato; a Roman senator, like Cicero; a medieval monk, like Thomas Aquinas; a seventeenth-century scientific pioneer, like Descartes; a German professor, like Kant; ... The philosophical problems of one age, like the cultural conflicts out of which they take their rise, are irrelevant to those of another."[13]

Whatever plausibility this denial of the historical continuity of problems has derives from an oversimple view of problems. Removable problems do change from age to age, and also within an age. But enduring problems do not. For enduring problems are occasioned by the unchanging aspects of human nature and our surroundings and not by the contingent historically variant aspects of our existence. The need to satisfy physiological urges, to know one's limitations, and capacities, to come to terms with the past and plan for the future, to develop ways of dealing with one's family, friends, enemies, with strangers and authority, to learn how to use power and how to obey, to have an attitude to nature, to form some view about whether the scheme of things is benevolent, hostile, indifferent, or neutral, to decide whether nature should be conquered, civilized, made use of, respected, submitted to, or dominated, these are not historically changing problems. All people in all ages had to face them and had to try to cope with them. Of course, the forms in which these enduring problems present themselves, the urgency of some and the luxury of being able to confront others in a leisurely way, do change from age to age, from society to society, from class to class.

There is here both historical continuity and historical change. In the case of enduring problems the continuity is important and the change superficial. Part of the benefit historical understanding yields is that we can penetrate with its help below the surface of superficial historical differences and perceive the identity of the problems confronted by various philosophers. We can peel away the obstructing layers of jargon, individual idiosyncrasy, the professional paraphernalia, and go to the heart of the philosopher's concern: to the problem he wanted to solve. Plato, Hobbes, Locke, and Popper are all concerned with the nature and justification of political authority. The Stoics, Spinoza, Kant, and Sartre have the analysis and understanding of individual freedom at the core of their ethical thought. Aristotle, John Stuart Mill, Frege, and Quine share the problem of logical necessity. Their motivation, vocabulary, rhetoric, and solutions differ. But the problems are the same. Part of what the historical understanding of a philosopher yields is the possibility of judging what is essential and what is only accidental in his thought, what is his contribution and what is due to past thinkers, what arguments are original never yet reckoned with and what are old stalwarts whose twists and turns have been explored many times before. In sum, historical understanding makes it possible to see the point of a philosopher's work by acquainting us with the problem the philosopher was trying to solve. Without this understanding one cannot judge the work, because one cannot judge whether the problem he was trying to solve has been solved.

Historical understanding, however, contributes something else as well. As I have noted many times before, philosophers do not just want to solve problems: they want to solve them in accordance with ideals. Perennial arguments concern the question of which ideals or which interpretation of an ideal should guide one's problem-solving. But the answer to that question depends not merely upon the identity of the problems and the nature and interpretation of the ideals, but also on the actual circumstances in which the problems are faced and the ideals pursued.

Consider as an illustration the problem of political authority. That there be such a thing is a necessary condition of social life: the problem is enduring. Two ideals for developing a policy for coping with the problem are what might be called the authoritarian and the libertarian. One aims to maximize political authority for the benefit of the society, the other aims to minimize it for the benefit of individuals. Plato in *The Laws* may be taken as a spokesman for the former, Mill in *On Liberty* as a champion of the latter.

Clearly, a reasonable person's judgment of which ideal to favor in any particular situation will depend in part on the nature of the situation. In a society tending toward tyranny, the claims of authoritarianism will be intellectually weak. Correspondingly, in a society on the brink of anarchy, libertarianism will exercise a limited rational appeal. Thus the historical circumstances in which ideals are pursued as solutions of problems have an unavoidable influence on the justification of the proposed solutions. The discovery of these historical circumstances depends on historical understanding.

One aim of this book is to show that perennial arguments lie at the core of philosophy. But historical understanding is crucial to the conduct and justification of perennial arguments. It follows, therefore, that historical understanding is crucial to philosophy.

Historical understanding is connected with philosophical justification on several different levels. The most fundamental one is that a philosophical theory must be understood before it can be justified, and understanding it requires historical appreciation of the problem the theory was meant to solve. On the next level, the justification of the solution must be judged. That judgment, however, must vary with the circumstances in which the problem and an ideal are connected by a policy. Historical understanding yields knowledge of these circumstances.

Historical understanding is a label for many things. Some are immediately relevant to philosophical justification, others have only an indirect bearing. The one with the most intimate connection with philosophical justification is provided by problematic history of philosophy. This is an approach to the history of philosophy which is internal, rather than external, special, rather than general, intellectual history dealing with cognitive ideas, rather than history of ideas dealing with all nontrivial ideas, and lastly, it is history of *ideas*, rather than of other things. Thus the approach shows what problems preoccupied a philosopher and does so from the point of view of philosophical significance.

This approach, however, cannot be relied upon at the exclusion of others. For the questions of why some problems rather than others worried a philosopher, what ideals or interpretation of ideals were available to him, what were the actual circumstances in which his solutions were presented, must also be answered. But answering these questions requires the consideration of the interaction between philosophical and nonphilosophical ideas, that is, of external and general intellectual history. However, since the circumstances of a period depend not only upon cognitive ideas, but also upon noncognitive ones, intellectual history must also be transcended and the history of ideas be considered. Nor is the consideration of the history of ideas sufficient, since circumstances are not shaped only by ideas. The fact is, however, that the further away one goes from internal and special problematic history of philosophy, the less philosophically relevant historical considerations are likely to become. The contribution made by historical understanding to philosophical justification ranges from the essential to the negligible. The existence of neither extreme should be denied in the application of the rule given at the beginning of this section.

III. *Historical Understanding and the Improvement of Worldviews*

The view I shall defend here is that historical understanding is necessary for the improvement of worldviews. Improvement is called for if the existing worldview is found to be inadequate. This may be due to the discovery of conflicting elements in the worldview or to the discovery of conflicts between the worldview and new developments. These can be coped with by revising the worldview so that the internal conflicts are overcome and the conflicts between the worldview and novelty are reconciled. It is a necessary condition of the removal of the conflicts that the inadequate worldview be known. And this knowledge is historical.

It depends on understanding the metaphysics, the anthropology, and culture of the worldview. But understanding, say, the twentieth century Western view of reality, the significance that it has for us, and the moral, political, and aesthetic ideals surrounding us, is inseparable from understanding the classic works which made the worldview what it is.

If the classics are philosophical, the understanding will be provided by problematic history of philosophy. As we have seen, however, the problems and ideals of a worldview are not usually philosophical. The problems are discovered and the ideals are proposed by politicians, artists, novelists, poets, prophets, scientists, critics, economists, and others. The discovery of a problem or the formulation of an ideal is partly what makes a work a classic. And many classics are not philosophical.

Newton, Darwin, and Freud, Burke, Rousseau, and Marx, Shakespeare, Milton, and T. S. Eliot, to mention only a few nonphilosopher authors of classics, for better or worse, formed our worldview, just as great philosophers have done. The ideas of these people and of others must also be understood to understand our worldview. So that while problematic history of philosophy is necessary to the achievement of an historical understanding of our worldview, it is not sufficient. It must be supplemented by intellectual history and the history of ideas.

The case I am making is that a consequence of the view of the nature of philosophy I have been defending is that philosophers must have historical understanding. For unless they understand their worldview, and understand it the only way possible: historically, they can not remove the conflicts which weaken it, and so they cannot perform their central task.

The achievement of historical understanding of one's worldview is what makes a person cultured: it is what ought to be the goal of a liberal education. Most people, including most philosophers, lack this. For most people this lack may not be a handicap in the exercise of whatever expertise they happen to have. Philosophers, however, are not so fortunate. For the consequence of their lack of understanding is failure in their expertise. One of the reasons for the contemporary low esteem for philosophy is that philosophers have thus handicapped themselves, so that even if they wanted to, they could not perform their task. Since, it seems to me, everybody, but philosophers, is aware of the urgency of having and justifying a worldview, the task is done by psychoanalysts, politicians, clergymen, literary critics, television pundits, and journalists. The result is that their efforts lack the rigor and sophistication which philosophical training provides, the task gets done badly, and we are all the poorer for it.

IV. *Historical Understanding and Sensibility*

I have argued in Chapter Five that the possession of a rationally justified worldview is necessary but not sufficient for the attainment of wisdom. Wisdom may result from having understood and accepted a rationally justified view of the nature of reality, the significance that view has for human beings, a set of ideals in accordance with which problems can be solved, and from having arrived at reasoned judgment about the actual problems confronting one, as well as at policies for coping with them. I say wisdom *may* result from these considerable cognitive achievements, because rational justification, understanding, the possession of good judgment, do not by themselves produce wisdom. Sensibility is also needed.

Sensibility is a combination of feeling and imagination. It is the development of an interior emotional climate. At the core of it are the ideals that a person accepts. His attitude to the ideals is not merely one of cognitive acceptance, resulting from a careful scrutiny of the epistemological credentials of ideals, it is also a feeling of their appropriateness and fittingness. Feeling and imagination commit a person to his ideals in the sense that he would feel great personal loss if the ideals would have to be given up because they turned out to be rationally unjustifiable after all. It is an attitude which makes it natural and pleasurable for a person to act in accordance with his ideals; his actions are done not only out of a duty, they are what he would have done even if he did not think that it was his duty. There is nothing grim in his pursuit of his ideals; acting in accordance with them does not require self-denial, strength of character, acts of will; he acts as his ideals prompt him to do, as a matter of course. What he thinks is right is the same as what he feels like doing.

Sensibility does not justify anything, and if there is a conflict between the cognitive and emotive attitudes to ideals, the cognitive one should prevail. For that is what determines whether the relevant problem can be solved in accordance with the ideal in question. But if there is such a conflict, wisdom is not yet attained. For wisdom is that felicitous state in which rational justification coincides with what one wishes, hopes, and desires to be true.

Sensibility, as I am using the term, is the opposite of alienation. Both attitudes are compatible with having a rationally justified worldview. But in the case of alienation, the person is made unhappy by his outlook, while the man of sensibility is made happy. He likes, approves of, welcomes what he takes to be the facts, their significance, and the ideals.

Needless to say, there is great scope for self-deception here. For a person may be dishonest in evaluating the rational arguments about the ideals he accepts. As a result, he may persuade himself that what he would like to be rationally justified is, even though a more dispassionate appraisal of the arguments would indicate otherwise. But the psychoanalytic view that reasoning is mostly rationalization, the existentialist claim that commitment to ideals can hardly avoid inauthenticity or be made in bad faith, and the Marxist thesis about false consciousness being involved in all but one system of ideals, seem to me to be mistaken. For there is a powerful curb on self-deception: self-interest.

If it is remembered that ideals are pursued because they are regarded as desirable ways of solving problems, and if it is not forgotten that the person who accepts and rejects ideals is the same one who has the problems, then it will be seen that it is in everybody's interest to be reasonable about what ideals to favor. For the penalty for unreasonability and self-deception is that the person so indulging himself will be left with unsolved or badly solved problems. Intellectual virtue, at least, will not go unrewarded, as intellectual vice will receive its comeuppance.

Sensibility is thus a good thing, and it is essential to wisdom. But what is the connection between historical understanding and sensibility? The connection is that historical understanding is one of the few ways in which one can develop sensibility.

At the core of sensibility lie ideals and the development of sensibility is partly the process of acquiring one's ideals. The acquisition of ideals may simply be a matter of inheritance or imitation; one may come to hold ideals as family hand-me-downs, or as a result of having accepted the opinions of people around oneself. But ideals may be acquired as a result of reflection, argument, and criticism. Their acquisition, then, is a matter of choice. This second is clearly preferable, for the more critical attention is paid to ideals, the more likely it is that the chosen ones will lead to successful problem-solving.

The desired critical attention to ideals is partly a matter of comparison between different and competing ideals. Making these comparisons requires imagination and emotional agility. For what the comparison amounts to is trying to imagine oneself being guided first by one and then by other ideals. What one has to do is to imagine himself to be in circumstances other than his own, face crises, be subject to pressures, fail and triumph, in imagined situations. Most people's imagination is insufficiently powerful to perform these tasks unaided. I can think of only a few ways of helping the imagination to make these comparisons.

One is through literature and such arts as the theatre and film. The other is by being intimately acquainted with a large number of people who are motivated by different ideals. The third is having anthropological knowledge of alien societies. The last one is historical understanding, and it is on that one that I shall concentrate here.

History is rich in societies, institutions, and people who guided by many different ideals faced many different problem-situations. One benefit of historical understanding is that it shows how the pursuit of different ideals works out in practice. It allows us to view history as an experiment in the exercise of human options. What we learn from it is not how to succeed or avoid failing, but what it is to attempt to solve a kind of problem in accordance with a particular ideal. We learn the likely pitfalls, the cost, the sacrifices that may be required, the risks that may have to be taken, the compromises that may have to be accepted, as well as the probable satisfactions, accomplishments, rewards, that are associated with the pursuit of particular ideals.

Of course, historical situations are different and they do not permit facile inferences. But types of historical situations are not all that different. We know that political revolutionaries must be prepared to kill, because we have learned that from the lives of Robespierre, Lenin, and Mao. We know that excessive concern with self-cultivation makes for political irresponsibility, because we have the examples of the early Quakers in Pennsylvania and the sad story of many German intellectuals from Humboldt to the early Thomas Mann. We know that millenarianism will lead to self-destruction and either to political tyranny or to anarchy because we have before us the examples of the heresy of the Free Spirit, the Albigensians, and the flagellants. We know that institutions and individuals in power tend to seek more power and unless checked will become arbitrary. Needless to say, none of this do we know infallibly. What we learn are tendencies. One's sensibility, however, is formed partly by welcoming or being repelled by the tendencies likely to be fostered by particular ideals.

So we may turn to history to help us shape our sensibility. But, of course, the adoption of ideals should depend on other things as well as on sensibility. Ideals must be rationally justified. I have emphasized here the role sensibility plays, because I was concerned with showing that historical understanding can make one a better person. The improvement comes about by the appreciation of many ideals, including ideals held by people with whom we disagree. Not only does this improve one's chances of solving his own problems, it is also likely to make him more appreciative and tolerant of other solutions.

V. *Conclusion*

I have argued in this chapter for the essential connection between historical understanding and the development and justification of worldviews. The argument was based on the recurring theme of this book that philosophy cannot be done well in ignorance of cultural influences. For cultural influences shape both the problems philosophers are trying to solve and the ideals they are trying to exemplify in their solutions. Understanding these influences is historical. Its possession is necessary for philosophical justification. Since unless one understands what a philosophical theory is supposed to accomplish, he cannot judge its success or failure. The judgment requires historical understanding of the problems and ideals of the theory. Furthermore, historical understanding is required also for the improvement of worldviews. Worldviews face both external and internal conflicts. Philosophical theories attempt to reconcile these conflicts. A necessary condition of their success, however, is historical understanding of the beleaguered worldview. Lastly, I have argued for the important role sensibility plays in the achievement of wisdom, personal happiness, and the good life. These great goods are the benefits the possession of a worldview can bestow on one. But the development of sensibility, their essential component, depends on both cognitive and emotive appreciation of human options represented by the various ideals and their interpretations. Historical understanding is one of the few ways of achieving that appreciation. So it seems to me that there is much to be gained from historical understanding in philosophy.

THE STATE OF THE ARGUMENT

The result of this part of the book is that it becomes possible to say a little more about the content a justified worldview in our age and society must have. The starting point of such a worldview is a problem-situation and its aim is the development of policies for coping with the enduring problems.

The development of policies, however, requires knowledge of the relevant facts. The common sense view of the world provides a set of facts which must be taken into account by any worldview. Consequently, the adequacy of the interpretations offered by the philosophical theories which are systematized in worldviews can be judged partly on the ground of whether they account for the facts of common sense.

The fundamentality of common sense introduces an unavoidable anthropocentric orientation into our worldviews. For what renders common sense fundamental is human nature. Given our bodies and their physiological and motor capacities and limitations, we must approach the world in our peculiarly human way. We can transcend the starting point, but the success and failure of such ventures must also be judged with reference to the very same set of facts above which we try to rise. Our perspective is necessarily human; to believe otherwise is an illusion.

But it does not follow from this that the human perspective cannot be rationally evaluated. Problem-solving and truth-directedness provide the standard with reference to which the rationality of our beliefs can be objectively and reliably judged.

Historical understanding is a necessary condition of judging them. For beliefs can be justified only if they are understood and understanding them requires knowledge of their problem-situation. The problem-situation is composed of the prevailing worldview, and either of some occurrence which appears anomalous from its point of view, or of some tension internal to the worldview. The adequacy of problem-solving attempts cannot, therefore, be judged without knowledge of the worldview. This knowledge involves consideration of cultural influences and historical understanding.

The emphasis upon common sense and historical understanding has been the constructive aim of this part of the book. But it also has a critical aim. This is the attempt to show that that contribution made by science to the construction and justification of worldviews is much less significant than contemporary philosophers are given to supposing.

My remarks about science do not aim to belittle its tremendous achievements and the resulting benefit for mankind. What I have been insisting on is the recognition that a successful worldview cannot be coextensive with even a utopian perfect science. For there is more to having a successful worldview than even a hypothetical complete science. There are enduring problems which cannot have scientific solutions and there are such areas of worldviews as culture, anthropology, diagnosis, and policy, which are not amenable to scientific treatment. What I have been insisting on is that science should be restricted to its proper sphere, the one within metaphysics. Its great contributions in that sphere are both undeniable and unexportable to other spheres.

NOTES

1. John H. Randall, Jr., *How Philosophy Uses Its Past* (New York: Columbia University Press, 1963), 77.

2. The position I am defending is a version of historicism. It originates, as far as I can tell, in Giambattista Vico's *The New Science* (Ithaca: Cornell University Press, 1970), tr. T. H. Bergin and M. H. Fisch. The best account of Vico's relevant ideas that I know of is Isaiah Berlin's *Vico and Herder* (London: Hogarth Press, 1976). Wilhelm Dilthey fundamentally influenced this tradition. For an English account of his thought see Rudolf A. Makkreel, *Dilthey* (Princeton: Princeton University Press, 1975); this work contains a full bibliography. Another major figure is Robin G. Collingwood, see his *An Essay on Metaphysics* (Oxford: Clarendon, 1962) and *The Idea of History* (Oxford: Clarendon, 1946). The most illuminating work I found on Collingwood is Louis O. Mink's *Mind, History, and Dialectic* (Bloomington: Indiana University Press, 1969). Two quite recent works in the same tradition are William B. Gallie's *Philosophy and Historical Understanding* (London: Chatto & Windus, 1964) and John H. Randall, Jr., *How Philosophy Uses Its Past, op. cit.* The position whose resemblance to my own is closest is Alasdair MacIntyre's "Epistemological Crises, Dramatic Narrative, and the Philosophy of Science," *The Monist*, 60 (1977), 453–72. The classic critique of historicism is Karl R. Popper's *The Poverty of Historicism* (London: Routledge, 1957). Not all forms of historicism are committed to the version Popper so devastatingly criticizes. The one defended here, for instance, is not. Penetrating accounts of the controversy are Maurice Mandelbaum's "Historicism," which is Part II of his *History, Man and Reason* (Baltimore: Johns Hopkins Press, 1971) and John Passmore's "*The Poverty of Historicism* Revisited," *History and Theory*, Beiheft 14 (1975), 30–47. Both have extensive bibliographies. A suggestive defence of historicism by an historian is John Lukacs' *Historical Consciousness* (New York: Harper & Row, 1968).

3. The distinctions are largely derived from Maurice Mandelbaum's "The History of Ideas, Intellectual History, and the History of Philosophy," *History and Theory*, Beiheft 5 (1965), 33–66.

4. This is Lukacs' phrase; cf. Note 2 above.

5. The distinction is John Passmore's in "The Idea of a History of Philosophy,"

History and Theory, Beiheft 5 (1965), 1–32. My descriptive history corresponds to his doxographical history. I am indebted to this article for many of my references.

6. Immanuel Kant, *Prolegomena to Any Future Metaphysics*, tr. L. W. Beck (New York: Liberal Arts, 1950), 3.

7. Ludwig Wittgenstein, *Notebooks 1914–1918*, tr. G. E. M. Anscombe (Oxford: Blackwell, 1969), 82e.

8. Kant, *Prolegomena*, 3.

9. Charles D. Broad, *Five Types of Ethical Theory* (London: Routledge, 1930), 1–2.

10. Robin G. Collingwood, *An Autobiography* (Oxford: Clarendon, 1939), 31.

11. Passmore, "The Idea of a History of Philosophy," 29.

12. Passmore, "The Idea of a History of Philosophy," 31.

13. John H. Randall, Jr., *The Career of Philosophy* (New York: Columbia University Press, 1962), Vol. I, 7.

PART FIVE

THE NATURE OF PHILOSOPHY: CONCLUSION

Chapter Twelve

Philosophy as the Construction and Justification of Worldviews

"In every state, not wholly barbarous, a philosophy, good or bad, there must be. However slightingly it may be the fashion to talk of speculation and theory, as opposed (sillily and nonsensically opposed) to practice, it would not be difficult to prove, that such as is the existing spirit of speculation during any given period, such will be the spirit and tone of religion, legislation, and morals, may even of the fine arts, the manners, and the fashions. Nor is this the less true, because the great majority of men live like bats, but in twilight, and know and feel the philosophy of their age only by its reflections and refractions."

SAMUEL T. COLERIDGE[1]

I. *Introduction*

This chapter and the next contain the overall description and justification of the view of the nature of philosophy I am concerned with defending. But these two chapters also constitute the keystone uniting two lines of argument in the book. The first is about perennial arguments, the second is about philosophical justification. The connection is that philosophy is concerned with the construction and justification of worldviews and its task is the philosophical justification of perennial arguments. Perennial arguments enable us to decide what ideals or what interpretations of ideals ought to guide us in solving enduring problems. The system formed of enduring problems, ideals for solving them, and perennial arguments aiming to justify particular ideals or their interpretations is what I am calling a worldview.

This description of philosophy is, of course, open to challenge and consequently it needs justification; that will be given in the next chapter. Since philosophy itself is an ideal, it too is subject to both external and internal perennial arguments. The justification of my view of philosophy, therefore, must consist in showing why one side should be taken in perennial arguments about philosophy.

II. *The Ideal of Philosophy*

My point of departure is a factual claim: "One of the broadest and surest generalizations ... about human beings is that no society is healthy or creative or strong unless that society has a set of common values that give meaning and purpose to group life, that can be symbolically expressed, that fit with the situation of the time as well as being linked to the historical past, and that do not outrage men's reason and at the same time appeal to their emotions."[2] I think that this claim is true, and what it calls for is a worldview. The ideal of philosophy is to provide it.

What needs to be done now is to describe this ideal in greater detail. The description should conform to the general characteristics of ideals given in Chapter Four. It was noted there that ideals are goals valued by people who have them; they represent desirable solutions to problems; they are significant; internally complex; variously assessable; open and modifiable; composed of presuppositions; and subject to both external and internal perennial arguments.

Let us begin with an extremely general description. Philosophy is an attempt to provide a rationally justified theory of reality and of the significance it has for human beings. A successful attempt yields a worldview. This ideal is clearly valued by people, for having an informed view of the facts and being able to judge their significance are necessary conditions for accomplishing whatever one wants. It is not clear, however, why knowledge of the facts and of their significance requires a worldview.

The answer is that a worldview is required by the universal need for solving enduring problems. The cluster of these enduring problems is that part of the human condition which forces people to act. If a person leaves enduring problems he faces unsolved, he will suffer. Ideals represent desirable goals in accordance with which particular enduring problems may be solved. Morality is the ideal way of dealing with other people, culture is the ideal way of providing oneself with an interesting and rich internal life, science is the ideal way of acquiring knowledge of nature.

Philosophy is also an ideal, but more comprehensive than others. It is the ideal way of solving the whole cluster of enduring problems. The worldview it aims to provide is systematic. It is not a random collection of ideals, but a coherent system formed of them. It aims to provide a coherent, consistent, harmonious framework for dealing with all three types of enduring problems.

The advantage of having a worldview over solving enduring problems piecemeal is the advantage of organization over disorganization.

Philosophy is a significant ideal. An ideal is significant if it represents a possible solution to enduring problems and if it is generally recognized as doing so. Significant ideals are the options in the consciousness of a particular epoch. When the ideal in question is philosophy itself, then its general recognition or public availability amounts to participation in a particular worldview. And that means that people in an intellectual epoch share a view about the form and urgency in which enduring problems present themselves and about the repertoire of available ideals for solving them. Their disagreements concern the choice among these ideals and the interpretation of the ideals upon which they agree. Thus, for instance, if we today face the enduring problem of how to deal with the claims of a minority in our society, their murder or enslavement are not live options. Whereas holding an election over the issue, referring their claims to lawcourts, or attempting to accommodate them by increasing their living standards are available ways of coping, and they are prompted by such ideals as equality, justice, or balanced distribution of resources.

Philosophy being a significant ideal, then, both excludes and includes certain considerations. It excludes private and personal aspirations and many historically influential ideals as well, for these are rarely publicly available. What it includes are the ideals in the public consciousness. The systematization and rational examination of these ideals is one of the main roles for worldviews.

Philosophy, however, cannot play this role unless it is prepared to take account of cultural influences. Only rarely do philosophers discover the problems or introduce the ideals which are encountered in an intellectual epoch. The philosophical task is the systematization and rational examination of the problems and ideals, a task which it is the role of perennial arguments to perform. Consideration of cultural influences is a necessary prerequisite of this, for it is through them that philosophers can learn what the problems and ideals are.

That there is a cluster of ideals available at any time in any epoch is not seriously arguable. The question about them is whether they are systematized and rationally examined. If philosophers are doing their job, the answer is affirmative. If they are failing, then we all suffer, because our attempts to solve enduring problems will be less successful than they might be. We run the risk, then, both of acting in accordance with intellectually dubious ideals and also that actions in pursuit of different ideals will conflict and thus jeopardize the chances of solving our problems. The systematization and rational examination of prevalent ideals is in everybody's interest, and that is why the construction and justification of worldviews is in the common good. The value of philosophy in any age depends on how well philosophers perform that all-important task.

The next feature of philosophy is internal complexity. The ideal is composed of many elements, each of which plays an essential role in the ideal. The internal complexity of philosophy is due to the five components of worldviews: metaphysics, anthropology, culture, diagnosis, and policy.

The ideal of philosophy is exemplified in the worldviews that prevail in particular intellectual epochs. Sometimes, though by no means always, there is a conscious effort made to formulate a particular worldview. These are the works of the philosophical synthesizers. Like everything else, this can be done well or badly. If done well, they become the great human options. Plato, Aristotle, Aquinas, Leibniz, Spinoza, Kant have done it superbly; Comte and Spencer poorly; and how well Hegel and Whitehead did it is arguable.

Not all philosophers aim to formulate worldviews. Many philosophers are concerned with criticizing them: Hume is the great example here. Others are interested in developing only parts of worldviews: Descartes' interests were largely metaphysical; John Stuart Mill's largely cultural and anthropological; Marx concentrated mainly on diagnosis and policy.

Thus my claim that philosophy is internally complex is the claim that worldviews are composed of five elements. Each contributes a necessary part to having a successful worldview. Metaphysics gives an overall explanation of such facts as science and other empirical inquiries provide. A successful metaphysical theory is thus necessary, for we have to have a reliable view of reality if we are to cope with it. The facts and explanations of metaphysics are meant to approximate as closely as possible the truth. The truth is independent of human wishes and desires. The world is what it is and would remain so even if mankind disappeared. But the immediate interest we, human beings, have in the world is that we must cope with it. Some facts help, others hinder this endeavor. Thus we are not indifferent to what metaphysics tells us. Some facts are important, relevant, surprising, grounds for hope or despair, others are not. Anthropology provides a way of interpreting the facts by imposing the inevitable human perspective from which we must think. But we do not only want to know what the facts are and how they help or hinder us in solving enduring problems; we also care about how these problems are solved. For some solutions are preferable to others. Culture is the repository of ideals in accordance with which we desire to solve the problems. But knowledge of the facts, their human significance, and the ideals do not by themselves solve enduring problems. We must also have a realistic estimate of our actual situation, of what form and urgency our problems have, and this is the function of the diagnosis. And lastly, we have to have a plan of action, a coordinated policy for translating ideals into practice, so that problems can be solved. If we have all this, we have a rationally justified worldview.

Various assessability is the feature of ideals which makes perennial arguments possible. What can be variously assessed is either the relative merits of different ideals for the solution of enduring problems, or the relative importance of the internally complex elements within an ideal. In the former case, various assessability results in an external perennial argument; in the latter, the consequence is an internal perennial argument. In both cases, however, the perennial arguments concern the suitability of a particular ideal for representing the best solution to an enduring problem. Philosophy is the battlefield on which the mettles of ideals get tested through perennial arguments.

There are different conceptions of philosophy because philosophy too is a variously assessable ideal. External perennial arguments about philosophy are conducted over its suitability for providing a worldview. Participants in such perennial arguments may recognize the desirability of having a worldview and deny that philosophy can provide it. Ideologues, for instance, may regard philosophical attempts at rational justification as the tricks of a ruling class anxious to maintain its dominance; mystics may think that only spiritual exercise, and not philosophical argument, can lead to an acceptable worldview; religious believers may suppose that the only true worldview has already been revealed, and philosophical attempts to provide a competitor are prompted by the Devil.

Internal perennial arguments occur among those who accept philosophy as the ideal way of constructing and justifying worldviews, but who attribute different importance to the various elements composing philosophy in solving enduring problems.

These arguments are perennial because to the question of how the elements should be ranked, there is no final answer. For the form and the urgency of enduring problems changes from period to period, and so must change the worldview, comprising the variously ranked elements, if it is to provide successful solutions.

But the absence of a final answer does not mean that there is not a right answer in every particular situation. For the test of an answer is not its endurance, but its capacity to do what it was meant to do: solve enduring problems in accordance with rationally justified ideals. Whether the Cartesians were right in emphasizing metaphysics and method and ignoring practically the rest of philosophy depends on how well the Cartesian worldview solved the enduring problems as they presented themselves to Western Europeans in the seventeenth century. Whether Marx was right in contending that "The philosophers have only *interpreted* the world in various ways; the point, however, is to *change* it,"[3] depends on how secure were the metaphysical, cultural, and anthropological grounds upon which this nineteenth-century diagnosis and policy for industrial societies depends. And whether the contemporary view of philosophy, resulting from the professionalization of the subject,[4] is correct depends on how well philosophy is fulfilling its traditional role: the construction and rational justification of worldviews.

The various assessability of philosophy means that it is an open and modifiable ideal. It can be adjusted to changing circumstances, because it allows for both flexibility and precision. Flexibility comes from the possibility of ranking the elements differently; precision can be attained by being clear about what we are doing.

What I have been aiming to do in arguing for a particular interpretation of philosophy has a negative and a positive side. The negative is to displace metaphysics from the privileged position it occupies in contemporary philosophical practice. The positive is to emphasize the importance of culture and anthropology. The justification for this is that the concentration upon metaphysics, inspired by the great success of science, leads us to pay attention to only one of the three problem-areas in which enduring problems occur. Our understanding and ability to cope with nature has increased manifold. Science and metaphysics are justly to be praised for that. But our understanding and ability to cope with problems connected with our relation to other people and society has not similarly increased. Nor has there been a noticeable improvement in people's self-knowledge and self-acceptance. We are not appreciably better off in solving these other types of enduring problems than our seventeenth century, scholastic, Roman, or Greek predecessors were. My emphasis upon culture and anthropology is justified, therefore, because balance needs to be restored.

It is more important for our contemporary worldview to have something illuminating to say about achieving the good life than to continue to trace the implications of quantum mechanics, or to ponder the implications of the discovery of yet another subatomic particle. And it is more important to consider and cope with the conflict between freedom and equality in contemporary democratic societies than to be conversant with the latest twist in the conflict between the expanding universe and steady-state theories. My point is not the absurd claim that the nature of reality is unimportant. Rather it is that the gain towards solving our enduring problems from additional information about reality is likely to be much less than the gain from deeper understanding of ourselves, other people, and society. I am recommending a shift from the one-sided philosophical concentration upon nature at the expense of humanity. And my recommendation is temporal: it is for our time. What was true in the past and what may be needed in the future are not questions I intend to consider.

But this recommendation is still too general. What needs to be done to further elucidate it is to show what the particular presuppositions are to which my ideal of philosophy is committed. I have argued in Chapter Four that the internally complex elements constituting an ideal are classificatory, existential, methodological, and axiological presuppositions. I need to say now what they are for philosophy.

III. *The Presuppositions of Philosophy*

The classificatory presuppositions of philosophy are the definitions and distinctions I have developed throughout the book. These form something like a conceptual grid which I have attempted to impose on the domain I take philosophy to occupy. They are the taxonomy of the problems, arguments, and ideals philosophy comprises. It would be tedious to restate them in detail, especially since I have had to appeal to them frequently and each appeal has involved some repetition.

The main existential presupposition of my view of philosophy is that metaphysics is the best guide to what there is. Needless to say, it is not an infallible guide or an unchallengable authority. For even the best metaphysical opinion may have to be revised. The point, however, is that what forces the revision is improved metaphysical opinion.

This is not a controversial presupposition. It becomes so when I explain how I am understanding metaphysics. Metaphysics, in my view, is an interpretive theory whose role is to interpret the facts and regularities provided by descriptive theories. So the content of metaphysics, apart from interpretations, is exclusively derived from theories whose primary concern is with the discovery and explanation of facts and regularities occurring in nature. Scientific theories, of course, are the most successful descriptive theories. But they are not the only ones. Historical, biographical, educational, legal, ethnographic, and many other theories also aim to discover and explain facts.

In much of this book I have stressed the discontinuity between science and metaphysics. But nothing I have said implies that there is a radical difference between them. Scientific theories and metaphysics have a common aim: forming a coherent view of reality. This aim is achieved only by conducting both descriptive and interpretive inquiries. If science is thought to concentrate mainly on the descriptive part of this aim, while metaphysics on the interpretive one, their continuity becomes evident. I have emphasized their discontinuity partly to guard against the common error of supposing that science is the only inquiry capable of producing truths about reality.

My claim, then, is that metaphysics, understood as the combination of facts, provided largely by science, but also by other descriptive inquiries, and of their interpretations, is the authority on the nature of reality.

The main negative implication of this existential presupposition is the exclusion of what might be called supernaturalism. Under this heading I include all claims about the existence of anything beyond what is ascertainable by descriptive-metaphysical research. Thus insofar as mystical or religious claims are made for the existence of a realm, or beings, or entities, or qualities which are not certifiable by descriptive-metaphysical research, so far my conception of philosophy is committed to rejecting them.

The argument for this conclusion is simple: the only way of coming to know anything about the facts is the descriptive-metaphysical way. This, of course, is not to say that there may not exist many things beyond the ken of contemporary or even all future descriptive inquiries and metaphysics. But if anything of this sort exists, we could not know about it. Nor is it to deny that we have a stock of problems whose solution requires going beyond contemporary metaphysics. For all I know, parapsychology may present such a case. The important thing is that what going beyond contemporary metaphysics means is trying to develop better metaphysics. The inadequacy of contemporary descriptive, explanatory, and metaphysical accounts is not an invitation to rely on insight, intuition, religious or mystical experiences, or faith. Thus the stock of unresolved problems cannot give support to the factual claims of mystics, theologians, spiritualists, and other advocates of supernaturalism.

The main positive implication of the presupposition is that metaphysics is the best authority about what there is. Following its recommendations, we have the best chance of solving our enduring problems in one problem-area: nature. The reason why the recommendations of metaphysics are the best in this area is that they are most likely to be true.

The third kind of presuppositions involved in my conception of philosophy is methodological. This concerns the question of how, by the use of what methods, can the task of philosophy, the construction and justification of worldviews, be achieved. The short answer is that it ought to be done rationally. But the short answer is unsatisfactory, because what rationality comes to in this area must be spelled out in detail.

To do this let us recall the distinction between the two contexts of justification discussed in Part Three: the first is that of introduction, the other of acceptance. In the context of intro-duction, justification depends on whether the theory is a possible solution of the problem for whose solution it was introduced. If the theory is a worldview, then its justification depends on whether it presents a possible solution for all the enduring problems which must be faced by a particular society at a particular time.

The enduring problems requiring a solution present themselves to a society through the inadequacy of the prevailing worldview. This inadequacy is noticed because the traditional ways of coping with enduring problems are no longer satisfactory. This may be due to inconsistency, the presence of incompatible elements, or the existence of tensions within the conventional worldview. Or it may happen because the worldview has difficulty in meeting enduring problems as they occur in new forms and with different degrees and rankings or urgency than before.

The emergence of these problems requires changing the existing worldview. The change may be piecemeal or comprehensive, depending on the success of the existing worldview in coping with the problems. Piecemeal changes may result in altering part of the prevailing view of reality; or revising the interpretation of its human significance; or replacing existing ideals; or changing the diagnostic and policy-making components of one's worldview. Such changes may be brought about by the success and failure of particular philosophical theories. Examples of such changes are the gradual recognition of the indefensibility of theism, vitalism, and perhaps dualism; the replacement of the Cartesian ideal of certainty with fallibilism; the probably fatal criticism of the view that there exist historical laws and historical necessity; the discovery that mathematics and science have a history and thus neither can be justifiably regarded as repositories of eternal truths; the breakdown of intuitionism in ethics; the great damage done to empiricism by the criticism of the analytic-synthetic distinction; and so on.

These piecemeal changes, however, may accumulate and force comprehensive changes in a worldview. Thus the Greeks undermined animism, Christianity replaced polytheism, Cartesianism led to the dissolution of the medieval outlook, and perhaps we are experiencing the breakdown of the Enlightenment-bred, optimism-filled, science-oriented, progressive-liberal worldview so well represented by logical positivism.

The justification of a worldview in the context of introduction thus depends on it being able to cope with those enduring problems its predecessors could, and, in addition, also with those which its predecessors could not handle. The standard of justification being appealed to in this context is problem-solving. If the required changes are piecemeal, the question of justification is raised and settled in connection with particular philosophical theories which compose parts of a worldview. The justification of the worldview as a whole is not likely to arise then, since in that situation it is functioning well and is deficient only in part. But if this is not so, and piecemeal changes are unlikely to save the worldview, then one must face the question of the justification of the worldview *in toto*. And that question is also answered with reference to providing possible answers to enduring problems, it is only that the justification of the worldview depends on providing a systematic solution to all the enduring problems which then require a solution.

I do not know how to answer the question of when piecemeal

changes are no longer enough and the worldview as a whole must be replaced. One can see in retrospect that this situation has confronted a society. But how to tell whether this is the case for one's own, is a profoundly difficult question. There are always doomsayers and apologists to listen to and only the not yet available historical perspective will tell which, if either, had his fingers on the pulse of history.

One thing, however, is crucial: historical understanding. For it is through it that we can grasp our problem-situation. The enduring problems we must solve are the ones for whose solution the preceding worldview is inadequate. Unless we understand that worldview, we cannot discover the source of its inadequacy and we do not know what would be an improvement upon it. This is one of the main reasons for the insistence on an intimate connection between philosophy and history.

Ideally, the context of introduction yields some worldviews each of which provides a systematic way of solving enduring problems. The next step is to choose between them rationally. The choice is made in the second context of justification, the context of acceptance. The standard of justification here is truth-directedness. The question that needs to be answered is: which of the theories whose introduction has been justified has the best chance of being true? The qualifying theory should be the one accepted. The truth-directedness of a theory is determined by comparing it to its rivals on the basis of their logical consistency, adequacy of interpretation, and capacity to withstand criticism.

Logical consistency consists in conformity to logical rules. Logical rules are extracted from successful practice, and what makes practices successful is that they help us to solve our problems in accordance with ideals. The explanation of why they help is that beliefs upon which the practice is based are normally true. In normal circumstances, success is due in part to verisimilitude. So logical rules guide practices which combine problem-solving in accordance with ideals and truth-directedness. The justification for conforming to logical rules is that they get us what we want.

The second test of truth-directedness in the context of acceptance is adequacy of interpretation. Theories solve problems by offering an interpretation of the relevant facts. What the relevant facts are differs from case to case. But there is a set of facts which must be reckoned with by any theory: facts vouchsafed for by common sense. I have argued in Chapter Nine that common sense is the inevitable and fallible foundation upon which all beliefs, theories, or knowledge rests. This has two implications relevant to the present context.

The first is that no philosophical, or any other, theory can provide a view which violates common sense and remain logically consistent. For the truth of common sense is assumed by all theories. So if a theory entails a conclusion which denies the truth of common sense, the theory is contradicting the assumption upon which it itself rests. This necessity to conform to common sense establishes a constraint upon the interpretations philosophical theories offer.

The implication of this for the view of philosophy I am defending is that one component of worldviews is more fundamental than the others: this privileged position is occupied by anthropology. If common sense, being contingent on human physiology, is basic and so all theories must assume its truth, then the human point of view is basic, and anthropology, representing it, must have the privileged position I claim for it.

The fundamentality of anthropology is important from the point of view of justification. Justification is an activity done by human beings. One task it has is to decide which solutions to our problems we should accept and act upon. But the problems are human problems. And the ideals in accordance with which we want to solve problems are human ideals. It should thus occasion no surprise that at the foundation of all of our cognitive ventures we find the anthropocentric perspective.

If this conclusion is sound, then my view of philosophy implies that a long-standing philosophical, and also religious, mystical, scientific, ambition is misdirected. If the human perspective is inescapable, then all attempts to form a view of the world independently of the anthropocentric view are doomed. The ambition to understand reality *sub specie aeternitatis* is unrealizable.

This brings us to the second implication the fundamentality of common sense has. It has long been assumed that if the anthropocentrism I advocate is true, then the impossibility of objective justification follows. If we cannot abandon the human perspective, the assumption is, then justification must be relative to human beings. Thus we can never find out whether our beliefs or theories correspond to reality as it is in itself without human mediation. I think that this assumption is false, and anthropocentrism is perfectly compatible with the possibility of objective justification.

What makes this possible is the pivotal notion of problems of life I have introduced in Chapter Three and made use of throughout the book. The possibility of objective justification depends on using problems of life as the external, context-independent standard with reference to which our theories must ultimately be justified. The explanation of success in solving problems of life is that the theory on the basis of which we acted is true. The reason why this explanation should be accepted is that it accounts for all the relevant facts and because all of its rivals can be shown either to presuppose it, or to amount to no more than the harmless claim that any explanation may be mistaken. I have argued for this in Chapter Nine.

Thus the use of adequacy of interpretation as a test of the truth-directedness of a philosophical theory commits my view of philosophy to anthropocentrism, to the fundamentality of common sense, and yet it allows for the possibility of objective justification.

The third test of truth-directedness is the capacity to withstand criticism. The employment of this test is warranted in the context of acceptance when there are available a number of philosophical theories which have been justified in the context of introduction, that is, theories presenting possible solutions to enduring problems, and whose logical consistency and adequacy of interpretation have been established. The test helps us to determine which of these we should accept.

But we need to ask at this point how worldviews or the philosophical theories which are parts of them can be criticized? One obvious way is by showing that they fail to be justified either in the context of introduction or in the context of acceptance. In the former case, they fail in problem-solving, in the latter, in logical consistency or adequacy of interpretation. This answer, however, does not go far enough, because the question of how the criticism of a worldview which is justified by these tests is possible still needs to be faced.

The answer is in terms of the distinction between descriptive and interpretive theories. This distinction is one of degree, not of kind. For the discovery of what the facts are involves interpretation and the correct interpretation of facts involves factual accuracy. Yet there are typical theories representing each of these two interests. Scientific and historical theories of low level of generality, concerned with discovering the cause of an event, are typically descriptive. Philosophical theories are typically interpretive. Worldviews, of course, are the extreme instances of interpretive theories.

So the question posed above becomes: how can such paradigmatically interpretive theories as worldviews be criticized?

Interpretive theories depend upon descriptive theories for the supply of the to-be-interpreted facts. Interpretive theories can therefore be critized indirectly, through the success and failure of the descriptive theories which provide their factual base.

This feature of worldviews explains why cultural influences must be considered by philosophers. For cultural influences include the factual base. They also include much else of importance for the construction and justification of worldviews, such as ideals. But without the factual base, worldviews could neither be constructed nor criticized. The other explanation that follows is that one main impetus for changing worldviews can now be identified. The factual base keeps shifting, because descriptive theories change. So the interpretations based on them must also change. And the accumulation of such changes will sooner or later result in having to change the worldview as well.

The methodological presupposition of my view of philosophy thus is this complex account of how the construction and justification of worldviews can proceed rationally. The process is intricate and slow, but it occurs. And if we are to solve our enduring problems rationally, it must occur.

The question of what axiological presuppositions philosophy has is ambiguous. It may be about the ideals implicit in a particular worldview, or about the ideal of philosophy in general. The former change from worldview to worldview, the latter does not. I am interested in the second interpretation of the question here. To put it plainly, what I am asking is: what is the value of philosophy?

I shall divide the answer into two. Philosophy aims to provide a rationally justified worldview and having such a worldview is both in the common good and valuable from the private point of view of each person participating in it. The common good provided by a worldview is that of having a rationally justified systematic way of solving enduring problems in accordance with ideals. What a worldview does is to provide a theoretical framework in terms of which people can conduct their lives. It yields understanding, a sense of values, a policy of action, and a forum for the rational discussion of the fundamental questions of life.

This last benefit is particularly important, because it characterizes philosophy uniquely. Religions, many ideologies, various brands of mysticism, also provide worldviews, but their answers to many fundamental questions are authoritatively given.

Acceptance of these authoritative answers is the price of participation in the worldview. And the thirst for having a worldview of one's own is so great that many people do not hesitate to pay this demeaning price. The acceptance of such answers not only demands self-deception, that being the way to lull one's critical faculties into silence, but it is also self-defeating. For the rational examination of all relevant questions is necessary to having a successful worldview. What makes a worldview successful is that it solves enduring problems. And what rational examination does is to maximize the chances of success by critically testing policies for action. If rational discussion of fundamental questions is eschewed, the possibility of having a successful worldview is undermined. The comfort provided by participation in an authoritatively founded worldview is thus false comfort, based on self-deception, and it leads to action against one's own interest.

Worldviews affording rational discussion maximize the chances of success, but they do not guarantee it. Rational discussion is the best way of testing the truth of one's view of the facts, their interpretations, and of the ideals one aims to realize. But human fallibility stands between the best efforts to reach truth and truth itself. So saying that philosophy is in the common good is saying that it aims to provide a benefit otherwise unobtainable, but it is not to say that it assures success. It is simply the best we can do.

The personal value of philosophy is that it makes the attainment of wisdom possible. Wisdom is a great human good, perhaps the greatest, and given human nature, everybody desires it, whether consciously or otherwise. Wisdom is a combination of intellectual, emotional, and imaginative elements. The intellectual component provides understanding; it comes from metaphysics, anthropology, and culture. Philosophical understanding thus unites a view of reality with an interpretation of its human significance and a system of ideals, all bound together by rational justification. A person who has it thus has a grip on the facts, a way of judging their importance, and a sense of values.

But wisdom is more than just this cognitive state. It has an emotional component as well, one that endows a person with sensibility. Sensibility comes from historical understanding of the ideals the worldview provides. It means that a person does not just assent to the ideals cognitively and is prepared to live according to them, but also that he feels their rightness. Thus his sense of values is not an externally imposed set of duties and obligations, but an internally motivated system of feelingful judgments. The man of sensibility has his values not merely because he recognizes that he ought to have them, but also because his emotional needs demand them. His understanding and senibility have been formed by the classic works of his culture. These show, as it were, the ideals in action. What he learns from them is what it is like to be guided by these ideals. And in times of crisis or doubt it is to these classics that he returns for strength, solace, and reinforcement.

Learning from the classics, and generally, coming to appreciate ideals, however, would not be possible without the third component of wisdom: imagination. For only through it can a person sympathetically entertain other options. And even more importantly, only by comparing one's own ideals to others can a person critically examine the ones he holds. The chances are that the stock of ideals during an intellectual epoch have impressive historical credentials. Few of them would have survived if they had not exercised powerful and lasting attraction upon men whose understanding was not appreciably poorer and whose sensibility was not much crasser than one's own. To reject such ideals and to prefer one's own are hollow gestures unless one appreciates the attraction of alternatives. Unexamined ideals are not worth holding. Imagination is the prime vehicle for their examination.

In the wise man, intellectual understanding, emotive sensibility, and imaginative awareness of ideals are thus combined. In possession of these, he has a chance to live a good life and be happy. Only a chance, though! For nature and society have a way of impinging on one's consciousness and infringing on even the noblest aspirations. But one thing is clear: the wise man has a better chance for the good life and personal happiness than anyone else. Participation in a justified worldview has personal value, because it increases that chance.

IV. *Conclusion*

In concluding this description of philosophy it may be illuminating to point out some things to which my view is not committed. There are a number of dichotomies or contrasts which it has been my purpose to make far less sharp. They do not disappear, but their importance is considerably attenuated.

The first of these dichotomies is between theory and practice. Given the central place of problem-solving in my account, the resulting conception of philosophy is bound to be practice-oriented. But it is very far from being exclusively so, for what policy one should follow is a theoretical question to be decided partly on the grounds of the relative truth-directedness of theories which suggest the policies. The point of theories is to aid practice, but practice could seldom be successful unless aided by theories. So what I find significant is not the difference between practice and theory, but their interdependence.

Another dichotomy that is minimized in my account is between facts and values. Ideals have both factual and axiological presuppositions. But these seem to me to be inextricably connected. Ideals are valued, but they are valued because they represent desirable ways of solving problems. And people have these problems because they and their environment are what they are. Problems are factual and ideals are evaluative. Yet the nature of problems has much to do with the justification of ideals, and the nature of ideals is dependent on what the problems are. I have found simply no need to consider the derivability of *ought* from *is* or to agonize over the supposed naturalistic fallacy.

Much has been written in contemporary philosophy about the impossibility of drawing a clear distinction between statements, beliefs, or theories which have in the past been classified as analytic or synthetic, empirical or conceptual, observational or theoretical, descriptive or interpretive. My account is committed to the illegitimacy of the supposition that these distinctions indicate anything more than a difference in degree, a point of emphasis. Interpretations without description are as impossible as descriptions without interpretations.

Lastly, I have denied the separability of philosophy from the rest of culture. The relevance of cultural influences makes the idea that philosophy can be done in isolation fundamentally wrongheaded. But the implication of this is not what many philosophers have feared: the loss of autonomy for philosophy. The autonomy of philosophy does not derive from a unique set of problems, ideals, or facts, but from a special task: the construction and justification of worldviews.

Having described my view of philosophy and labored its attraction, I now recommend it for acceptance. If I am right, its acceptance is dictated both by the common good and self-interest.

NOTES

1. Samuel T. Coleridge, *Essays on His Own Times*, ed. by His Daughter (London: Pickering, 1850), Vol. 3, 708–9.

2. Clyde Kluckhohn, "Culture and Behaviour," *Collected Essays of Clyde Kluckhohn*, ed. R. Kluckhohn (New York: Free Press, 1962), 297–8.

3. Karl Marx, "Theses on Feuerbach," XI, in Marx and Engels, *Basic Writings on Politics and Philosophy* (New York: Doubleday, 1959).

4. An excellent account of how the conception of philosophy changed in a certain place during a particular period is Bruce Kuklick's *The Rise of American Philosophy: Cambridge, Massachusetts: 1860–1930* (New Haven: Yale University Press, 1977).

Chapter Thirteen

Philosophy and Perennial Arguments

"On the one hand, philosophers, more than any other type of investigator, persistently work at what appear to be the same unchanging problems. On the other hand, although these problems appear not only to be unchanging but to admit of rational or even necessary solutions, yet the history of philosophy presents them as the centers of unending conflicts and debates, punctuated briefly from time to time by claims that a revolution has taken place and that philosophical problems will now be speedily wound up—after which things go on again very much as before. This picture is not presented in irony or in cruel mockery of philosophy. On the contrary, I have claimed that the never-ending debates over the central concepts of philosophy provide a clue to their special nature ... and their peculiar function, which is to ensure intellectual vitality across the whole spectrum of human knowledge."

WILLIAM B. GALLIE[1]

I. *Introduction*

The relation between philosophy and perennial arguments has two aspects. The first is that perennial arguments play an essential role in the construction and justification of worldviews. Perennial arguments are the methods through which what I take to be the business of philosophy is conducted. The second aspect of the relation is that philosophy itself is one of these ideals about which there are perennial arguments. External perennial arguments about philosophy occur because it is doubted that philosophy is suitable for solving enduring problems. Religion, mysticism, and science are some of the competing ideals. Internal perennial arguments about philosophy begin with granting that philosophy is a worthwhile ideal, but they are generated by disagreements about the proper interpretation of the ideal.

The task of this book can now be expressed as the development of a particular interpretation of the ideal of philosophy and the defence of that interpretation from challenges presented by both external and internal perennial arguments about philosophy. In the previous chapter I have given an overall description of this interpretation. Here I shall defend it from both kinds of challenges. They jointly constitute my defence of the interpretation.

It may be thought that the dual relation between philosophy and perennial arguments makes the justification of my interpretation of philosophy circular. Philosophy is supposed to be the discipline whose method is perennial argumentation; but that philosophy is this discipline is itself a matter for perennial argumentation. So, a critic might claim that if the second claim is true it follows from it that the first claim must be controversial and it cannot be rendered immune to reasonable challenge.

This objection rests on two mistakes. The first is the supposition that if an ideal is subject to perennial argumentation, then particular interpretations of it cannot be justified. The supposition is erroneous because justification depends in part upon the suitability of the contested ideal for solving enduring problems in some particular form. The forms as well as the urgency of enduring problems change and so must change the judgment about the suitability of a particular interpretation of the ideal. Thus the possibility of justification and the need for the reconsideration of previously justified interpretations are both constant and in no way incompatible features of perennial arguments.

If the ideal is philosophy, the situation does not change. The interpretation I have offered is justified or not depending on whether viewing philosophy as the arena of perennial argumentation does indeed best solve the enduring problem of constructing and justifying a worldview. And even if the answer is favorable, it is so only for our time. If, for instance, in the future a worldview becomes a deadening orthodoxy, then the problem-situation will have changed and philosophy should perhaps be reinterpreted as a critical enterprise. Problem-solving makes justification relative to problem-situations. But it does not follow that there is no justifiable solution in any particular problem-situation.

The second mistake upon which the above objection depends is a confusion between interpretation and justification. The claim that philosophy is the subject devoted to perennial argumentation and the claim that philosophy being this subject is itself the object of perennial argumentation aim to offer an *interpretation* of the nature of philosophy. The interpretation is circular. But from this interpretation the *justification* of the interpretation must be distinguished. The justification of my interpretation of philosophy is that by adopting it we maximize our chances of solving our enduring problems. There is no circularity involved in this justification. So I readily admit, indeed insist, that the ideal of philosophy and my interpretation of it are subject to perennial argumentation. It should be clear, however, that the justification of interpretations can only be determined in particular situations. I have endeavored to justify my interpretation in our situation.

The last point I shall consider in this introductory part is the fit between my view of philosophy and contemporary philosophical practice. Obviously, if what I claim philosophy is does not tally with philosophical practice, then something is amiss. However, I do not think that the question of how close is the fit is amenable to a simple answer.

To begin with, the practice of individual philosophers is not what is meant by philosophical practice. There are hundreds of productive philosophers who would scoff at the idea that they are engaged in constructing and justifying a worldview. And it is clear that they do not intend their work to have this consequence. The cunning of reason, however, has not diminished since Hegel took notice of it. For regardless of their intentions, philosophers do contribute to the construction and justification of worldviews.

The overwhelming majority of philosophers are engaged in work within a tradition. They are followers of Quine, Popper, Marx, Sartre, Heidegger, and so on. These traditions, however, do form worldviews. Insofar as philosophers work on problems that arise within these traditions, they do contribute, albeit unwittingly and only incidentally, and hence minimally, to the construction and justification of worldviews. This is so even if their contribution is critical.

The practice of particular philosophers, therefore, has the perhaps unintended consequence of making philosophy the kind of enterprise I take it to be. So what I mean by philosophical practice is the picture that emerges when one reflects on the results of the aggregate formed of the practices of individual philosophers. It might be argued, however, that even in this sense of philosophical practice, my account does not do justice to it.

What, it might be said, does the immense literature that has grown up, for instance, around the Gettier-problem, possible world semantics, the derivability of ought from is, the justification of induction, have to do with the construction of worldviews? The answer is: a great deal! For the Gettier-problem is about the ideal of knowledge, possible world semantics involves rethinking the ideal of logic, the derivability of ought from is is about the nature of value in general, and the justification of induction is about the possibility of science. Ideals such as these are the desired goals in accordance with which the enduring problems of a particular epoch are solved. These technical philosophical questions are in fact questions that arise in the course of perennial arguments about some of the ideals of worldviews.

At the same time, I must concede that my view of philosophy is unlikely to fit philosophical practice perfectly. It is possible to find philosophical preoccupations which cannot be readily accommodated by my account. I would handle such instances in one of two ways. There must be practices overlapping philosophy and other inquiries; there must also be borderline cases; and idiosyncratic, unclassifiable works. To any general thesis there are such exceptions. Their mere occurrence is not an objection to the accuracy of the description. They would become objectionable only if they occurred in such large numbers that they ceased to be exceptions and had to be regarded as standard features requiring inclusion in the description. But I do not think that there are such exceptions to my thesis.

The second strategy for handling deviations between philosophical practice and my account of it is to state plainly that my account is not only descriptive but also evaluative. There are some bad philosophical practices. That my account does not include them as exemplifications of the ideal of philosophy is not a defect but a virtue: the opposite of promiscuity. When, for instance, philosophical practice degenerates into scholastic squabbles about pedantic minutiae whose resolution is neither possible nor desirable, for their resolution contributes to the solution of no enduring problem, then I would call that bad philosophy. Or, to take another case, when a worldview is defended by declamation posing as argument rather than by genuine argument, then once again bad philosophy is being done. Cases in point will readily occur to readers.

II. *External Perennial Arguments about Philosophy*

There are external perennial arguments about philosophy because there are doubts about the worthwhileness of the ideal represented by philosophy. Of course, what that ideal is changes. The kind of external perennial arguments there are about philosophy, therefore, also changes. I shall consider here some of the grounds upon which philosophy, interpreted as the ideal of constructing and justifying worldviews, is challenged. I make no claim to an exhaustive consideration of all possible challenges. My interest is in identifying the main challenges to my interpretation of philosophy and showing how they can be met.

The typical form of an external perennial argument is that the participants agree about the general description of an ideal and disagree about its value. Critics of the ideal may deny that the ideal has been rationally justified. This denial may have two general sources. One is that rational justification of ideals is impossible. The other allows for the possibility of rational justification of ideals, but denies that it can be or has been done in the case of a particular contested ideal. However, when the contested ideal is philosophy itself, understood as the ideal of rationally justifying other ideals, then challenges to it must be of the first kind. Thus external perennial arguments about philosophy take the form of denying that worldviews can be rationally justified. I shall label collectively all positions embracing this denial as fideism.

If the fideistic challenge to philosophy could not be met, prospects for civilized life would be bleak. For what fideism amounts to is the view that rational choice between conflicting worldviews is impossible. If that were so, we would still have to choose, but since we could not choose rationally, we would have to choose arbitrarily. One disastrous consequence of such a choice would be that conflicts between worldviews could not help but become contests between arbitrary authorities and result in settlement the only way possible: by force. The other dismal result would be that worldviews could not be appraised as problem-solving ventures. Hence they would be unreliable guides to handling the vicissitudes of life. And since they are the only candidates for rationally justifiable strategies, if fideism were correct, we would be in a sad state. These unpalatable consequences are not arguments against fideism, for truth may be unpalatable. But the recognition of the consequences may lead to an enhanced appreciation of the importance of defending philosphy against external perennial arguments.

Fideism is a general position and it may take many forms. In each of its forms, as an argument against the ideal of philosophy, it is based on challenging some presupposition of the ideal. I shall discuss three such challenges: supernaturalism, based on denial of an existential presupposition; relativism, resting on denial of a methodological presupposition; and positivism, committed to the failure of both a classificatory and an axiological presupposition.

Supernaturalism is the view that we can have reasons for supposing that there exists a realm, or entities, or qualities beyond what can be ascertained by the joint enterprise of descriptive theories and metaphysics. Supernaturalism rejects the existential presupposition that metaphysics is the authority about what there is. Or, alternatively, the thesis of supernaturalism can be expressed as the assertion that the domain of metaphysics is not exhausted by the information provided by descriptive theories and the interpretation of the information. In the former case, the challenge to my view is the denial that metaphysics is the authority about what there is; in the latter case, the challenge is that while metaphysics does have that authority, my conception of philosophy errs about the nature of metaphysics. It does not matter how the challenge is formulated: its point is that there is more to reality than what science and other descriptive theories reveal.

Supernaturalism has always exercised a powerful attraction, as the many forms of mysticism and religion demonstrate. This attraction is not fully explainable by charging those who have succumbed to it with mystery-mongering, obfuscation, yearning for extra-mundane authority, a desire for faith in something, or an inability to live without reposing hope in a benevolent design informing brute facts. For it is perfectly reasonable to suppose that what we know, and perhaps can know, does not exhaust what there is. If supernaturalism amounted only to a reminder of human limitations, it would be a salutary doctrine. Such a reminder, however, does not provide a challenge to having a rationally justified worldview. Pointing out that metaphysics is unlikely to yield omniscience is compatible with accepting it as the authoritative guide to reality.

Supernaturalism challenges my view because its adherents go on to claim that rationally justifiable knowledge does not exhaust what can be known. They suppose themselves to have arcane knowledge of the existence of things which escape the possibility of rational comprehension. And they go on to claim that what really gives meaning and purpose to life, what ultimately justifies some ideals and shows the hollowness of others, is this supernatural realm.

What is wrong with this view is that there is not and cannot be a shred of evidence for it. For whatever evidence there is or can be is provided just by those descriptive theories whose authority supernaturalism aims to undermine. From the fact that there may exist seemingly inexplicable predictions, problems apparently closed to rational solution, events whose occurrence is presently incomprehensible, it follows that our knowledge is limited. It does not follow that there is a supernatural explanation. That conclusion would not follow even if the predictions, problems, and events remain forever impenetrable to our cognitive powers.

Thus the reason for rejecting supernaturalism as an alternative ideal for solving our enduring problems is that it rests on the totally unsubstantiated claim that the key to problem-solving lies in a rationally incomprehensible realm. If there exists such a realm, nothing about it can be known, not by us, nor by supernaturalists. For to know anything is to bring it within rational comprehension. It would be self-defeating, therefore, to look to such a realm for guidance in solving our enduring problems. So in this external perennial argument I claim victory for my side on the grounds that the other side could not even begin to solve enduring problems.

The next external perennial arguments I shall consider is based on challenging the main methodological presupposition of my conception of philosophy. This presupposition is that particular worldviews can be rationally appraised, and some may be rationally justified, on the basis of a context-independent, objective standard of rationality: problem-solving. The challenge rests on the assumption that there are no such standards. I shall refer to all the many forms of this challenge as relativism.

Relativism may take the form of scepticism. The sceptical argument is that the justification of standards of rationality is both required and impossible. It is required because unless the standards are justified, their acceptance is arbitrary. Rational justification, in that case, is just as much a dogmatic appeal to some unsubstantiated belief held on faith as is any other form of fideism. But the required rational justification of standards of rationality is impossible, for it involves appeal to another standard which must also be similarly justified, and thus infinite regress follows.

Or relativism may appear as a sociological or anthropological argument to the effect that we are all immersed in a particular ideology or society and the standards to which we appeal and the arguments we find persuasive are part and parcel of the ideological or social superstructure which pervades our lives and informs our consciousness. We can perhaps make the supreme effort and challenge our own ideology or society, but if we do so it is only to replace it with another. Rational justification is possible within an ideology or society, but ideologies or societies cannot be rationally justified.

Or relativism may be given a psychological twist and maintain that rational justification properly understood always turns out to be rationalization. That is, rational justification is the work of our superego, or the result of successful socialization, or a function of the role we find ourselves playing. It always amounts to a pretence to make appear intellectually respectable what we want to do or are impelled to do anyway. Relativism is the current orthodoxy in sociology, anthropology, and psychology.

Thus relativists would perhaps accept my description of philosophy as the attempt to construct and justify worldviews, but they would deny that justification is possible. The ground for their denial is that justification can occur only within a worldview, thus worldviews themselves cannot be justified. They would regard the philosophical search for a standard of justification outside of particular worldviews as an illusion incapable of realization.

My response to the relativistic challenge is to charge it with being based on an absurd view of human nature. It is absurd because it flies in the face of facts whose existence no reasonable person would deny. These facts are that human beings always, everywhere share certain basic characteristics. Indeed, they are identifiably human because they have these shared features. They have human bodies with human sensory, physiological, and motor capacities and limitations; they have to obtain the necessities for survival from their environment; they form social groups and live in the midst of other people; they are capable of psychological and physiological pleasure and pain; they can remember the past and plan for the future; they are capable of learning from experience; and so on. These features are universally human, historically constant, and culturally invariant. Having them occasions what I have called problems of life. All human beings have problems of life.

The significance of problems of life is that their existence and the need to solve them in some manner or another provides just that objective, context-independent standard whose existence relativism denies. For the standard of justification outside of worldviews by which worldviews can be judged is their success in solving problems of life.

The fundamental error of relativism is to be so impressed by the differences among people that they overlook the glaring facts of their similarities. These differences manifest themselves in the many different ways in which people in different societies and historical periods solved problems of life and other problems as well. But these differences occur against the background of just those similarities which make beings of our kind human. It is a strange irony that the dominant doctrine of contemporary social sciences, devoted to understanding humanity, overlooks the most salient features of being human.

The third challenge to my conception of philosophy comes from positivism; it denies two presuppositions. The denial is not so much an attempt at deliberate refutation, it is more of a tacit assumption that the presuppositions do not obtain.

By positivism I mean the general view which regards science and the employment of scientific method as the paradigm of rationality. Other inquiries and methods are judged to be rational to the extent to which they approximate the scientific paradigm. It is perhaps surprising to include positivism, along with supernaturalism and relativism, as a form of fideistic challenge, for positivism has the reputation of tough-minded rationality. But while this reputation is earned in one problem-area, nature, it is totally unmerited in the other two: one's attitude to humanity and to oneself. In fact, the hallmark of positivism is the failure to distinguish between different problem-areas. All problems are treated as if they were scientific ones. Consequently, positivism has nothing to offer, and can have nothing to offer, towards a rational solution of such nonscientific problems as arise in the two problem-areas it ignores.[2]

Positivism is a form of fideism because it is committed to the impossibility of rationally justifying solutions of problems which are not amenable to scientific treatment. Since these problems must still be solved, and since they cannot be solved scientifically, and thus rationally, they will be solved, it follows from positivism, unscientifically and thus irrationally. The tough-minded rationalism of positivism towards nature is consequently combined with fideism in human affairs.

The first presupposition whose denial follows from positivism is the classificatory one distinguishing between removable and enduring problems. Positivism treats all problems as if they were removable. As a result, they overlook the existence of problems whose solution does not result in the disappearance of the problems, but in the development of a policy towards coping with it. These problems will not disappear, they are not removable, because they stem from unalterable conditions occasioned by human nature and the world being what they are.

Positivism conflicts with my conception of philosophy because the reason for constructing a worldview is to solve just these enduring problems, problems whose very existence positivism denies. And the reason why the positivistically inspired fideism regarding the solution of enduring problems is unwarranted is that policies for solving them can be rationally appraised, although they cannot be scientifically appraised. The appraisal depends on the comparative success of these policies in solving enduring problems.

The second presupposition denied by positivism is the evaluative one that the ideal of philosophy, or the value of philosophy, can be rationally justified. The ground of this denial is not any specific doubt about philosophy itself, but a general doubt about the possibility of bringing ideals within rational control. This general doubt is caused by the combination of the true belief that ideals cannot be scientifically justified and the false belief that only scientific justification is possible. The result of this combination is the disastrous view that political, moral, personal, and public ideals are incapable of rational treatment, that choices in these areas are arbitrary, that there is no better and worse in this domain. At best, positivism may result in an unreflective tolerance for all ideals. But not all ideals are tolerable. Some, like slavery, racism, wanton cruelty, the tyranny of a self-perpetuating group, are evil. If one had no rational way of showing that they are such, tolerance would perhaps be the least suicidal policy. But since ideals can be rationally appraised on the ground of their propensity to solve enduring problems, it is possible to justify the rejection of some and the acceptance of others.

The defence of my ideal of philosophy against these fideistic attacks upon it has been to show that the fideistic alternatives leave our enduring problems unsolved or badly solved, while they are tractable on the ideal I favor. This follows in the case of supernaturalism, because it looks for the justification of ideals to a supernatural authority whose existence is unknowable, and because it denies the reliability of the only method we have, the descriptive-metaphysical one, for obtaining knowledge of facts. Relativism, in turn, denies the possibility of rational justification and this results in endorsing whatever ideals of problem-solving happen to prevail. That this conservative conclusion follows from that hotbed of radicalism, the social sciences, is obvious if one recognizes that the impossibility of rationally appraising ideals prevailing in a society from a vantage point outside of the society is a consequence of relativism. On my view, there is an objective standard upon which such appraisal can depend: the universal problems faced by humanity. The positivistic challenge fails, because it not only leaves unsolved our enduring problems, it even fails to recognize their existence, and it fails to see also that the ideals with reference to which solutions would be possible are open to rational justification and criticism.

III. *Internal Perennial Arguments about Philosophy*

I shall consider here the main alternative to my conception of philosophy: the dominant view held by philosophers in America and increasingly also elsewhere, though there are some pockets of resistance to it. But since the editorial policies of many publishers and learned journals, the personnel policies of most philosophy departments, the education of doctoral students, the criteria for the award of prizes, grants, and fellowships, largely reflect this official view, reasoned and responsible dissension, or indeed, dissenters, are becoming increasingly rare. I have not been persuaded that this is due to the intrinsic excellence of the emerging orthodoxy.

In Chapter Twelve I have begun describing my view of philosophy by a quite general and neutral characterization of the subject. Philosophy, I have claimed, is an attempt to provide a rationally justified view of reality and of the significance it has for human beings. My position can be characterized by the emphasis it places upon providing a rationally justified account of the human significance the theory of reality has and by its lack of emphasis upon further developments of the theory of reality. The dominant position which I am opposing, reverses this emphasis. It is concerned primarily with having a rationally justified theory of reality and only incidentally with the significance the theory has for human beings. The argument between these two conceptions is an internal perennial argument because, while both sides agree about the value the ideal of philosophy has, they disagree about the interpretation of the ideal. My opponents stress the importance of metaphysics, I stress the importance of culture and anthropology.

The stress placed upon metaphysics is closely connected with the great success of science. The dominant view is that the distinction between science and philosophy, understood as a theory of reality, is arbitrary. Russell, for instance, expresses this point by writing: "Philosophical knowledge ... does not differ essentially from scientific knowledge; there is no special source of wisdom which is open to philosophy but not to science, and the results obtained by philosophy are not radically different from those obtained by science."[3] And Quine, perhaps the most authoritative contemporary spokesman for the dominant view, echoes this sentiment: "The relation between philosophy and science is not best seen ... in terms of give and take. Philosophy ... is an aspect of science."[4]

To illustrate this interpretation of philosophy consider how Quine responded when asked: "What about such questions as how man orients himself to the world of his experience, what meanings he finds in events, what values he aspires to, what standards guide his choices in all he does?" He replied: "If you and I were today to find a way of allaying major political and social evil ... then I think we would be duty-bound even now to quit our respective posts and join in the good new cause. But this responsibility would hinge no more on the nature of my present work than on that of yours. Nor, I venture to say, does the nature of my present work make me any likelier to discover that social remedy than the nature of your present work makes you. The fact that mine is partly allocated under a corner of that blanket word 'philosophy' is neither here nor there."[5] Philosophy, according to this view, does not provide wisdom, it is not concerned with the question of meaning and purpose of life, it is not interested in values and standards that guide us in private and social life. What philosophy is interested in is the construction of "a canonical idiom" for "the statement of one's scientific theory ... all traits of reality worthy of the name can be set down in an idiom of this austere form if in any idiom. ... It delimits what counts as scientifically admissible construction, and declares that whatever is not thus constructible ... must either be conceded the status of one more irreducible given term or eschewed."[6]

In contrast, I think that while philosophy must provide a theory of reality, it has done so for our time, and thanks mainly to science, we have a very serviceable one. What we do not have and badly need is wisdom, a rationally justified set of ideals to solve our enduring problems, and a worldview to give meaning and purpose to our lives. What reason is there for preferring my view to the dominant one?

There are two reasons. The first is that the dominant view is dangerously onesided. It concentrates on one problem-area, nature, at the expense of the other two, humanity and oneself. As a result, urgent enduring problems remain unsolved or badly solved. The second is that the development of a theory of reality, the aim of the dominant view, depends upon the cultural and anthropological components of worldviews, components which the dominant view ignores. The view I favor, on the other hand, offers a more balanced approach to solving our enduring problems and it goes deeper, because it emphasizes the need to rationally justify the unexamined presuppositions of the dominant view.

These reasons can be spelled out in detail by considering the implications of the three chapters which comprise the fourth part of this book. In two of these chapters I have argued constructively, while in one my thesis has been critical. The constructive argument is that, due partly to the fundamentality of the common sense, anthropocentrism is the unavoidable feature of all cognitive inquiries. This is the reason why the dominant view's concentration upon metaphysics is misplaced. Metaphysics rests upon culture and anthropology: the necessarily fundamental anthropocentric perspective. The other part of the constructive argument is that for the rational justification of cultural and anthropological ideals we must have historical understanding. The critical argument is that the justification of science, the pillar of the dominant view, rests upon common sense and historical understanding, the two pillars of my conception of philosophy. Thus where the dominant view stresses metaphysics, my view stresses culture and anthropology; where the dominant view favors science, my view favors common sense and history. The justification for my stress and favor is that they will aid us in solving enduring problems as we find them now.

What is at issue between the dominant view and my own is partly the perspective from which reality ought to be viewed. The aim of the dominant view is to establish an impersonal, nonhuman standpoint. The justification of pursuing this aim is the supposition that unless such a standpoint is established rationality and truth become impossible ideals. I think that the aim of the dominant view is unattainable. For the fundamentality of common sense makes anthropocentrism, the personal and human standpoint, unavoidable. Because we have our physiological, sensory and motor capacities, because scientific instruments must be designed and calibrated with reference to our senses, and because theories about reality must be constructed and tested by human beings, the achievement of the perspective aimed at by the dominant view is impossible. Part of the burden of the argument in Chapter Nine has been to show how science presupposes the anthropocentric perspective, and therefore neither it nor any other cognitive inquiry can be used to discredit the anthropocentric foundation upon which it rests.

At the same time, and this is crucial to my case, I deny the supposition implicit in the dominant view that rationality and truth become impossible if anthropocentrism is true. In the third part of the book, devoted to philosophical justification, I have offered a theory of justification which combines the possibility of rationality and truth with anthropocentrism.

So part of my reason for rejecting the dominant view is that its aim, the achievement of an impersonal, nonhuman standpoint, is impossible of attainment, and the benefit which the achievement of the aim was supposed to yield, rationality and truth, can be obtained otherwise. My view offers a combination of a theory of justification which makes rationality and truth obtainable and the recognition that anthropocentrism is unavoidable.

Another fundamental issue between the dominant and my view concerns the strategy to be adopted in pursuit of rationality and truth. I emphasize the importance of historical understanding, the dominant view emphasizes the importance of science. What is the justification for my emphasis?

The justification is that historical understanding is a necessary condition of the justification of philosophical theories. The attainment of rationality and truth, the common aim of the dominant and my own view, is impossible without such understanding. Furthermore, the employment of science for justification is warranted only after historical understanding of the relevant situation has been achieved.

This consequence follows from the distinction between the two contexts of justification. In the context of introduction, the question that must be answered is: what justification is there for the introduction of a theory? What we want to know there is why a particular theory should be considered at all. In the context of acceptance, the relevant question is: what justification is there for the acceptance of one among all the available theories? As we have seen in Chapters Seven and Eight, the first question is answered by appealing to problem-solving as the justification of the introduction of a theory, while the answer to the second question is given in terms of the truth-directedness of the theories whose introduction has already been justified.

The introduction of a theory is justified if the theory provides a possible solution of the relevant problem. Normally, the problems philosophical theories aim to solve directly are enduring problems of reflection. These problems, however arise against the background of a worldview. A problem arises either because there are tensions, conflicts, inconsistencies within a worldview, or because the growth of knowledge, changing circumstances, the emergence of novelty makes it necessary to revise the worldview so as to accommodate new developments. The problem is solved if these external and internal conflicts are overcome. Thus justification of the introduction of a philosophical theory is that the theory offers a possible reconciliation.

Historical understanding is a necessary condition of offering such a reconciliation, because, as we have seen in Chapter Eleven, historical understanding is the only way the worldview can be known. The recognition of something as problematic, the consideration of a theory as a possible solution, the categories available for the formulation of theories, the methods by which conflicts could be solved, all depend upon historical understanding of the traditional worldview. And even the decision to reject the traditional outlook of one's society depends on historical understanding, for only on that basis can the inadequacy of the worldview be judged.

My criticism of the dominant view is that it ignores the importance of historical understanding. It proceeds as if the only context of justification were the context of acceptance. It is true that in that context historical understanding does not play an important role. But this is so only because in the other context of justification, that of introduction, it has performed the main role. One can solve a problem only if it is understood, and it must be understood historically if it is an enduring problem of reflection.

What underlies the dominant view is its failure to draw a number of crucial distinctions. If it recognized the difference between removable and enduring problems, it would not regard science as the touchstone of rationality, for enduring problems cannot be solved scientifically. If it recognized the existence of problem-areas apart from nature, it would have to acknowledge that the philosophical task is greater than the construction and justification of a theory of reality. If it recognized that we do not just want to solve problems, but solve them in accordance with ideals, it could not fail to see that the attempt to find rational and true solutions is inseparable from the justification of ideals. If it recognized that the problems and ideals which theories aim to connect are human problems and ideals, it would not try to achieve an impersonal, nonhuman, and in any case impossible, perspective.

The dominant view is mistaken because it fails to recognize these points.

IV. *Conclusion*

In Chapter Twelve I have described my view of philosophy and in this chapter I have defended it against criticism. My claim is that the proper interpretation of the ideal of philosophy in our age is that it is an attempt to construct and justify a worldview. The justification for this interpretation is that it has the best chance of solving the enduring problems as they present themselves to us. The consequence of the failure to embrace this ideal or this interpretation of the ideal is that the enduring problems will remain unsolved or badly solved.

NOTES

1. William B. Gallie, *Philosophy and Historical Understanding* (New York: Schocken, 1968), 2nd ed., 7.

2. For a criticism of positivism similar to my own consider: positivism "is an attempt to consolidate science as a self-sufficient activity, which exhausts all possible ways of appropriating the world intellectually. In this radical positivist view the realities of the world—which can, of course, be interpreted by natural science, but which are in addition an object of man's 'extreme curiosity', a source of fear or disgust, an occasion for commitment or rejection—if they are to be encompassed by reflection and expressed in words, can be reduced to their empirical properties. Suffering, death, ideological conflict, social clashes, antithetical values of any kind—all are declared out of bonds, matters we can only be silent about, in obedience to the principle of verifiability. Positivism so understood is an act of escape from commitments, an escape masked as a definition of knowledge. ... Positivism in this sense is the escapist's design for living, a life voluntarily cut off from participation in anything that cannot be correctly formulated." Leszek Kolakowski, *The Alienation of Reason* (Garden City, N. J.: Doubleday, 1968), tr. N. Guterman, 204–5.

3. Bertrand Russell, *The Problems of Philosophy* (Oxford: Oxford University Press, 1967), 87.

4. Willard V. Quine, "Philosophical Progress in Language Theory," *Metaphilosophy*, 1 (1970), 2.

5. Willard V. Quine, "A Letter to Mr Osterman," in *The Owl of Minerva*, eds. C. J. Bontempo and S. J. Odell (New York: McGraw-Hill, 1975), 227 and 229.

6. Willard V. Quine, *Word and Object* (Cambridge: MIT Press, 1960), 228–9.

NAME INDEX

SUBJECT INDEX

Aesthetic sensibility, 17, 18, 24, 46, 50, 55
Aestheticism, 97
Alienation, 11, 175
Analysis, 10
Analytic-synthetic distinction, 84–88, 201
Anomaly, 32, 118
Anthropocentrism, xvi, 103, 131, 143–145, 161–162, 196–197, 213–218
Anthropology, 8, 213–218
  and common sense, 143–145
  as a component of worldviews, 60–61, 63–64, 143–145, 158, 196–197
  and metaphysical sentiments, 69–70
  and metaphysics, 60, 143–145
  and science, 160–162
  and wisdom, 61, 65
Arts, 10, 18, 41, 152
Astrology, xiii
Astronomy, 7, 8
Atheism, 24, 66–67, 68–69
Attitude to oneself, 33–34, 39, 152
Avowals, 98

Basic beliefs, 96–98, 131–138
Bibliography, 150
Biography, 149, 152
Biology, 7, 8, 148, 149

Categories, 82
Chemistry, 8
Classics, 10, 173–174, 200
Classicists, 24
Clear and distinct ideas, 98
Coherence, 85–88, 96–98
Coherentism, 96–98, 99, 107–108
Commitment, 12, 22, 27
Common sense
  and anthropocentrism, 143–145
  and basic beliefs, 131–138
  and the context of acceptance, 139, 141
  and the context of introduction, 139, 141
  and facts, 144–145
  and human nature, 131–138
  and ideals, 139
  and interpretation, 135–138

justification of, 138–145
  and metaphysics, 143–145
  and philosophy, xv, 131–146, 195–197
  and pragmatism, 140–141
  and problems, 139–140
  and problem-solving, 141
  and scepticism, 136, 142–143
  and science, 144–145, 160–162
  and worldviews, 131–146, 179–180
Conceptual
  inquiries, 82–88
  truths, 82–88
Conditional necessity, 83
Conservatism, 103
Context
  of acceptance, 99–102, 111–125, 126–127, 139, 165
  of discovery, 80–94, 126–127, 165
  of introduction, 95–110, 126–127, 139, 165
  of justification, 80–94, 126–127, 139, 165
Copernican cosmology, 97
Correspondence, 85–88, 92, 99, 107–108
Criticism, 12, 115, 116–118, 121–122, 197–198
Cultural influences, xvi, 79–80, 82, 91–92, 102, 109, 115, 120, 126–127, 165–166, 198, 201
Culture, 17, 20, 46, 201, 213–218
  as a component of worldviews, 61–62
  and history, 158–159
  and ideals, 61–62
  and science, 158–159
  and sensibility, 62

Deduction, 98
Democracy, 11, 17, 18, 20, 22, 24, 41–42, 46, 47, 48, 50
Descriptive arguments and theories, 27–28, 71, 119–120, 197–198
Determinism, 103
Diagnosis, 62–63, 64, 158
Dialectic, 28
Dialectical Materialism, 28, 151
Discovery, 80–94, 165

221

226   INDEX

Truth-directedness, 99–102, 106–107, 111–127, 195–198
Truth-possibility, 113–115
Tyranny, 18

Utilitarians, 24

Values, 11, 18–19, 201
Verbal arguments, 23–29
Verifiability principle, 98
Vision, 66–67

Western tradition, xiii
Wisdom, 3, 4, 11–12, 13, 61, 65–70, 174–177, 199–200
Witchcraft, xiii
Worldviews, xiii, xv, 4, 9, 13, 58–74, 179–180
  and adequacy of interpretation, 115–118
  and anthropocentrism, 131, 143–145
  and anthropology, 60–61, 63–64, 106, 143–145, 158, 160–162
  and change, 63–65
  and common sense, 131–146, 179
  components of, 59–65
  construction of, xiv, xv, 11, 12, 185–202
  and continuity, 63–65

and criticism, 116–118
criticism of, 11
and culture, 61–62, 64, 106, 158–159
and diagnosis, 62–63, 158, 159–160
and historical understanding, 164–181
and ideals, 3, 98
initial plausibility, 104–109
and internal tensions, 102–107
justification of, xiv, xv, 11, 12, 64–65, 95–127, 185–202
and logical consistency, 111–115
and metaphysical sentiments, 67–70
and metaphysics, 59–60, 63–64, 106, 143–145, 158
and perennial arguments, 43–44, 58–65, 73–74
and philosophical theories, 58, 65
and philosophy, xv, 3, 43–44, 70–72, 185–213
and presuppositions, 98
and policy, 63–64, 158, 159–160
and problems, 58–65, 73–74, 186–191
replacement of, 12
and science, 131, 147–163, 179–180
and theory of reality, 3
and vision, 66–67
and wisdom, 3

The Library
University of Saint Francis
2701 Spring Street
Fort Wayne, Indiana 46808

WITHDRAWN